LANDMARK COLLECTOR'S LIBRARY

A History
of Crich

J. G. Dawes

LANDMARK COLLECTOR'S LIBRARY

A HISTORY OF CRICH

J.G. Dawes

Landmark Publishing

Published by

Ashbourne Hall, Cokayne Ave
Ashbourne, Derbyshire DE6 1EJ England
Tel: (01335) 347349 Fax: (01335) 347303
e-mail: landmark@clara.net
web site: www.landmarkpublishing.co.uk

1st edition

ISBN 1 84306 082 5

© J. G. Dawes 2003

The rights of J. G. Dawes as author of this work
has been asserted by him in accordance with the Copyright,
Design and Patents Act, 1993.

All rights reserved. No part of this publication may be reproduced,
stored in a retrieval system or transmitted in any form or by any means,
electronic, mechanical, photocopying, recording or otherwise without
the prior permission of Landmark Publishing Ltd.

British Library Cataloguing in Publication Data: a catalogue
record for this book is available from the British Library.

Printed by Bookcraft, Midsomer, Norton, Bath

Design & reproduction by Simon Hartshorne

CONTENTS

Maps and References
Note on Extent of Crich Parish
Foreword
Preface
Acknowledgments

PART I : THE SOCIAL STORY

1. The Beginning — 10

2. Aristocrats, Squires and Landowners — 12
2.0 Precis — 12
2.1 The Manor of Crich — 12
2.2 The Manor of Wingfield — 15
2.3 The Manor of Wakebridge — 15
2.4 Tudor Times — 16
2.5 The Civil War and Afterwards — 18
2.6 The Manor of Alderwasley — 19
2.7 The Manor Houses in Crich — 20
2.8 Important Landowners — 24
2.9 Humbler Crich People — 26

3. Village Government — 31
3.1 In Anglo-Saxon Times — 31
3.2 After the Conquest — 31
3.3 The Sheriffs — 32
3.4 Manorial Courts — 33
3.5 The Constables — 35
3.6 The Justices — 39
3.7 Wage Control — 40
3.8 Tithes — 41
3.9 The Relief of the Poor — 41
3.10 Other Duties of the J.P.s — 43
3.11 Musters, Militias and Volunteers — 45
3.12 Workhouses — 49
3.13 The 1834 Poor Law — 51
3.14 The End of Tithes — 53
3.15 Elected Local Government — 54
3.16 Postscript on Local Government — 54

4. Travelling — 58
4.1 Early Tracks — 58
4.2 Cattle Drovers Routes — 59
4.3 Causeways — 59
4.4 Packhorses — 60
4.5 Cross Routes — 61
4.6 Metalled Roads — 63
4.7 Turnpikes — 64
4.8 Canals — 68
4.9 Railways — 68
4.10 Changing Times — 69

5. Meetings — 71
5.1 Introduction — 71
5.2 The Church of St. Mary — 71
5.3 Chapels and Assemblies — 78
5.4 Schools — 81
5.5 A Celebration on the Hill — 85
5.6 Public Houses — 86
5.7 Clubs — 89
5.8 Crich Reading Room — 90
5.9 Footnote — 91

PART II : THE STORY OF WORK

6. Farming — 92
6.1 Villeins & Freeholders Lands — 92
6.2 Use of Woodlands — 94
6.3 Effect of the Black Death — 95
6.4 Life on the Medieval Farm — 96
6.5 Tudor Inflation — 97
6.6 New Farming Practices — 98
6.7 The Formal Enclosures — 100
6.8 The War with Republican France — 101
6.9 The Times of George IV, William IV and Victoria — 104

7. Quarrying — 110
7.1 Early Quarries — 110
7.2 Building Stone — 110
7.3 Limestone — 111
7.4 The Butterley Company Quarries — 111
7.5 The Cliff Quarry — 113

8. Lead Mining — 116
8.1 The Liberty of Crich — 116
8.2 Getting the Lead to Market — 117
8.3 The Miners and their Work — 118
8.4 Some Crich Lead Mines — 120
8.5 The Twilight of the Industry — 121

9.	Manufacturing	124	Appendix		163
	9.1 For Parish Use	124	Tables		164
	9.2 Stone Products	126	A	Service Reservoirs 1987	149
	9.3 Barge Building	127	B	Location of Manor &	
	9.4 Pots	127		Canon's Court	164
	9.5 Various Mills	128	C	Places near Manor &	
	9.6 The Hat Factory	131		Canon's Court	165
	9.7 Framework Knitting	134	D	Principal Landowners : 1786	166
			E	Principal Landowners : 1847	167

PART III : THE TWENTIETH CENTURY

			F	Landholdings in 13th Century	168
			G	Field Names in mid 19th Century	170
10.	Remembering	144	H	Weekly Money Income : General	171
	10.1 Introduction	144	J	Weekly Money Income :	
	10.2 Fairs and Farming	145		Framework Knitters	172
	10.3 Manufacturing	146	K	Field Name Groups : 1847-49	173
	10.4 Public Services	146			
	10.5 Reservoirs	148	Figures		
	10.6 Travelling	150	Fig.1	Main Features of Crich District -	
	10.7 Schools	151		Mid 20th Century	174
	10.8 Welfare	152	Fig.2	Crich Parish - Mid 20th	
	10.9 Clubs	153		Century	175
	10.10 Shopping	154	Fig.3	Lead Mines	176
	10.11 Entertainment & Holidays	156	Fig.4	The Northern limits of Crich Parish	177
	10.12 Singing Hymns	157	Fig.5	Wages and Price of Wheat	178
	10.13 Bellringing	158	Fig.6	Location of Manor and	
	10.14 Quakers	158		Canon's Court	179
	10.15 Quarrying	159	Fig.7	Principal Landowners	180
	10.16 Wars	160	Fig.8	Land Enclosed by 1786	
	10.17 Epilogue	161		Commission	181
			Fig.9	Populations	182
11.	In Conclusion	162	Fig.10	Wage Rates	183

MAPS AND REFERENCES

Six-figure National Grid references are given throughout the text. They can all be preceded with the SK prefix.

Endnote numbers are in square brackets in the text and details are to be found at the end of each section.

Cross-references to other sections of the text are in round brackets.

NOTE

In the Domesday Survey Wessington is said to be "in the jurisdiction of Crich". Wirksworth, Lea and Tansley - though paying taxes in the Wapentake of Wirksworth - are said "to lie in Crich". Certainly until well into the 19th century Tansley and Wessington were joined administratively with Crich. Thus as late as 1851 the Parliamentary Census Return numbers, for Crich, 3670 inhabitants of whom 1118 were returned for Tansley and Wessington. The grouping persisted until 1862. In 1934 an area including Bullbridge in the Parish of Crich, part of the Belper Rural District, was transferred to the Parish of Heage - part of the Ripley Urban District.

For the purpose of this book, Crich is taken to include Bullbridge, but not Tansley, Wessington, Dethick or Lea.

The present-day boundaries of Crich Parish are shown in Figures 2, 3 and 4.

FOREWORD

Geoff Dawes was born in Crich and has spent much of his life living in the parish, with homes in Crich and Fritchley. However, he currently resides in Stone, Staffordshire. Before he retired he wrote a delightful, anecdotal book about Crich characters which was published by Scarthin Books. It was called "The Crich Tales" and enjoyed commercial success.

After his retirement, for reasons he sets out in the following preface, Geoff turned his attention to the present, more serious, work, and completed it in 1988. He chose not to have it published at that time and contented himself with reproducing about 50 copies. These were judiciously distributed to friends, interested parties and bodies which have duties to collect and preserve local histories.

The Crich Heritage Partnership came into existence in 1999 and in the following year Geoff generously presented the Committee with one of the few remaining copies of "The Tale of Crich". He hoped it would be useful to CHP as a reference source. The Committee soon formed the view that the book deserved a wider audience than it had had and resolved to get it into print and make it available to those with an interest in, and affection for, Crich and its neighbourhood.

Geoff was consulted on this suggestion and was content to let CHP take on the job of revising and tidying the manuscript and finding a publisher. A debate was held about whether the account of Crich should be brought 'up-to-date' and Geoff certainly favoured this if someone could be found to do it. But the Committee - and it has to be said, the publisher - felt that the original end-date of September 1988 should remain so that the work was unquestionably that of one author. The story of Crich from that date must await another chronicler.

Ken and Val Jackson took on the job of reformatting the book on behalf of Crich Heritage Partnership. We have done some 'nipping and tucking' and retyping, and have provided and researched the photographs. The text has been changed as little as possible and then simply to prevent the reader reaching wrongful conclusions because of the passage of time between completion and publication. Occasionally we have felt the need to insert clarification on minor points of fact and these editorial inserts are, we hope, clearly attributable to us.

Ken and Val Jackson
April 2003

PREFACE

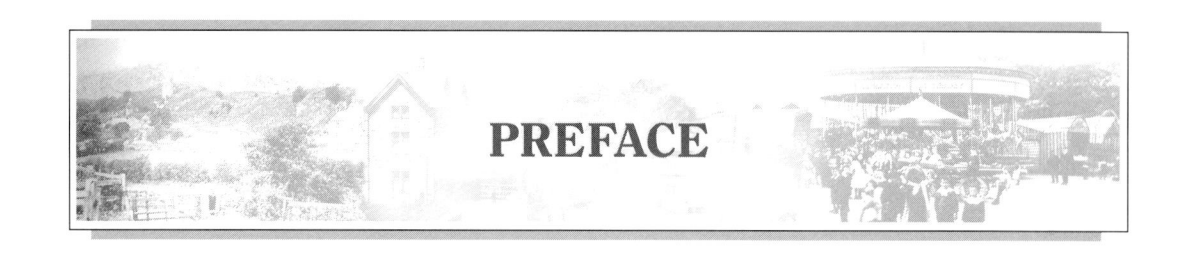

When preparing the prologues to the various groups of "The Crich Tales" I delved into some old books about Derbyshire - in particular those discussing topics of interest to the area round Crich. Many statements of 'the truth' are recorded and sometimes they disagree. But then, as new evidence becomes available and as they think more deeply and with experience, even modern professional historians and antiquarians change their minds.

So, I hope with no touch of gall, I here present, as an amateur, an ordered collection of documented gossip about people and events in Crich.

Sources, too often secondary and sometimes presenting conflicting 'facts', are given and an attempt has been made, here and there, at inducing coherence, at interpreting observations and at setting local events in a wider context - even if only at the level of school-boy history.

Parts I and II cover the years up to about 1900 A.D. and an attempt has been made to identify the origin of all the 'facts' included.

Part III is different. No serious attempt is made to use documentary sources. It would be a task for a scholar - and a scholar with more time than I have - to present an adequately complete story of the village in the 20th century. The amount of material is vast: official records and statistics, newspapers, records of local societies and clubs - and so on. What is attempted in Part III is the recording of things known directly or told to me by relatives, friends and acquaintances, which may not be easy to find in 'official' records - but which give some of the flavour of local life in the first half of the 20th century - especially to the newer generations who, for instance, may not appreciate the importance to the poorest people of Crich in the 1930s of local charities - administered by the Church and the Parish Council - some of which had been established hundreds of years previously.

After 1951 when TV signals could be received from Sutton Coldfield not only was a new form of entertainment introduced (which spelled the death of the Crich Cinema, which closed in 1955-56) but TV also gave the native parishioners a view of the world which before long integrated them with the global village generated by the comprehensive communications of the end of the 20th century.

Also, in the 1950s, there was a rapid rise in the 'standard of living' in the United Kingdom and expenditure on food was no longer, perhaps, the dominant item in the wage-earners' budget (See Figure 5).

These things together have changed the Crich village way of life forever and Part III of this book hopes to preserve some facts and some memories of older days.

In spite of unavoidable uncertainties, I hope that this "Tale of Crich" is roughly right and will afford some interest and some pleasure to the reader.

J. G. Dawes
April 2003

ACKNOWLEDGMENTS

My first recognition of debt must be to Arthur Watkins of Fritchley - who died in 1954. He had prepared a sketch for a local history called "The Manor of Crich" which was typed by his daughter Joan Johns and was made available to a number of local people who were thought to be interested. It is a fascinating document and it first stimulated my own interest in the history of Crich. Without its inspiration this book would probably never have existed.

I also want particularly to thank Mrs. Joan Wragg of Crich for many useful leads to events in the past. Everyone locally who is interested in the history of our area is indebted to her: I am, greatly so.

My thanks are also gratefully offered to the staff of the County Library at Belper and especially Miss Rosemary Hall who has been a staunch ally.

Without the staff and facilities of the Local Studies Library at Derby and the County Archives at Matlock and the willing and pleasant assistance provided, where would we local 'researchers' be?: their assistance too has been invaluable!

My brothers Peter and Terence have also been able to help me because of their specialised knowledge in local government and agriculture respectively.

Irene Sinclair of Tor View has earned not only my thanks but also my admiration for the excellent drawing she has devised using a photograph of the painting which shows Roger Beler's Manor House (see title page).

If I offer my special thanks to Miss Alma Mason of Sydney, Australia towards the end of my catalogue of pleasure - it is because she deserves special attention. She earns thanks not only from me, but from all who, I am sure, will be intrigued and given pleasure by the opportunity to share part of her grandfather's experience when he came to Crich from Australia in the 1860s.

Although this book is about a particular village, it also presents, to the non-professional historian, a picture of things as they were over the years in the country as a whole. It could interest much more than a local audience. For this reason not only am I, but many could be, grateful to the Crich Heritage Partnership – and especially to Ken and Val Jackson – for taking the initiative in the production of this edition of my original exploration of the history of Crich. Landmark Publishing also deserve thanks for producing such an elegant volume.

Finally, I fondly thank my wife Lorna for her encouragement - and for her forbearance in a period when I am sure I have neglected many things - from painting the kitchen ceiling to sending her a Valentine card - and have been known to get irritated about going visiting and shopping. Ah well - no excuses in future!!

J. G. Dawes

PART I

THE SOCIAL STORY

1. The Beginning

Crich Parish in mid-Derbyshire contains not only the village of Crich but also Fritchley, Bullbridge, Thurlow Booth, Whatstandwell, Crich Carr, Robin Hood, Coddington, Wakebridge, Shuckstone, Wheatcroft, Plaistow, Parkhead and Culland (Figures 1 and 7). It is bounded by the Derwent Valley to the west, the Amber Valley to the east and by their confluence to the south. To the north lie the commons of Dethick and the moors of Tansley and Beeley. Crich rests on one of the south-eastern foothills of the Pennine Range and its name, which has been spelt in many ways, simply means "Hill". [1]

Crich can be thought of as beginning three hundred million years ago when the Carboniferous limestones and sandstones were being deposited on the sea bed. With time the strata were raised and folded - the folds being filled underneath with a volcanic rock, locally called "toadstone". At this time the fissures in the folding limestone strata were flooded with hot mineralising fluids from the deep earth. They cooled there and settled as veins and pipes of ore and the area around what is now Crich Hill [343555] and particularly between Wakebridge [338557] and Plaistow [349557] was crossed by rakes and veins of lead. Eventually, within the last two million years, as the glaciers of the Ice Ages eroded the surface of the land, the limestone dome that formed Crich Hill and underlies much of the old village was scoured of the overlying shales and gritstones and exposed.[2] The edges of gritstone strata can readily be seen along the Tors [349536] at Edge Moor [354553] where Ashover Grit appears above the shales and near Robin Hood [332550] and Coddington [339548] where the Chatsworth Grit -a finer stone - forms the exposed dome above Benthill [340544].

The Dimple Valley [356537], which drains the uplands above Benthill and to the east of Crich Hill down towards the River Amber, is filled with the boulder-clay formed in glacial times and in the quarries at the side of the Dimple -particularly in the "Old Quarry" [357542] great lumps of Cumberland Granite carried down from the north by the glaciers have been found.[3] Two such egg-shaped boulders in the Old Quarry weighed more than a ton each.

Early men avoided both marshy valleys and too-exposed high places and one of the earliest traces of men in the parish is in Lindway-Spring Wood [358580] to the north-east of Crich Hill at a height above sea-level of between 500 and 600 feet. Here are to be found the remains of stone-lined pits in which Stone Age men of 4000-2000 B.C. made their homes. There are two rows of pits of circular form - called the Pitsteads.[4] One row contained twenty-five, the other twenty-eight, extending two hundred and fifty yards in length: most of them were about fifteen feet in diameter and six feet in depth.

At a later time, from about 1800 B.C. to 500 B.C. (during the Bronze Age) the ridges parallel to the Derwent Valley -and especially those near Crich where 'The Hill' provided a useful landmark -attracted travellers making their way north and south. A main 'high-ground' route was established and this highway, with its successors, had a strong influence on the later life of the

The Beginning

parish.

The route north out of Crich passed by Shuckstone [343572] - a place separately identified in the Domesday Survey. Here, at a junction with a path coming up from Robin Hood and Wakebridge, was to be found Shuckstone Cross[5] where, in 1788, an earthen pot of copper Roman coins was found. (A shuck was a robber and a murderer and this lonely place would be a hunting ground for such!). It is known,[6] following the discovery of six pigs of lead near Brough on the Humber and of four others at Pulborough in Sussex marked with the inscription LUT (for Lutadorum -a place not identified with any precision but thought to be near Matlock), that the Romans were engaged from about A.D.117 to the third century in exploiting local lead deposits. Evidence of the presence of the Romans in the parish, and presumably they came to exploit the Crich lead ores, has come from the discovery of hoards of Roman coins and other artefacts. Apart from the earthen pot at Shuckstone a collection of Roman 'copper' coins was found in the foundation of a small building on Crich Cliff in 1761- as well as some tiles.[7] The coins had been struck in the reigns of Domitian, Hadrian and Diocletian. Then in 1778 a find of silver coins (denarii)[8] from the reigns of Hadrian, Diocletian and Constantine was made at Culland [364542]. Another find of coins was also made on Edge Moor.[9] Around 1900 a great number of pieces of broken Roman pottery was found on Crich Hill - a little below the position of the Old Stand.[10]

The finds at Culland and Edge Moor were on routes away from the ore-field and towards the Roman fort on Castle Hill between Pentrich and Oakerthorpe and on Ryknild Street - the Roman road running from "Little Chester" in Derby up to Chesterfield and on to Templeborough - from whence there is easy access to the Humber and so to the sea and to Rome.

Although there are these early indications of human activity in Crich, it is not until Norman times that enough evidence becomes available on which to base a reasonably reliable story. When the Normans settled in Derbyshire, Crich was in the Duffield Frith - a largely wooded area put under the control of Earl Ferrers of Duffield Castle.

[1] Fraser W. (1947) *Field Names in South Derbyshire* Ipswich, Adland, pp.1, 105.
[2] OS Geological Map
[3] Watkins A. (1952) *The Manor of Crich* : Manuscript pp.4, 34.
[4] Hackett R.R. (1899) *Wirksworth and Five Miles Round* Wirksworth. Brooks. p.111
[5] Ordnance Survey 6 inch / 1 mile
[6] Nixon F. (1969) *The Industrial Archaeology of Derbyshire.* Newton Abbot, David and Charles. p.24
[7] Kirkham N. (1968-69) *Lead Mining in Crich.* Manchester Association of Engineers Session 1968-69 No.5 p.14
[8] Pilkington J. (1789) *View of the Present State of Derbyshire* . Derby. James Pilkington p.239
[9] Watkins. Ibid. p.1, 8.
[10] Ibid. p.9

2. ARISTOCRATS, SQUIRES AND LAND OWNERS

2.0 Precis

For readers who find genealogies and the succession of inheritance and of purchase less than fascinating, this section presents a brief outline of the material recorded in detail in the remaining nine sections of this chapter - which such readers may prefer to skip through or over !

Before the Norman Conquest, Crich was one of the Manors held by the family of Godwin the Saxon Earl of Wessex and at the time of Domesday it had passed to Ralph Fitzhubert. The first Baron of Crich was Ralph's son, Ralph FitzRalph who was succeeded by his nephew, Hubert FitzRalph. Hubert's daughter, who inherited Crich, married a Frecheville and it stayed with the Frechevilles until Ralph (Hubert's great-grandson) sold out to Sir Roger Beler. This Roger was succeeded by his son, also Roger, whose daughter married a Swillington who became Lord of the Manor of South Wingfield. Her son left both Crich and South Wingfield Manors to his sister and from thence it passed by marriage into the hands of the Cromwell family - to Ralph, Lord Cromwell, who was Treasurer to Henry IV. Cromwell sold Crich and South Wingfield Manors to the Talbots, who held title as the Earls of Shrewsbury. On the death of Gilbert, the 7th Earl of Shrewsbury, the rights of the Manors were divided amongst his three daughters who eventually sold out, mostly to commoners.

The Manor of Wakebridge and its distinguished Lord at the time of the Black Death, Sir William de Wakebridge, was subordinate to the Manor of Crich. Through Sir John Pole, whose mother was Sir William's only surviving sister and relative, and Pole's descendant German Pole, whose widow married John Claye, the Claye family acquired an important role in the village in Tudor times. John Claye's daughters, by marriage, brought the Willoughbys of Wollaton, the Curzons of Kedleston and the Dixies of Bosworth into Crich affairs and they were joined later by the Wilmots of Chaddesden. After the Civil War these families and the yeomen like the Smiths, the Bennetts and the Wrights who had purchased parcels of rights in the Manor exercised power in the village and they, in due course, were joined by the Turtons, Travises and the Towndrows and by such neighbouring 'squires' as Richard Arkwright of Cromford, Peter Nightingale of Lea and the Strutts of Belper who all owned tracts of land in the village.

Another local squire - the Lord of the Manor of Alderwasley - also had a considerable influence in the village. The Hurts of Alderwasley - over two centuries, both by their benefactions and by their ownership of property in the parish, were long regarded in Crich with great respect. Indeed the man spoken of locally as the last real 'Squire of Crich' was Francis Cecil Albert Hurt of Alderwasley who was born in 1878. After his death in 1930, his successors emigrated to Africa and so the last of the local 'aristocrats and squires' left the parish scene.

2.1 The Manor of Crich

An early written reference to Crich is in the 'Domesday' survey of 1086 A.D. where it says that Ralph, son of Hubert, (Ralph FitzHubert) held the land which had a plough in the lordship and which also had a lead mine - being of value 40s. 0d before 1066 and, in 1086, of value 30s 0d.[1] Ralph FitzHubert became involved in the civil war between Matilda (the Empress Maud) and Stephen and was hanged by a partisan of Matilda in 1140.[2] He had a son Ralph FitzRalph, who became the first Baron of Crich, and two daughters. One, Matilda, married Ralph FitzEudo, the other daughter married Edward of Salisbury.[3]

Ralph FitzRalph, in the reign of Stephen (1135-54), gave lands at Hartshorn, south of the Trent, to the Knights Templars of Jerusalem whose order had been founded in 1118. In 1154-59, Ralph FitzEudo - one of the wealthiest magnates in Derbyshire - gave Crich Church and its appendages at Lea, Dethick, Ible, Tansley, Wessington, Ogston and Succethorn (Shuckstone) to the Canons of Darley Abbey - with the consent of Earl Robert de Ferrers.

Hubert FitzRalph, son of Matilda and Ralph FitzEudo, succeeded as Baron of Crich and is on record as having paid, in 1166, the levy on 30 knights fees* for his rights in the Manor of Crich[4]

In 1175 Hubert FitzRalph, as the result of a well-documented lawsuit tried before Roger, the Bishop of Worcester (who had been appointed by Pope Alexander III) confirmed his gifts to Darley Abbey and, in addition, granted the Canons rights in part of Crich Wood (see the Appendix) - all in exchange for the renunciation by the Canons of their claim to payment for the pasturage of swine (pannage) and from the profit for doing this (agistment), throughout all the woods of the Manor. Albinus, the Abbot of Darley, accepted the ruling.

In 1200 Hubert FitzRalph paid 30 marks (£20) to King John to be allowed to make his woods in Crich a free chase and to have hounds and deer of his own.[5] Crich Chase - so called to this day - is easily found on Figure 2.

In 1204 Leonia, widow of Robert de Stuteville, daughter of the Earl of Salisbury and granddaughter of Edward of Salisbury (who had married a sister of the first Baron of Crich), paid 200 marks to Hubert for rights in the Barony of Crich. When, in 1205, there was a levy from the Crown of two marks for each knight under the control of the Barony in lieu of personal service (scutage), Hubert paid for fifteen and Leonia covered the remaining fifteen. Two marks was, in value, equal to £1-6s-8d, i.e. 320d - perhaps about a year's pay for a labourer (see Figure 5).

Apart from giving Darley Abbey rights in part of the Wood of Crich Hubert FitzRalph gave the Canons numerous parcels of land and facilities in Crich for "the safety of his soul" and for the souls of his first wife Edeline and of his second wife Sara.

Hubert died before 1219. His daughter Juliana, who had married Anker (Anthony) de Frecheville (I) (who was also dead by 1219), lived until 1221. Her son, Ralph de Frecheville, succeeded as Lord of the Manor of Crich. In 1229 he still retained fifteen of the knight's fees and was summoned to Parliament as representative of Crich in 1241. Over the period from 1242 to 1258 he was involved in a long series of court cases - both Royal and Ecclesiastical. In the King's Court in 1242 he disputed the rights on two knights fees held by the Abbot of Darley and another case on this was heard in 1258. In 1244 and 1254 he confirmed the gifts of his predecessors to the Canons of Darley and made agreements with Abbot Walter on the Canon's rights in Crich.

In 1260 Ralph de Frecheville (I) died and was succeeded by his son Anker (II) who lived until 1268, being succeeded by his son Ralph de Frecheville (II). This Ralph - who was 22 in 1287 -

---

* One knight's fee was basically a unit of land sufficient to keep one knight fully armed and supported in the field for one campaigning season. The number of knight's fees for which a tenant-in-chief was responsible was, therefore, related to the extent and value of his holding. If the services of the knights were not called on the levies (in money) exacted by the Crown were used to finance the King's Court.

was involved in that year in a legal contest about homage and service for a tenement in Wessington and in 1297 was summoned to Parliament to represent Crich. In 1309 Ralph II lost a law contest with the Abbot of Darley who recovered the freehold of common pasture in Crich which Ralph had enclosed. He was in the King's Court again in 1315 and was required to acquit the Canons of Darley Abbey of the services of two knights fees which they held in the Manor of Crich: this was an old dispute which had started in his grandfather's day.

In the 1320s Ralph II, in a contest with the family of Thomas Lord Beler of Kirby Bellars in Leicestershire about the Manor of Boney in Nottinghamshire, acknowledged that it - with its 'appurtenances', but with the exception of the homages and services of the Abbot of Darley - belonged to Sir Roger Beler. As the result of the fine levied by the Kings Court, and at the command of the King (Edward II), Ralph II in 1325, and for a consideration of 200 marks, transferred the ownership to Sir Roger Beler, not only of the dues from the Abbey of Darley but also his rights in his part of the Manor of Crich.[6] The Belers were directly descended, on the female side, from William the Conqueror.[7]

In 1325 too, the rights of Sir Roger Beler - the new Lord of the Manor - in the King's lead mine at Crich, were confirmed by Edward II. Thus Crich became a 'Liberty'[8] i.e. a lead-ore field outside the jurisdiction of the Crown and able to establish its own rules [9] (Section 8.1)*.

In 1326 Sir Roger Beler (I) was murdered; his son Roger then being only seven years old. Sir Roger Beler (II) reached his majority in 1339 and then inherited full rights in the Manor of Crich. This Roger lived until 1380. Before then he had enclosed a park stretching from Plaistow [352565] along Edge Moor to Culland [364542] and embracing Parkhead [361546]. It was Sir Roger (II) who sanctioned, in 1368, the Chantry in Crich Church dedicated to the friends, servants and parishioners of Sir William de Wakebridge who founded it (his second donation of a chantry to the Church) (Section 5.2).

By this time it was not only the senior gentry who were making gifts to Darley Abbey - "for the safety of their souls"[10]. Quite a number of bequests were made to the Canons by less exalted families. Thus Peter, son of Geoffrey of Crich granted to the Canons his rights in the toft and croft which his father held in Crich.

Another typical gift was by Richard, son of William Bylbot, to the Canons of "4 $^1/_2$ acres in le Lewes in Crich with the adjoining meadow lying between the land which John Culbil held and that of Ralph of Wakebridge towards le Dumpel"[11] (the Dimple - a deep, shady dell) [356537]. Although some properties were worked by their servants (probably based on their Court near St. Thomas' Mount - Section 2.7) - who also exercised the rights of gathering wood for building, hedging and fuel in parts of Crich Wood - a large part, probably the greater part, of the revenues of the Canons derived from the various bequests to them in the form of money rents (Section 6.1).

2.2 The Manor of Wingfield

Sir Roger Beler (II) left the Manor of Crich to his daughter Margaret. She had married Robert de Swillington who was Lord of the Manor of South Wingfield. Their son, Sir John Swillington, who died in 1405, left it to his sister. There had been much intermarriage between the local aristocratic families (at several levels of seniority in each family) and detail of the conveyance of manorial rights is cloudy.[12] Over 100 years earlier Ralph de Cromwell who had served with the army of Edward I - (when he returned from the Crusades and spent the period 1275-1285

---

* The Section numbers in round brackets refer to Chapters and Sections in the text.

contesting sovereignty with the Scots and especially the Welsh) had a daughter Joan who married Alexander of the Frecheville family (Section 2.1) which held Crich Manor until, in the 1320s, the rights passed to the Beler family. Through this link, and after the Swillingtons, the manorial rights in both Crich and South Wingfield passed eventually to Ralph, Lord Cromwell - Treasurer to Henry IV.[13] This Ralph was not only Chancellor of the Exchequer (in modern parlance) but also Master of the Royal Hounds and Falcons and Steward and Keeper of Sherwood Forest. In 1440 he started to rebuild the Manor House at South Wingfield and then in 1455 the Cromwell estates at Crich and Wingfield were sold to John Talbot, the 2nd Earl of Shrewsbury who was living at Wingfield in 1458-9, and was succeeded by his son in 1474.[14] Eventually the Manors passed to George Talbot, the 6th Earl of Shrewsbury and husband of Bess of Hardwick. George was charged by Queen Elizabeth I with the custody of Mary Queen of Scots and for a time Mary was held prisoner in the Manor at Wingfield (Section 2.2). On the death of Gilbert, 7th Earl of Shrewsbury, the rights of the Manors of Crich and Wingfield were divided up amongst his three daughters and co-heiresses Mary, Countess of Pembroke; Elizabeth, Countess of Kent and Althea, Countess of Arundel.

2.3 The Manor of Wakebridge

The 2nd Baron of Crich Hubert FitzRalph had, in addition to Juliana whose son Ralph de Frecheville became Lord of the Manor of Crich, another daughter (Alice or Emma - there is some confusion) who married Peter de Wakebridge.[15] He was a Knight of the Shire with a Manor at Wakebridge (on the site of the present-day Wakebridge Farm [338557]) and was summoned to Edward III's parliaments.

His son, Sir William de Wakebridge fought with Edward III in the 100 Year War with France, possibly at Crecy. He was not only a soldier however. In his later years he was also a busy administrator. He became 'Commissioner of Oyer and Terminer' for Nottinghamshire and Derbyshire, i.e. a judge on circuit dealing with criminal cases and boundary disputes. He was Cloth Trade Commissioner for Nottinghamshire and he was appointed a Justice to deal with cases arising from the Statute of Labourers in 1349 (Section 3.7). He served Parliament as a Knight of the Shire at times between 1353 and 1363 and not only served Edward III and Queen Phillipa as an official but was appointed in 1353 as Sergeant at Law to the Black Prince in Cheshire, Flint and elsewhere (at an annual fee of £5). He was still active in the service of the Black Prince in 1364 and he received a bonus of £4 out of the profits of the circuit court (the eyre) held in 1358 in the forest in Cheshire. Probably the most traumatic event in Sir William's life was the decimation of his family in the Black Death of 1348. Within three months he lost his father, his wife, three brothers, two sisters and a sister-in-law. Only his sister Cecilia was left.[16] In the years following Sir William enriched Crich Church by endowing two chantries there. He was not able, it seems, to use much of his Manor of Wakebridge as the basis of his endowment but instead was able to purchase lands in Crich and nearby settlements for that purpose.[17] It is likely that, from his public services, he had accumulated quite a fund of 'liquid assets' and when, after the Black Death land values became very depressed (Section 6.3) he was able to pick up a number of bargains to sustain his chantries. He needed permission from the Crown to do this and indeed obtained it - paying a fine of 10 marks (£6.$^2/_3$) to the King to transfer ownership of the lands involved for the purpose of endowment. Sir William's tomb is in the north aisle of Crich Church and has been frequently described[18].

Sir William de Wakebridge's sister Cecilia married Sir John de Pole of Hartington and on William's death the Manor of Wakebridge passed to Sir John and his son succeeded him.

2.4 Tudor Times

Another son of Cecilia, Sir Peter, founded the Poles of Radbourne one of whom, Reginald, became a Cardinal.[19] * Sir Peter was ward of the daughters of Robert Dethick of Dethick and one of those married Sir Thomas Babington - who took over the Manor of Dethick. After the Dissolution of the Monasteries the "Great Tithes" of Crich were granted by Henry VIII to the Babingtons of Dethick[20] and the 16th century barn at Dethick may have been built to hold the offerings.

In 1584 Anthony Babington - a descendant of Sir Thomas - sold, to John Claye of Crich, his land in Crich, Plaistow Green and Edge Moor and also the tithes, to support his attempt to free Mary, Queen of Scots, who was held a prisoner in Wingfield Manor for a total of about six months after 1569 - on the last occasion in 1584 before she was taken to Tutbury by Sir Ralph Sadler.[21] Before setting out Sadler sent off a scouting party of two men "to see if there were any way passable with coach and carriage" if he went by Mercaston. They reported "there was no other possible way for a coach but the common way and scant that at that time of the year by reason of hills, rocks and woods". Sadler then explored the way himself and actually built some bridges "to avoid many evil passages" but he was driven to use the road by Derby that was very little better.[22]

There is a local legend that in order to get Mary out of Wingfield Manor, Anthony Babington and his accomplices started to dig a tunnel some distance away from the Manor with the object of burrowing under the walls and coming up into the suite where Mary was being kept.[23]

The Crich Manor House just below Edge Moor, known in more recent times as the "Pot House" [353565] had a room in it called the "Queen's Room".[24] This had an ornate plaster ceiling and elaborate wall panelling and, it was said, was prepared to receive Mary when she escaped from Wingfield Manor. No evidence for the existence of Babington's tunnel to Wingfield Manor has been found. Nevertheless when the Pot House was being demolished in the late 1950's the workmen thought they'd found a tunnel heading towards Wingfield Manor. This tunnel turned out to be a large drain or sough passing under the house. At a later stage in the demolition when the lower part of the Queens Room was being knocked down, the workmen found steps leading downwards to a passage heading towards Edge Moor.[25] It was blocked by a fall before it reached the line of Dark Lane and its exit on the hillside has not been discovered. Had Mary been in the Pot House (the Crich Manor House) and had it been surrounded by the Earl of Shrewsbury's men it would have been possible - if the passage towards Edge Moor emerged in the shrub and trees under the Edge - to escape along this route. It is possible that this passage was the source of the legend of Babington's escape tunnel. Whatever the historical foundation of the legend, what is known is that Babington's conspiracy was discovered and it failed. Anthony Babington and six others were executed for high treason in September 1586.[26] As is recorded on a memorial in Dethick Church, the traitors were hung, drawn and quartered. Mary, Queen of Scots, was herself executed in February 1587.

When Anthony Babington's estate was sequestrated at the time of his execution two farms at Crich were granted to Sir Walter Raleigh (they had been omitted from Babington's sale to Claye) but Raleigh sold them quite soon.[27]

---

* Reginald Pole opposed Henry VIII's divorce and fled the country to Rome. His mother, Margaret, Countess of Salisbury was beheaded - together with other relations - by Henry VIII for conspiracy against Henry; but when Mary Tudor ascended the throne Reginald returned to England to become Archbishop of Canterbury.

A descendant of William de Wakebridge's heir, Sir John Pole, was German Pole (nowadays Jermyn). He married Margaret, daughter of Edward de Ferrars (a member of the same family as the Earls of Derby). German Pole died in 1588 and Margaret married John Claye whose first wife Mary had died in 1583 and whose father had been 'Chief Cock Matcher and Servant of the Hawks' to Henry VIII. Nevertheless, when Margaret died she was buried in Crich Church in the same tomb as German.[28] A plaque showing both German and Margaret dressed in Tudor gowns and ruffs is fixed to the north wall of the chancel at the east end: it was originally part of their tomb.

John Claye (whose grandfather John came from Chapel-en-le-Frith and had also lived in Crich) built a manor house[29] next to the north-west corner of the Churchyard [347547]. In 1597 John Claye (then said to be 'of Wakebridge') was one of the gentlemen of Derbyshire who was 'requested' to make a 'loan' to the Crown.[30] These loans were requested from Counties by the Privy Council acting on behalf of Elizabeth. The Earl of Shrewsbury delegated the job of collecting the money from Derbyshire to John Manners and on an earlier occasion on 7th May 1589 he had written to John Manners, his brother-in-law, to say that he was "troubled to hear of slackness of those gentlemen who ought to be most favoured to do the Queen's Pleasure" - and he recommended that new 'privy seals' be delivered to those in arrears and warning them of the need to make payment by an early date. The Privy Seal was the official document demanding the particular share of the 'loan' assigned to a particular person, sealed with the royal privy seal, and sent down to their local agent in the provinces by the Council. John Manners was beset with requests from many of those to whom privy seals had been addressed - one such being John Claye. Later that year (1589) the Earl of Shrewsbury was informed from the Court that "sums of £50 imposed under a Privy Seal on John Claye of Crich be reduced to £25 - as they have large families and are in debt".[31] Building the Manor House and buying the tithes from Anthony Babington must have upset Claye's cash-flow.

In 1606 there is, in the Talbot Papers, a record of an examination of one John Dakin concerning a report that John Claye of Crich, Gentlemen, had made certain slanderous speeches accusing the Earl of Shrewsbury of being forewarned of the Gunpowder Plot and of absenting himself from Parliament "under cover of his happy gout".[32]

Claye had three daughters Susanna, Mary and Elizabeth on whom, in 1612, he settled his estates[33]: he lived until 1632. He was a man of great local reputation: about thirty years later a building used to house a party of 41 'Friends' from Eyam being taken to Derby jail was referred to as Squire Claye's barn[34]: it could have been the barn to the north of the early 20th century graveyard.

Each of Claye's daughters married. Susanna married Robert Clark of Mansfield and Mary, Timothy Pusey of Selston. The third daughter Elizabeth married Sir William Willoughby of Wollaton Hall in Nottingham. (An earlier Sir William Willoughby had married Alice the daughter of Richard Curzon of Kedleston in the mid 15th century).

Elizabeth and William Willoughby had two children. One, Sir William, the heir to the baronetcy, died without issue and his estates passed to his sister Mary Willoughby who, in 1652, married Beaumont Dixie. Sir Beaumont - the 2nd Baronet and son of a former Sheriff of Leicestershire - had a son Wolstan who was father of the notorious 4th Baronet Sir Wolstan Dixie who, in 1731, briefly employed Samuel Johnson as an 'undermaster' in the school on his estate - Bosworth Park near Market Bosworth in Leicestershire.

2.5 The Civil War and Afterwards

Crich was not directly involved in the Civil War although many of the local families were. With their 'Roman' sympathies it is not surprising that the Babingtons of Dethick and the Poles of Wakebridge were on the side of the Royalists. So too were the heirs of John Claye. Beaumont Dixie's father, the lst Baronet - Sir Wolstan Dixie - was especially so, and "zealously espoused the royal cause at the breaking out of the rebellion of 1641"[35]. It may have been their influence which resulted in the naming of two local public houses - the "Kings Arms" and the "Royal Oak". Certainly some of the local gentry were punished "for malignancy" by the Puritan Parliament for their support of King Charles.

German Pole of Wakebridge had a comparatively small fine of £255. Timothy Pusey - who had married Mary Claye was charged £967 - which he was allowed to reduce by £500 on condition he paid £50 a year to Crich Church 'forever'.[36] Sir Wolstan Dixie the lst Baronet - who was father-in-law to Mary Willoughby (Elizabeth Claye's daughter) was fined £1835.

Not all the local aristocrats were on the side of the Royalists, however. Mary, the eldest daughter of the 7th Earl of Shrewsbury (Section 2.2) had married Phillip, the 4th Earl of Pembroke, and it was she who, on Gilbert's death, inherited Wingfield Manor. Pembroke supported Parliament in the Civil War and often represented it in negotiations with the King.[37] He defended Wingfield Manor but it was taken by the Earl of Newcastle in December 1643 and then retaken in the following year for Parliament by Sir John Gell of Hopton Hall. Great damage was caused by the four 36-pound cannons with which Gell bombarded the Manor and it was dismantled for military use in 1646.[38]

After the Restoration of Charles II Wingfield Manor passed to Immanuel Halton in 1678. He had been, at one time, Auditor to the Earl of Arundel and, after a fashion, repaired and refitted part of it. Eventually - much to the disdain of antiquarians - the Haltons used much of the masonry from the site to build a large house in the valley below the Manor. Immanuel Halton, who was both an astronomer and a mathematician, was living at the Manor in 1666 and in 1675 he observed a solar eclipse on which he wrote a treatise. It was he who encouraged John Flamsteed of Denby by trying to teach him mathematics.[39] Flamsteed became one of the most notable astronomers of his day.

At the time of the Restoration of Charles II the families of the three Shrewsbury heiresses - presumably to meet their losses in the Civil War and its aftermath - in 1660 began to sell their lands and manorial rights in Wingfield and Crich.

The Hon. Henry Howard, son of the Earl of Arundel, sold his share in 1660 to Anthony Bennet and Ralph Smith for £3270.[40] The deed of sale mentions the property as including one third of each of:

>the Chase of Crich
>Culland Park
>a limestone quarry
>a red-lead mill
>a water corn mill

Bennett and Smith sold two-thirds of their mineral rights - which were divided up into many shares then owned by separate individuals including Thomas Wright of Fritchley. (Section 5.2) The Countess of Kent passed her share to her uncle Edward, the 8th Earl of Shrewsbury. The lands were sold in 1710 and then soon afterwards were resold in comparatively small lots to local people. The manorial rights were sold - one third of the Manor of Crich - in 1711 to a William Sudbury and others. In 1841 they were in the possession of, amongst others, Samuel Travis of Crich, Gentleman; Richard Arkwright Esquire of Willesley Castle; Samuel Towndrow of Crich, Yeoman; Thomas Towndrow of Crich, Farmer and the Topham families of Ripley and Belper. (Section 5.2)[41]

The Countess of Pembroke's one third share of her father's estate passed to the Earls of Thanet who held some mineral rights in Crich at least until 1841 and who, at the time of the Enclosure Award in Crich[42] in 1784, also retained some lands in the parish (in the Thorpe Hill - Culland area).

In 1724 the then Lord of the Manor of Wakebridge, John Pole, died and the manor passed to his great nephew, whose brother and heir Edward sold it to Peter Nightingale of Lea (a forbear of the famous Florence). (Section 2.7)

2.6 The Manor of Alderwasley

There was another local family which had great influence in Crich - the Lords of the Manor of Alderwasley. Alderwasley, part of Colebrook Ward in Duffield Frith, had been given, in the 13th century, as a dowry to Margaret de Ferrars and after the Simon de Montfort rebellion, when the Ferrars were dispossessed, it went to John of Gaunt, Earl of Lancaster and so to the Crown.[43] Anthony Lowe I, who died in 1555 and who had then served Henry VII, Henry VIII, Edward VI and Queen Mary, was made Lord of the Manor of Alderwasley by Henry VIII as a reward for services rendered.[44] Anthony Lowe was a descendant of Thomas Lowe who had married the heiress of the Fawne family in 1471. The Fawnes were Lords of the Manor of Shining Cliff - which was originally granted to William Fawne in 1285 by Edmund, Earl of Lancaster.[45] Thus Anthony became Lord to the two adjacent Manors of Alderwasley and of Shining Cliff.*

Just below Shining Cliff [334523] there is a survival of one of the ancient forges of Duffield Frith which were common at places not far from Belper and which gave rise to the industry of the Belper Nailers. (Section 9.1).

One of Anthony Lowe's descendants, Elizabeth Lowe, who had married Nicholas Hurt of Casterne in Staffordshire, inherited the manor of Alderwasley from her father John Lowe after the death of her brother John in 1690 (he was 39 years old). Elizabeth died in 1713 aged 62.

It was the Hurt family who established Crich Stand. It was originally a wooden structure with a platform from which the countryside could be viewed. Then, in 1785, the Francis Hurt of that time (there were between 1722 and 1878 five Francis Hurts in the family succession), rebuilt it as a stone, conical tower with a wooden platform on top. This was in ruins by 1843 and it was dismantled six years later and rebuilt in 1851, at a cost of £210 as a round, stone tower[46] (photographs of which exist today). This was struck by lightning in 1908 and was badly damaged. The present Sherwood Foresters memorial was built in 1923 (Section 10.16).

Not far from the peak of Haytop [333534] and between it and the Deercote in Alderwasley Park there are today the remains of an ancient yew tree - known as "Betty Kenny's Tree". In the late 18th century, Luke Kenyon - locally pronounced as Kenny - built a cabin roofed with turf

---

* Shining Cliff - in the early 20th century - was notable for being covered with rhododendron. In Spring it really did shine, but it must have shone for some other reason long before rhododendron were introduced into the United Kingdom in 1656. The Himalayan types of rhododendron were not brought to England until their introduction by Sir Joseph Hooker in 1849-51.

(which was used as a bedroom) near the hollow yew tree which served as living space and he and his wife Kate - also known as Betty - brought eight children into the world in this 'home'.[47] It is said that a hollowed-out section of one of the branches was used as a crib by each of the babies in turn - one of whom died in infancy and was buried nearby in the wood. Luke was a charcoal burner from Papplewick in Nottinghamshire and, according to an 18th century account book (held by an Ambergate farmer who recorded charges for moving Luke's equipment and goods about the countryside) he operated both in Alderwasley Woods and in Crich Chase. It is likely that one of his principal customers was Hurt's Ironworks at the "Forge" [341523] alongside the Derwent (Section 9.1).

Early in the 19th century the Hurts arranged for James Ward R.A. to paint portraits of both Luke and Betty. Luke, who was then 96, complained that he found the room in the Hall where he was sitting for his portrait to be "draughty". Luke died after he and his wife had been assaulted - whilst still living in the tree - and robbed of their life savings of £10. Betty is supposed to have taken part in a dance at the Hall after her hundredth birthday.

The Hurts were considerable benefactors to Crich, contributing to the 'restoration' of the Church in 1861[48] and the erection of the Fritchley Mission Church and School in 1870.[49] In 1859 they demolished the old "Hob Hall" [342537] and erected the present house Chase Cliffe[50] on the site*. The Misses Hurt, who were so active in 'good deeds' in the parish lived there - and are commemorated by a stained-glass window in the south wall of the chancel at Crich Church. The house is the nearest modern equivalent in the village to a Manor House. Even after the Hurts left Alderwasley Hall in the 1930s and until the 1939-45 war there were deer roaming in Alderwasley Park[51].

Nowadays there are not many rhododendron on Shining Cliffe and Hay Top but, before World War II - when there was a disastrous fire - the whole of the east bank of the Derwent up to Alderwasley Park was a glorious sight in early summer when the rhododendron, covering the whole area, were in bloom.

2.7 The Manor Houses in Crich

As is to be expected, with many links over the centuries between aristocratic families and what is now the Parish of Crich, there have been, at one time and another, several important "houses" in the area.

Information on FitzRalph's Manor (later occupied by Ralph de Frecheville) and the Canon's Court - which was, clearly, not far away from it - is given in the Darley Abbey Cartulary.[52] The main clues to their location are given in Table B and the items mentioned there are associated, in Table C, with field names listed in the schedule to the 1839 Crich Rating Survey.[53]

A starting point for trying to determine where the 13th century Manor and Court were is the location of St. Thomas' Mount - so named in the late 12th or early 13th century after Thomas a Beckett had been assassinated in 1170. It is reasonable to suppose (and such an assumption fits in well with the 'picture' developed below) that the small hill on which the Church is built is St. Thomas's Mount. It is clearly identifiable as a separate 'hillock' from several directions - for instance from Hog Nick [354553] or from Stones [345545].

According to the Cartulary, FitzRalph's demesne (or home farm) included a "furlong" (Section

---

* There is a figure on a gable at Chase Cliffe representing a stag pierced by an arrow. The legend is that the first member of the family to be called Hurt was so called because when out hunting with the King, when the King's arrow hit a stag, the King claimed a kill and his equerry said "No Sire - tis only hurt". He was, on the spot, dubbed "Hurt".

6.1) stretching from St. Thomas' Mount to the front of the grange of the Canons of Darley Abbey. This was adjacent to the Canon's Furlong which stretched from St. Thomas' Mount to the Merewelsiche.[54] The word ending 'siche' (perhaps attached to a well on the way to Morwood) indicates a piece of land beside a stream ('sick' is the modern equivalent and is not uncommon on Ordnance Survey Maps of North Derbyshire). It is consistent with other data (see below) to suppose that the stream concerned* is the one which drains the land to the east of Crich Hill and flows down to the Dimple Valley by the eastern edge of the Old Quarry.

It could have been this stream which fed the 'fish pond' commemorated in the name of Fishpond House [349550]. It was the habit of religious houses in medieval times to cultivate carp and other fish in ponds or stews (which were tanks for keeping live fish for the table - the canons being fond of tasty protein on Fridays !). It is reasonable, then, to suppose that the Canon's Court was not far from Fishpond House - if not actually on its site.

In Figure 6 the stream and the church, on the summit of St. Thomas' Mount, are shown. There are also areas shown which, it can be supposed, were, in medieval times, common fields, pastures and meadows for the whole village.

Until the 1786 Enclosures there were areas along the route of the old Ridgeway ((Section 4.1) shown in Figure 6) which were common ground and were not, until then, enclosed. There is also evidence that the area to the north of the present day "Ten-Acre-Lane" (running from the bottom of the lane up the hill to the Stand on to Sycamore House) was a common field of strip-holdings between Cliff Side and Plaistow Green. Along each of the boundaries of the land being enclosed in 1786 are shown, on the Enclosure Map (See Figure 8), the names of the proprietors of the adjacent lands. There are many such - and at frequent intervals - as indeed would happen if there had been, in the area, a 'strip-field-common' which had already been enclosed before 1786. Thus the name of Nathaniel Curzon appears five times between Sycamore House [351554] and Plaistow [350565]. It also appears five times on the boundary to the east of the land enclosed in 1786 on the Cliff side between Wakebridge and the Cliff Inn. On the south side of the Ten-Acre-Lane there are two "Town Fields" and Wig Meadow. Wig meadow could be the Wigesbuttes mentioned in Cartulary 554 (Table C). 'Wiges' may have been corrupted elsewhere to 'Wicks' which, in more recent times, is the word used to describe the outlying part of a farm and the "buttes" was a site used for practising archery, which would probably be on the edge of the common ground of the village. Again on the other side of the stream shown as the boundary of Hays Land there are two fields known as "Undertown Field" (Figure 6). Hays Land is a more modern version of the medieval "Le Hey" which meant a fenced-in piece of land or a part of a forest enclosed for preserving game.

Le Hey (perhaps owned by Hubert FitzRalph) would stand between the 'village pastures' (Undertown Field) and the 'common pastures' (Wig Meadow and the Town Fields adjacent to the medieval village strip holdings to the east of Stand Lane) mentioned in Cartulary 551.**

The "road to Wessington" (Cartulary 543 and Figure 6) is most probably the path used by Wessington villagers coming through Hog Nick to Crich Church - which still exists and on part of which (in 1987 at least) the remains of a causeway through the Wig Meadow were still to be found (Section 4.3).

---

* It is, nowadays, much less vigorous than it was before the Hollins Sough and the Fritchley Sough (Section 8.4) took away water from Crich Hill.
** All references to Cartulary are taken from the 1945 publication "The Cartulary of Darley Abbey", edited by R. A. Darlington. Page numbers are given.

If, as in Table C and Figure 6, it is supposed that:

i) the three Parsons Closes are the six acres given by Hubert Fitzralph to the Canons (Cart.543)

ii) the Canon's Furlong included Bottom Piece and Hall Croft (Cart.545)

iii) the "Three Acres" is Ralphs furlong abutting his garden and running from St. Thomas' Mount to Merewelsiche (Cart.554)

iv) the two fields named Hall Croft suggest the presence of at least one important building nearby

- then it is implied that the Manor was just to the north of the Church - as indicated by the symbol on Figure 6.

The position of the Canon's Court cannot be postulated with the same confidence. It could have been on the site of the present-day Fishpond House for the exchange of land in Cartulary 554 for part of what is now Fishpond Close for land in Wig Meadow Pingle would have been reasonable if the Canons wanted to enlarge their court on the site of Fishpond House: also, of course, a site favourable for building tends to get re-used if it is not too remote. No traces of another building in the same area are known, but if the Canon's Court was not at Fishpond House it can reasonably safely be assumed that it was somewhere near or in "Near Parsons Close": the symbol in Figure 6 is, of course, only indicative.

To revert to FitzRalph's Manor. The building of Crich Church started in the 12th century,[55] probably while FitzRalph was living in his 'manor'.[56] Until at least the early 18th century (recorded by Bassano) there was a door* in the north wall of the church opposite to that now covered by the present-day porch on the south wall.

Such a door would be a preferred entrance to the Church from buildings between it and the present-day "Folds Yard" [347547]. It would be made during the building and rebuilding of the church in the 13th century (Section 5.2). This was long before John Claye - in the later part of the 16th century had his manor** near or on the same site as the FitzRalph and Frecheville manor. If this was indeed the site of the original Crich Manor House - the core of the Lord of the Manor's demesne - it would not be unexpected that there would be a sheep fold nearby (Folds Yard) nor that in ground running down the Mount toward the Merewelsiche there would be a dovecote and a calf croft (see Figure 6).

The fact that the FitzRalph Manor could be on such a prime site should not be surprising. It had easy access to water at the Holywell [345546] (vandalised and destroyed in the 1970s) - even if it did not have its own well - and it was near to the church.

From a Manor on that site it would be possible to take long views over the surrounding countryside with aspects open to the Tors, and to the Canons Wood (Appendix), to Culland Park, to Plaistow and Edge Moor and to Crich Hill, which would be a good look-out post in time of trouble - and westwards over Benthill. It would also be possible to overlook most of the common land in the village (Section 6.1) - before there were any significant enclosures at all. For all these reasons then, it is deduced that FitzRalph's Manor was located as suggested by the symbol in Figure 6.

---

* The northern doorway could be traced in the masonry until the 1980s when an Annex to the Church was erected just outside it with access from the main body of the church through the wall at its position.

** Parts of a building of the 16th century can be identified in the dwelling at present on the site - see below.

There was also, in the immediate vicinity to the north, an area of comparatively level and well-drained ground between it and the foot of Crich Hill. This could have formed the basis of the demesne's arable land and, overall, it was not too exposed. A minor consideration was that there would be a fairly easy journey around the edge of the common land to the east of Crich Hill to the Manor of Wakebridge.

When Ralph de Frecheville II parted with his manorial rights in the Parish of Crich (Section 2.1) to Sir Roger Beler in about 1325 it is possible that he retained his residence in the village. This could have been the reason why Sir Roger Beler built a new Manor House in a more sheltered and separate place down on what is now the Market Place - out of what was then the centre of the village.

A picture of Sir Roger Beler's Manor House (on the site of the present-day Baptist Chapel) was painted in about 1728 and remained in the manor house - then called Wheeldon House (Section 5.3) until the property was sold to the Baptists in the latter part of the 19th century. The picture - once owned by Denis Bower of Crich - is now in Chiddingstone Castle in Kent. It shows the 'cliff' at the north end of the Tors, what is now Bown's Hill, the building itself, its gardens and roads in the vicinity at the time. In the present context, particularly, it indicates that most of the buildings in the village were located around the Church, which, even as late as the beginning of the 18th century was still, obviously, the 'centre of the village'.

Years after Beler had built his Manor House and after the Frechevilles had left the Crich scene it is within belief, when John Claye came to establish himself as a 'local squire' and married into the family owning the Wakebridge Manor estates (Section 2.3), that he should build on the site of FitzRalph's original Manor House at the north-west corner of the churchyard. He might, indeed, have incorporated parts of the older Manor House into his own.

There is no doubt about the location of Sir William de Wakebridge's Manor House.[57] The foundations of the old manor house can be traced in the turf behind the present-day Wakebridge Farm [338558]. After the Black Death when Sir William devoted himself to religious activities he built a chapel at his Manor House "garnished" with an "orgayne and other costly devices"[58] and an inventory of the chapel's possessions is given in the Crich Cartulary under the date 1368. The east window of the chapel which had been incorporated into a barn was still in place in 1818 but in about 1850 it was taken out and taken to the Nightingale residence at Lea. Peter Nightingale had bought the Wakebridge estate in 1717 and had demolished the old manor but had left the chapel intact. There was, however, a relic of the Manor House in the Wakebridge Farm building at least as late as the 1920s. This was a 15th century door made of oak which was then in use in the farm kitchen. It was panelled in the linen-fold pattern and had a band of ornament resembling that on the tower parapet of Crich Church. A drawing of the door is given by Tudor.[59]

One of the Crich Manor Houses stood on Dark Lane [353564] below Wheatcroft. This curious-looking house (again a drawing is given by Tudor)[60] was obviously constructed over several periods of time - the levels of the windows on the upper floors are quite different on the two sides of the facade on either side of the main doorway. The earlier-built unit may have been the house prepared to receive Mary Queen of Scots - had she been able to get out of Wingfield Manor.[61] The ceiling of the "Queen's Room" is also illustrated by Tudor. In the mid-19th century the building, then known as the "Pot House" was bequeathed to Mary Marshall (Section 2.9). A modern house has been built on the site.

There was another, minor, house of importance and still occupied, at the north side of the Dimple Green [351542]. It was built as the croft house to the Beler Manor and a lintel dates it as of 1667. The inscription on the lintel says:

> "Remember thy time
> All flesh must die"

and there is a similar motto on the stone overmantel on the fireplace in the sitting room of the house. Attached to the end of the house was the original, Victorian, Chapel Sunday-School Reading Room.

Again, at the foot of Bown's Hill [350542], is a building known as the "Mansion House" which dates from the 17th century and, at the top of Bown's Hill a house called "The Mount" - both of these houses are to be seen on the 1728 painting now in Chiddingstone Castle.

2.8 Important Landowners

After the sales of land and manorial rights in Crich Parish in the late 17th century (Section 2.5) there were many resales, divisions and amalgamations of holdings. The pattern of land ownership at the time of the 1786 Enclosures is indicated in Table D. Figure 7 shows the areas of the parish used in the Table to locate the various holdings and allotments. Landowners of note were :

> The Duke of Devonshire
> The Hurts of Alderwasley
> The Smiths
> The Bowmers
> Sir Robert Meade Wilmot
> Hon. Nathaniel Curzon

The Duke of Devonshire had inherited land through the Shrewsburys (Section 2.2); the Hurts had 'bought-in' to Crich from their neighbouring Manor of Alderwasley; the Smiths - through Ralph - had purchased land and rights from the Howards in 1660 (Section 2.5) and the Bowmers had been yeoman farmers in the Wingfield Park and Fritchley areas for generations (there was a Thomas Bowmer at Barn Close Farm, Fritchley in 1661).[62]

Sir Robert Meade Wilmot, the 2nd Baronet, was the owner of what was formerly known as "Dixie-land".[63] This was an area along Edge Moor and Plaistow Green. It had passed into the hands of Dame Mary Dixie who had inherited through her mother (also Mary) who was Elizabeth Willoughby's daughter (Elizabeth was daughter of John Claye (Section 2.4)). Dame Mary was great-grandmother of Sir Wolstan Dixie the 5th Baronet (1737-1806) who retained the grant of the living or 'benefice' (the advowson) of Crich Church.[64] Lady Dixie sold her estate in Crich to a Thomas Morley - a potter (Section 9.4). In turn Morley sold several parcels of land to various people and the remainder to a Mrs. Millicent Fuller of Nottingham, who was a widow. She left it to her grandson Robert Musters also of Nottingham. Musters and his wife - around 1747 - sold part of their property to an officer of excise, Dehurst Bilsborough and the remainder to Edward Wilmot - the Dr. Wilmot who was to become Sir Edward Wilmot Bart in 1759 (Section 3.14).

The other notable landlord in 1786, the Hon. Nathaniel Curzon, was a member of the old Derbyshire family descended from John Curzon of Kedleston who was High Sheriff of Derbyshire and Nottinghamshire in 1437. His son, Richard of Kedleston (d.1496) married Alice, a daughter of Sir Robert Willoughby of Wollaton in Nottinghamshire.[65] His daughter Elizabeth was

Prioress of Kings Mead (St. Mary de Pratis) in Derby from 1514 to her death in 1525. The convent, not far from present-day Friargate, was small - but famed for its school where young Derbyshire ladies were educated. In 1514 Elizabeth leased, for 60 years, to John Pole (son and heir of Ralph Pole of Wakebridge)[66] the field called "Nunsfield" above Millgreen on the Dimple [358535]. After the dissolution of the monasteries, Henry VIII granted the field to John Bellowe and Robert Bygott*.

It is, perhaps, of some relevance that Alice Curzon's grandson - also a Richard - married, in the 1520s, Helena - a daughter of German Pole of Radbourne. German Pole of Wakebridge - first husband of Margaret Claye (Section 2.4) - had, for his first wife married his relative Jane, daughter of German Pole of Radbourne.[67] This is another link with the Claye family !

Altogether then there were several associations between Crich and the Curzons of Kedleston. Furthermore, junior branches of the Curzon family were also linked with the parish. One connection was with George Curzon of Croxell.[68] He was the brother of Joan Curzon who was burnt at the stake in 1557 by Queen Mary who abhorred her Protestantism. George married Katherine Babington - sister of Anthony, the archetypal Catholic who had owned the Great Tithes and much property in Crich Parish. After Babington's properties were sequestrated (Section 2.4) some remnants were 'enjoyed' by Francis Babington - either a brother or nephew of Anthony - who settled in Leicestershire. Property in Crich may have reached the Curzon family thereby. The Nathaniel Curzon shown as owner of much land, in various parts of Crich Parish in the 1786 Enclosure Award (Table D) was to become Baron Scarsdale. He appears as Lord Scarsdale in the 1847 Tithe Apportionment (Table E). Of course Crich had very old connections with the Hundred of Scarsdale.[69] Although in Morleystone and Litchurch, Crich is on the border of Scarsdale and as early as 1215-22 Hubert FitzRalph had given the advowson of Scarcliff to the canons of Darley Abbey "for the souls of himself, Edelina his first wife and Sara his second wife".[70] Again, in 1569 Wryley noted that Amicia Musard had married Anker de Frecheville (Section 2.1) and that Anker who held the Manor of Crich in the 13th century (he died in 1268) also held the Barony of Staveley in the Hundred of Scarsdale in his wife's right. Eventually the Hundred of Scarsdale passed to the Countess of Kent, Joanna, and when she died without issue in 1442 it passed to Richard Nevile the Earl of Salisbury through his wife Alice. Their line also failed and in the reign of Edward IV Richard, Duke of Gloucester and Anne, his wife (who was cousin and heir to Alice) gave Scarsdale to the King in exchange for property in Yorkshire (which included Scarborough Castle).[71] By exchange again, the Hundred of Scarsdale passed to George the Earl of Shrewsbury - who had it when he died in 1592. Once again then, the Manors of Crich and Scarsdale were in the same hands. George's son Gilbert - the 7th Earl - sold the Manor of Chesterfield and the rights of the Scarsdale Hundred to William Cavendish, Earl of Newcastle in 1612.

There is another noble family linked with the Cavendishes who are recorded as holding rights in Crich Parish. The Earl of Thanet appears as Lord of the Manor in the 1786 Crich Enclosure Award and he was granted an allotment on the Cliff. He also was joint owner of some land down the Dimple. The Earls of Thanet were mostly associated with Westmorland[72] - although Thomas Tufton, Earl of Thanet and Lord Clifford, married, probably at Welbeck in 1684, Catherine the daughter and co-heir of Henry Cavendish - who was associated with the Shrewsburys through Bess of Hardwick, whose second husband was a Cavendish.

---

* In both the 1839 Rating Survey and the 1849 Tithe Apportionment, Nunfield Close is shown as owned by John Bowmer. In 1839 there was a house and garden occupied by one William Peat about half-way up the field from Millgreen

The line became extinct in 1849 with the death of Henry Tufton. Before then, however, he had sold his mineral rights on Crich Cliff in 1841 (together with Samuel Travis, Richard Arkwright, Samuel, Thomas and David Towndrow, John Topham and others) to a consortium including George and Robert Stephenson, Sir Joshua Walmsley and George Hudson (Section 7.5).[73]

2.9 Humbler Crich People

With the exception of the Hurts - who acquired land and manorial rights in the parish - in the hundred years on from the Civil War and possibly as a result of it, the influence locally of the old aristocratic families, based on their manors and inherited rights, with their records of succession and possession, began to wane; even though they retained some mineral rights and some church patronage. 'Control' of village life by the Established Church also became less comprehensive as non-conformism became more widespread and more acceptable.

From about the beginning of the eighteenth century local initiatives increasingly passed to the humbler local people engaged directly, either as 'owner-managers' or 'workers' in farming, in lead mining and stone working and eventually in manufacture. Their story is more diffuse and anonymous even though baptisms, marriages and burials are recorded in Church Registers.[74] In Crich the registers date from 1564. Between 1572 and 1587 and again from 1593 to 1600 pages of the register are missing and even when records are available the peculiar style of writing means that they are not easily decipherable. Nevertheless, names appear which - in recent times - still identify local families.

Such are :

Babington	Flynte (Flint)
Bunting	Daws (Dawes)
Curzon	Wetton (sometimes written Wotton)
Claye	Wylde
Bryan	Poole
Smith	Redfern
Radford (sometimes written Redfort or Redford)	

The register from 1600 to 1654 is fairly complete but the entries on the parchment pages, from age and exposure, are now almost indecipherable. However, some of the entries at intervals may still be read and the names of :

Bollington	Boamer (Bowmer)
Bembridge	Sellars
Ludlam	Holmes
Haslam	Allyn (Allen)
Martyn (Martin)	Berrisford
Piggin	Fritchley
Cowlishaw	Greener (Greenough)

appear. Families with these names were still resident in Crich Parish in the first half of the 20th century.

By a happy chance a copy of a diary kept by one Denman Mason has become available and it gives some insight into middle-class affairs in Crich in the mid-19th century.[75] Denman's father Edwin Mason was, it seems, an easy-living man who had frittered away his property. In a diary note of 20th March 1868 Denman recorded that his father was just recovering from a drinking bout which had lasted about three weeks. (Such bouts were not at all uncommon in Victorian and Edwardian times and - as noted in "The Crich Tales"[76] - were still occurring in the 1920s and 1930s). Moreover Edwin had sold two cows, his pony and trap and other things - "for a supply of drink". Denman said of his father that he had been "nothing but a scatterer during the whole of his life". Denman's mother was Julia. Her father had been Ralph Wheeldon Smith, who was a direct descendant of the Ralph Smith who, in 1660, had acquired part of the property and some of the manorial rights in Crich from Henry Howard - of the House of Arundel.

Two of Julia's brothers, Rupert and Thomas, emigrated to Australia and it seems that Julia had sent Denman out to Australia to live with his uncles hoping to give him a better start in life than he might expect in Crich. But times in Australia were hard. The uncles were farmers and butchers and on 8th April 1868 Denman recorded in his diary that, although butchers in Crich could sell second quality beef at 8d a pound and mutton at $7 \frac{1}{2}$ d a pound, in Melbourne, Australia it was reported that good mutton was only fetching 1d or 2d a pound. In the hope of restoring their fortunes, Uncles Rupert and Thomas sent Denman back to England to progress the settlement of his grandfather's estate. He arrived in Crich on 31st August 1866 and his diary covers the period from then to July 1869.

His grandmother, now Mary Marshall, was a widow and in her eighties and was living in a cottage near Dial Farm [352535]. Mary had married William Marshall after the deaths of her two previous husbands; John Mason (father of Edwin) and Samuel - brother of Ralph Wheeldon Smith. Denman also had an uncle Ralph W. Smith living in Crich - at Fishpond House [348530] at the foot of the last peak of Crich Hill.

William Marshall had bequeathed the Crich Manor House below Edge Moor - the "Pot House" - to Grandmother Mary. When this was put up for sale of 16th October 1866 Denman Mason was given authority, as her agent, to receive the monies from the sale.

Ralph Wheeldon Smith had owned much property in Crich and at one time lived in Roger Beler's 14th century Manor House on what is now Crich Market Place and which was renamed Wheeldon House. The Smiths also owned Fishpond House; "the Common House", where Aunt Smith had entertained John Wesley a century earlier: land on the Nether, the Upper and the Middle Cliff as well as rights (lot and cope - Section 8.1) in a local lead mine, fishing rights on the Derwent and so on. Some of these were sold - as a step towards settling Ralph Wheeldon Smith's estate - on 25th February 1867 at the "Jovial Dutchman" at Crich Cross. The last sale of R. W. Smith's property also took place at the "Dutchman" about a year later on 14th January 1868. On that occasion the Butterley Company bought the Cliff Land for £62 per acre and S. Radford of Bullbridge bought the Common Farm for £751.

Ralph Smith, who had been living at Fishpond House when his son, and Denman's cousin, Joseph Smith had died there (aged 18) on 29th August 1867, moved to Wheeldon House in February 1868. (It had been standing empty for over three years). Denman Mason helped his cousin Susannah to tidy-up the old front garden, which was in a very bad state. He contrasted it with its condition when his Grandmother - as wife of Sam Smith - took pride and tended it with so much care.

Ralph Smith owned the "Jovial Dutchman" and on 23rd March 1868 Denman drew up an agreement for letting the inn to a Mr. Boole from Sheffield. Ralph also had the rent from Fishpond House and he drew an income of £1 a week (and travelling expenses) from the Crich Co-operative Society - a company of butchers - for "buying in and selling out". Denman thought this good pay for about three days work. Later, property-owner Ralph began working 'physically'. He started slaughtering cattle for the Co-operative Society and Denman used to help his uncle. For instance, on 5th March 1868 together they killed a cow and two sheep and on 12th March 1868 another cow. On 4th April 1868 Denman records helping his uncle in his shop (they had killed a 600 lb bullock on April lst). On 8th April 1868 they killed a calf and a sheep. Denman must have felt he had acquired skill as a butcher for, on 25th May 1868 he "wrote to Messrs. Money Wigram and Sons for a situation as butcher for the voyage out to the Colony".

He was ready to return to Australia but before he went he, on 30th September 1868, helped his Uncle Ralph by painting at the "old house on the green" (i.e. the Market Place) and he noted that Ralph had given-up butchering for the Crich Co-operative Society and was now in business for himself "in the old shop on the green". On 9th October 1868 Denman and Ralph slaughtered two cows and five sheep for Crich Fair. Ralph "sold out all the Wakes beef and has killed another cow, making his share three. I think Crich people are noted for beef eating, especially at the Wakes for this time there was 16 slaughtered in all".

In an earlier part of his diary Denman noted on 2nd September 1867 that Squire Hurt (of Alderwasley) and Squire Wass (of Holloway) had spent the day shooting on Crich Common and had called at the Mason house for refreshment - giving Denman "full permission to fish their rivers any time I thought well". The next day, 3rd September 1867, he recorded that he and his brother had a good day's sport - fishing on Gregory Pond (nowadays called Gregory Widehole on the Cromford Canal [328555]) on Squire Nightingale's land. They caught thirty-two roach and several perch. A few days later Denman "received a present of three brace of birds and one rabbit from Sir H. F. Every, Egginton Hall, as a return for the privelege of shooting over the Inkermill land" and on 13th September 1867 he had "a hare and brace of birds from Squire Buxton, being his annual present for the privelege of sporting over the Hilton Common land - now in the occupation of Mr. Blood". Both these were family properties.

So, although the Smiths and the Masons were no longer so prosperous as formerly, they were obviously in easy social contact with the local squirearchy - and recognised as "gentry".

[1] Phillimore (1978) *Domesday Book (27) Derbyshire* Chichester, Phillimore. p.10
[2] Cox J.C. (1879) *Notes on the Churches of Derbyshire*. Chesterfield, Edmunds. p.33
[3] Darlington R. A. (1945) *The Cartulary of Darley Abbey* Kendal. And other sources.
[4] Darlington Ibid p.xvi
[5] Craven M. (1987) *The Ancient Families of Derbyshire* Derby. Derbyshire Life and Countryside. Feb, Mar and April. II 60.
[6] Glover S. (1829) *History of the County of Derby* Derby, Mozley. Vol.II p.316
[7] Watkins A. (1952) *The Manor of Crich*. Manuscript p.13
[8] Glover Ibid. Vol.I p.73
[9] Watkins Ibid p.12
[10] Darlington Ibid p.560-570
[11] Cameron K. (1959) *The Place Names of Derbyshire* Cambridge, Camb.Univ.Press. p.437
[12] Burke (1967) *Peerage and Baronetage* London, Burke. p.655
[13] Tudor T.L. (1926) *The High Peak to Sherwood* London. Scott. p.257
[14] Saltman A. (1976) *The Cartulary of the Wakebridge Chantries at Crich* Derbys Arch.Soc.Record Series. Introduction.
[15] Cox J.C. (1879) *Notes on the Churches of Derbyshire* Chesterfield, Edmunds. p.42
[16] Cox Ibid p.44 Jeayes I.H. (1906) *Derbyshire Charters* London.Bemrose.
[17] Cox Ibid p.55

[18] Done A.B. (1912) *History of St.Mary's Church Crich* Belper. G.Gibson. p.7
[19] *Chambers Biographical Dictionary* (1984) Edinburgh, Chambers. p.1070
[20] Watkins Ibid. p.17-18
[21] Tudor Ibid. p.258
[22] Watkins Ibid. p.19
[23] Tudor Ibid. pp.244,246,259.
[24] Dawes J.G. (1983) *The Crich Tales* Cromford. Scarthin.
[25] Wragg J. (1985) Lecture : Fritchley OAP Friendship Club
[26] Chambers Biographical Dictionary. Ibid. p.75
[27] Glover Ibid. p.320
[28] Firth J.B. (1905) *Highways & Byways in Derbyshire* London.Macmillan. p.429
[29] Cox Ibid. p.58
[30] Cox J.C. (1890) *Three Centuries of Derbyshire Annals* Derby. Bemrose. Vol.II p.105
[31] Batho G.R. (1968) *A Calendar of the Talbot Papers* Derbys.Arch.Soc.Record Series Vol.4 G.417
[32] Batho Ibid. M.380
[33] Cox Ibid. p.59
[34] Davidson T. (1901) *Margaret Lynam:Quaker* Derby. Sainty. p.2
[35] Burke (1967) *Peerage and Baronetage* London Burke p.763
[36] Watkins Ibid p.26
[37] Clarendon (1703) *The History of the Great Rebellion* (OUP for the Folio Soc. 1967) p.237
[38] Watkins Ibid p.267
[39] Derbyshire Characters (1977) *Derbyshire Countryside* p.14
[40] Glover Ibid p.318 and in Hackett R.R.(1899) *Wirksworth and Five Miles Round* Wirksworth Brooks
[41] Garlick S. L. (1966) *Further Notes on Crich* Vol.3.8 Derbyshire Miscellany p.13
[42] Crich Enclosure Award (1786) Derbyshire Record Office. Q/RI 2
[43] Tudor Ibid p.239
[44] Hackett Ibid p.53
[45] Tudor Ibid p.240
[46] White (1857) *History Gazetteer and Directory of Derbyshire* Sheffield. White p.255
[47] Channon H. P. (1949) *Alderwasley and Shining Cliffe* The Derbyshire Advertiser 29.6.1949
[48] Done Ibid p.20
[49] *Kelly's Directory of Derbyshire 1908 Crich*
[50] *Kelly's Directory of Derbyshire 1895 Crich*
[51] Watkins Ibid p.12
[52] Darlington Ibid
[53] *Crich Rating Survey* (1839) Derbyshire Record Office D.1281/PI
[54] Field J. (1972) *English Field Names* Newton Abbott, David and Charles p.247
[55] Cox Ibid p.62
[56] Done Ibid p.15
[57] Cox Ibid p.66
[58] Cox (1879) Ibid p.65
[59] Tudor Ibid p.248
[60] Ibid p.244
[61] Dawes Ibid p.36

[62] Davidson Ibid p.1
[63] Watkins Ibid p.46
[64] Glover Ibid II p.353
[65] Craven M. (1987) *The Ancient Families of Derbyshire* Derby.Derbyshire Life and Countryside. Feb.Mar.April
[66] Jeayes I.H. (1906) *Derbyshire Charters* London.Bemrose.p.923-4
[67] Cox (1879) Ibid p.56
[68] Craven Ibid
[69] Darlington Ibid p.542
[70] Cox Ibid p.62
[71] Cox (1890) Ibid p.86
[72] *Complete Peerage* Vol.XII (White) p.695
[73] Garlick Ibid p.15
[74] Done Ibid p.17
[75] Mason D. (1866-69) *Diary*. (From Miss A. Mason of Sydney, Australia)
[76] Dawes Ibid p.44

1. Ambergate in the nineteenth century. The Hurt Arms stands on the left with outbuildings which are now gone. Also gone is the substantial toll booth which dominates the three-way road junction in this picture. The Cromford and Belper Turnpike Trust was established in 1817 to build a new road along the Derwent Valley

2. Crich Cross
This picture was taken before the Jovial Dutchman pub was given a major facelift and still had a thatched roof. The cross was refurbished in 1871, so the photo is no older than that

3. VILLAGE GOVERNMENT

3.1 In Anglo-Saxon Times

Before the death of Alfred the Great in 889 A.D. it was established[1] that the responsibility for keeping "The King's Peace"* [2] - the legal name for the normal state of society - fell upon the people in each locality.

The vill - which consisted of a village or an adjacent collection of settlements[3] - was the smallest unit of social government and one of the important functions it acquired was the 'policing' of the district. The problem was to discover and punish those evil doers whose actions disturbed the local society. The solution adopted was to require every male person, unless excused through high social position or property, to be enrolled in a group of about ten families - known as a tything - headed by a tythingman.

If any member of the group committed a crime the group could be fined or called on to make compensation if they could not produce him for trial. There was also an obligation on all members of the tything to join in pursuit of a felon who avoided or escaped arrest [hue and cry (Section 3.5)].

Groups of tythings were formed into a Hundred (or wapentake), the head man of which was known as the Hundred man, or reeve, and he exercised administrative and judicial powers through a 'Hundred Court'. This was under the supervision of the shire-reeve - or sheriff - who had the general responsibility, under the King, for preserving the peace of the shire. Canute, who in 1016 became king of what became the 'Danish Empire' in Britain, ordained that enrolment in a tything was compulsory: "And we will that every freeman be brought into a hundred and into a tything - as soon as he is 12 years old".[4]

Before the Norman Conquest in 1066, the local community in Crich was under the control of Leofric and Leonoth who were, it is thought, kin of Godwin the Saxon Earl of Wessex who died in 1053.[5] Between them they held thirty-two manors between Dinting in Longdendale and the Trent.[6] They were taxable on four bovates of land [Section 6.1].

3.2 After the Conquest

The Normans, the conquerors, hated and feared by the English, took over the tything system for maintaining peace but also introduced a system called 'frankpledge'. This imposed a charge for bail on a tything, fixed for individuals - not after their arrest for some crime, but as a safeguard in anticipation of it. It was a means of holding the natives in repression. The system was supervised by Sheriffs, who were Royal Officers and who held a special court

---

* A recent definition of the "King's Peace" was given by Newsam in 1954 - as follows: the maintenance of conditions under which the normal functions of civilised government can be carried on, where obedience to the law is adequately secured and the people are free to pursue their lawful ends without threat of interference.

which sat twice a year to make sure that all who ought to be enrolled in a tything and pledged for good behaviour were, in fact, covered by the frankpledge.

Originally members of a tything only had to produce one of their number when demanded as a 'hostage' by the authorities, but additionally the Assize of Clarendon of 1166 required villagers to report to the Sheriff's court of scrutiny - or 'tourn' - any suspicions they might harbour about one another, together with anything affecting the affairs of the vill. These 'presentments' were made by the tythingman to a jury of twelve free men of the Hundred, who forwarded serious accusations to the Sheriff. Information was not only demanded about felons but also about any suspicious characters "such as sleep by day and watch by night, and eat and drink well, and have nothing".

The system of 'bail-in-case-of-crime' and of informers was exploited by the Normans to keep the 'natives' under submissive control. As with so many conquerors (and not only in the military field) the Normans masked their nervousness by barbarity: many activities of the royal sheriff's tourn prompted revulsion. Men were deprived of their property and then killed - by 'legal' execution. Many were mutilated - having eyes gouged out either for minor offences or even when patently innocent in the eyes of their peers.

Eventually, as a result of intermarriage between Anglo-Saxons and Normans and in reaction to the excesses of the unpopular tourns, the 'royal' courts of the hundred were superseded by manorial courts - or courts leet - and there was a reversion to the Anglo-Saxon principle of locally-determined law-enforcement, when the freemen of the vill, sitting in the court-leet, decided on guilt and whether or not the case should be referred to a superior court.

3.3 The Sheriffs

Immediately after the Conquest the Sheriffs were direct royal appointments but as the Sheriff's tourn was deprived of its jurisdiction a new type of Sheriff, elected by all the principal inhabitants of the County, was given power*.[7]

Formerly the Sheriff was entrusted with all the business of the Sovereign in the Shire (at one time Nottinghamshire and Derbyshire were, together, under the same Sheriff - at Nottingham). The 'executive' government of the County was vested in the Sheriff**;[8] the Royal Warrant entrusted him with "the custody of the County". Specifically he:

- was the chief conservator of peace in the Shire
- executed the sentences and processes of the sovereign's court - both 'criminal' and 'civil'
- was the principal executive officer (at a later date) of the elections to the King's Parliament.

Eventually (Section 3.11) he was assisted by a Lord Lieutenant, who was head of the local military forces in the County, but even so the Sheriff could, even until the 19th century, summon the whole force of the County - a summons which each and every able-bodied commoner was required to obey under penalty of fine or punishment.

---

*In later centuries the Sheriff was again appointed by the Crown but this time out of a list of three or more men recommended by the judges and other higher officers of state.
**In 1361 Roger Beler of Crich was Sheriff for two years and in 1369 was appointed for another four years. In 1442 John Pole of Wakebridge was also appointed Sheriff of the County.

The Sheriff's Court - presided over by the local Sheriff - who was often the local Earl - was the main place in which all official business in the County was co-ordinated and through which royal writs were executed. Subordinate to it were the Hundred (or wapentake) courts and the monthly meetings of these courts heard cases concerning breaches of the peace, levied taxation and transacted business brought to them by private citizens. The manorial courts brought the more serious cases to the Hundred Court for consideration and were responsible for promulgating - at the level of the village - the requirements of superior legislation.

3.4 Manorial Courts

At the time of the Domesday Survey, the tenant-in-chief at Crich was Ralph FitzHubert. He, and his successors, who eventually became known as Lords of the Manor, did not actually 'own' the land in that they could do with it and its produce as they liked: but they were in control of it and were entitled to certain dues from its occupants. Ralph held his land on behalf of the Crown and was responsible immediately to the Sheriff of the County. In exchange for his possession of the estate he was required by the King to provide, on request, the services of an agreed number of 'knights' for military service. These armed serving men were kept, by the Lord of the Manor, about his hall. In 1166 the Crich Manor was held to be of value equal to 30 knight's fees (Section 2.1)

Usually when a knight's position became permanent he was given a parcel of land to provide him with an income. His 'farm' would be occupied by serfs who were required to work it for him.[9] Other people of the manor would include freemen - who were quite independent and could even choose under whose lordship and on which manor they would live. There were tenants of sokeland (sokemen) who were comparatively independent farmers (though they may have kept well in with the Lord of the Manor by giving him presents): however, although not required to labour on the Lord's demesne (or home farm)[10] they were bound to the land and were under the control of the Lord's manorial court - where they were required to serve and where they went for justice. In the 11th century there were, in Crich, three parcels of 'sokeland'.[11] The majority of the Crich villagers (ten plus two smallholders) would be villeins or lower orders of peasant and serf (Section 6.1). Such were required to provide labour-service to the Lord.

As time went by the elements of personal service - of the Lord of the Manor to the King; of knights, sokemen, villeins and subordinate classes to the Lord of the Manor - were replaced by money dues of one kind or another. The feudal landholder paid a money 'fine' (called scutage) to the Crown in lieu of personal service to the King and Knight's Fees were paid for release from the requirement to provide fighting men for the King (Section 2.1) The knights, no longer on direct call for military service, would pay rent for their land to the Lord of the Manor and through him to the King. Within the manor the sokemen were usually subject to a charge on their farm (a 'feorm') or annual food rent also due to the King. Such were early forms of 'national taxation'.

By the 12th century even villeins were paying 'rent' to the local Lord rather than labouring for him (Section 6.1).[12] By the end of the 13th century Lords everywhere were receiving more from tenants by way of rents - in money or in kind - than by way of service. In nearby Yorkshire perhaps no more than 10 percent of dues to the local landlords were in the form of actual personal service.[13] In Crich the proportion would probably be similar.

The local government of a parish or manor such as Crich was carried out through the local Lord's court, the court-leet or manorial court. National levies, for instance, the tribute known as 'custom' - in origin a food rent - at the time of Domesday were normally paid in coin and were handled through the manorial court. In 1086 Ralph Fitzhubert's dues for Crich were assessed at 30s 0d. Such courts dealing with the affairs of the local community - or vill - had the right from the Crown not only of collecting 'dues' (or taxes) but also of receiving fines for misbehaviour.*

One of the benefits the local Lord derived from the Manorial Court was that the 'profits' arising from fines on villagers went to him.[14] Under the Normans there were fewer freemen than there had been in Anglo-Saxon times and the contests in court were usually between the Lord of the Manor - or his agents - and peasants and serfs under his control.[15] The types of 'civil' case disputed in manorial courts and as such resulted in fines on villeins were for :

- not grinding corn at the Lord's mill
- diverting a water course
- paying rent in bad money
- delay in doing their service on the Lord's home farm or hall
- letting a daughter trespass in the corn

In some cases, records are available for fines exacted. Two examples are :

- 6s 0d for not going to wash the Lord's sheep
- 40s 0d for damage and 20s 0d for dishonour for unlawfully striking a certain Hugh de Stanbridge and dragging him by his hair out of his own proper house[16]. (This fine was imposed on the wife of a local notable's son - and her accomplice).

The scale of those fines - and the benefit to the local Lord can be judged when they are compared with a typical day's wage. At the end of the 13th century a day labourer (like a thatcher's mate) could earn 1d a day and a skilled man - a carpenter or a mason could, perhaps, earn 3d or 4d a day (see Figure 5).

A minor note of interest showing the range of the Manorial Courts is the payment to the Court (i.e. to the Lord of the Manor) by one Walter Hulle of 13s 4d (a mark) for a licence "to dwell off the manor so long as he shall live".

When the manorial courts took over the responsibility for keeping the Kings Peace locally from the Sheriff's tourn they also assumed the responsibility for electing, annually, the officers who were to serve their turn in assisting the Lord of the Manor to regulate the affairs of the community. The senior of these officers was the constable - an office dignified by that title in a statute of 1252[18] - others included the ale taster, the bread weigher and the swine ringer.

3.5 The Constables

The Statute of Winchester of 1285 had, as its objective : "to abate the power of felons", and it established the principle that it was the duty of everyone to maintain the Kings Peace and made it open to any citizen to arrest an offender.[19] It was the principal regulation covering the policing of the country between the Norman Conquest and the Metropolitan Police Act of 1829. Unpaid, part-time, constables had the special duty to arrest offenders and present them for judgement to the local court. Although somewhat later (Section 3.6) the village constable was put

---

* In 1086 Crich was under the jurisdiction of the Morleyston Wapentake - later combined with Litchurch to form the Morleyston and Litchurch Hundred.[17] A wapentake is a division of a Shire with its own court: equivalent to a Hundred in other parts of the country.

under the more direct control of the Justices of the Peace, his immediate supervisor was the Chief Constable of the Hundred. The village - or petty - constables were required to execute 'warrants' with which they had been charged by the Chief Constable (see below) and they had a number of 'standing responsibilities' including :

(i) organisation of the village 'watch and ward'. All able-bodied men of the village were put on a roster for regular service to provide for a due watch being kept in the village between sunset and sunrise.[20] The one acting for the constable on such occasions had the full legal powers of the constable, such as arresting till morning. The constable was in charge of the village lock-up - where there was one - used to retain a prisoner after arrest. (The Rating Survey of Crich of 1839 records that the parish was then required to pay rates on the village prison* - which was a small building of stone at the northern end of the block in which the Parish Room was to be found).[21]

(ii) starting a 'hue and cry', This was a way of dealing with alleged offenders who resisted arrest by the constable or one of his watchmen and who escaped. The fugitive was to be pursued by the whole population. Work had to be laid aside and anyone failing to respond to the call was regarded as siding with the fugitive and was himself restrained if necessary by a further 'chase'. (The progenitor of the Wild West 'posse' !)

(iii) the state of the parish stocks.

(iv) the presentation, eventually to Quarter Sessions, of lists of freeholders who could be called to give jury service to the Justices.

(v) the summoning of jurors within their parish.

In the early days after the Statute of Winchester was promulgated each male in the community between the ages of 15 and 60 was required to keep in his house "harness to keep the peace". Men of superior rank had to have "a hauberke and helm of iron, a sword, a knife and a horse": poor people were to have bows and arrows available.

In each Hundred two high constables were appointed by the Hundred Court to make a six-monthly inspection of arms so that, if called on, the citizens were equipped to take part in a hue and cry.

An oath used to swear-in a constable has been preserved on record. It requires the office-holder to keep the Kings Peace and, within the law, to "arrest all those who shall make any contest, riot, debate or affray in breaking said peace .... and bring them to the house of one of the Sheriffs .... and if you shall be withstood by strength of such misdoers, you shall raise upon them hue and cry and shall follow them from street to street and from ward to ward until they are arrested. And you also shall search at all times when you shall be required .... for the common nuisances of the ward until they are arrested".[22]

Although originally subordinate to the court-leet which appointed him, the constable eventually became the 'Justices man', even though he still remained the agent of the manor or parish. Like other officers, he was unpaid - though he could claim certain customary fees and expenses. Often the office of village constable was filled in rotation by occupiers of premises listed in a certain order and sometimes in rural areas it depended on the tenure of certain land - depending on the local traditional customs. Refusal to accept office was punishable by fine. The constable's symbol of authority was his staff or baton (there was no uniform) which he could hang outside his cottage door and which, if necessary, he could use as a defensive weapon.[23]

---

* The Village Pound, where stray animals were restrained under the control of the Constable was also itemised in the 1839 Rating Survey. It was opposite, and to the south of, the Church where there is today a house called "Penfold" - the local name for the pound. In it there is a strongly-built room with no windows which, it is believed, was used as a lock-up by village constables.

In Tudor times it became the custom for the constable to ask a Justice to grant 'hue and cry' before instituting pursuit of a fugitive - the document then issued has been known since the 18th century as a 'warrant'.

In later years private and public complaints on a whole range of issues were brought to court by the village constable: criminal offences, public nuisances, and offences against the community. Four times in his year of office the constable would have to make his way to attend quarter sessions and much of his unpaid work was concerned with 'presentments' - when he was again acting as the representative of the parish.

Two early appointments in Crich were of William Gresley in 1562 who was elected "Petty Constable" and of William Bowler in the 1630s.[24] It was William Bowler who, in 1634, presented six Crich parishioners:

William Meacocke
Francis Burton
Henry Burton
Robert Ibberson and Elizabeth his wife
Margery Smith - wife of George Smith

to the Quarter Sessions - "in that they and every one of them have been absent from their Parish Church of Crich three Sabbath days last past". Some other offences presented by the constables to Quarter Sessions were :

Selling ale without a licence
Keeping a disorderly house
"Keeping Mans sones and servants in his house at inconvenient times, in the night, he beinge an alekeeper"
Denying to sell any ale without her house
"Unlawful gameinge on the Sabbath Day"   (1634)
Making and baking of bread on the Sabbath   (1666)
Lodging rogues and beggars
Not serving time of apprenticeship
Neglecting watch and ward
Refusing to help mend highways when commanded by the constable
Keeping greyhounds and guns without license
Hawking or droving without license
Not taking oaths of fidelity   (1698)
Assault and battery
Obstruction and nuisance on the highway
Not repairing the market place
Not repairing the stocks
Befouling a common well
Breaking the pound
Working at a trade without having served an apprenticeship
"Tracing of hares in the snow"   (1668)
"Turning a scabed mare on the common whereby other men's goods are in danger of being affected"[25]

This list gives an impression of the degree of regulation existing in the 17th century. The constable, as well as presenting alleged offences against the person and against property for consideration by the Justices, had oversight of activities nowadays the concern of numerous government departments (most with local representatives) - agriculture, the environment, employment, trading, transport and civil responsibilities.*

The lot of the village constable was by no means enviable, particularly because he was supposed to act as public accuser of the parish should there be any failure to satisfy the requirement of the law. He held the responsibility to disclose and bring to punishment every breach of the laws by which the village was bound and if there was any failure in this it rendered the villagers vulnerable to a collective fine payable to the Crown as well as a compensation payment to the injured party. Further, the constable himself could be 'presented' to court by the Chief Constable of the Hundred for negligence and from time to time the Chief Constable himself would be urged by the Justices to 'stimulate' the petty constables into greater activity.

In these circumstances, when it became the turn of wealthier members of the community to act as village constable, there was a tendency for them to pay a deputy to carry out the duties for them.[26] It was easy if you had money to pay somebody else to do the unpleasant work and to incur the risk of being presented to court for inadequate or negligent performance. From about the end of the 16th century this practice increased and the deputies paid by the wealthier tradesmen and farmers themselves began to pay deputies to act in their place. As a result in some places the office came to be filled by those who could find no other form of employment and so served more or less permanently as parish constable from year to year on a menial wage and the office sank lower and lower in public esteem, especially in the towns. By the time that George I was on the throne no man who could afford to pay his way out of serving as constable (certainly in the towns) neglected to do so.[27] In 1714 Daniel Defoe said "the imposition of the office of constable is an unsupportable hardship and takes up so much of a man's time that his own affairs are frequently neglected, too often to his ruin". Defoe himself paid £10 in 1721 (about six months wages for a labourer, Figure 5) "to be excused from serving parish offices" in Stoke Newington.

As the pace of industrial life grew in the 18th century, and especially in the towns, the old principles of community service broke down. After perhaps twelve hours hard toil in a factory - or operating a framework knitting machine at home - men simply could not serve twice a year in the court leet to appoint a constable or serve in rotation as night watchmen - never mind about calls for hue and cry after a fugitive offender. There was simply no-one to keep order, mend or pave the streets or light them - or even to clear away the accumulating filth and refuse. The former collective effort monitored by the parish constable simply broke down.

There was an influential school of thought in the 17th and 18th centuries described by Critchley "which insisted on drawing a distinction between the dissolute ways of the wealthy - which harmed no-one but themselves - and those of the poor, which if persisted in deprived the nation of the produce of their toil and, shall, therefore be penalised".[28]

---

* Even with expert help the author has been unable to discover the names of any Crich "Petty Constables" - or of information about their presentments - later than those listed by Cox - (Gresley and Bowler). Sydney and Beatrice Webb in their classic studies of local government in the United Kingdom noted that the presentments made by the petty constables to Quarter Sessions were usually 'scrawled' on scraps of paper of all shapes and sizes and often in virtually illegible condition. It has been suggested that at the time Cox and his assistants were preparing material, most of the presentments to the Quarter Sessions at Derby, Chesterfield and Bakewell were separated from other official records and are now lost.

This philosophy, developed at a time when collective responsibility for the common well-being was waning, persisted and the poor suffered.*

The wealthier, as crime increased in association with the more evil aspects of the Industrial Revolution, banded together to protect themselves by forming voluntary societies to provide funds for the capture and prosecution of felons. One such was the 'Association for the Prosecution of Felons' based on South Wingfield in which Joseph Bowmer, Thomas Travis and Sam Turton (all of Crich) took an active part (Section 5.6).

Nevertheless, in rural areas such as Crich, even after the Industrial Revolution and the Napoleonic Wars, there was still some dependence on the court leet;[29] for instance, in Crich (Section 8.1) the court leet acted as the agency for maintaining the Crich Mining Laws.

The local Lords of the Manor and the local Justices of the Peace were still in control of the parish constable, and there was no superior organisation for policing the local community. The situation was most unsatisfactory and change was inevitable.

The first radical change took place in 1827 when an Act abolished all obligation of high or petty constables to make presentments of "popish recusants, persons not attending church, rogues and vagabonds, profane swearers, servants out of place, false weights and measures, highways and bridges out of repair, riots and unlawful assemblies and whether the poor are well provided for and the constables legally chosen".[30] Thus the duties of the village constable were restricted more towards what today we would regard as the proper duties of the police.

Even so, in 1828, Robert Peel, the Home Secretary, who had initiated a country-wide reform of police, was impelled to remark, when addressing those who lived in country districts :

"Why, I ask, should we entrust a grocer, or any other tradesman, however respectable, with the direction and management of a police for 5000 or 6000 inhabitants ? Why should such a person, unpaid and unrewarded, be taken from his usual avocations and called upon to perform the laborious duties of a night constable?"[31]

The upshot was the passing into law of the County Police Act of 1839.[32] Although this allowed Justices in the Counties to establish Police Forces if they thought it necessary, and the Derbyshire Justices were in favour of doing so, the 'powerful' members of the population of the County were against the idea on grounds of cost; it would have cost a penny rate ! A compromise was adopted. The Parish Constable was retained and the paid office of Superintendent Constable was introduced. These men were charged with overseeing and assisting the Parish Constable and they usually lived at the lock-up (like the one on Crich Market Place). The Superintendent Constable had to provide his own uniform coat and this had to meet with the magistrate's approval; but he was supplied with the official buttons !

Over the whole County, eleven Superintendent Constables were appointed in 1854 and they were each paid £140 a year. They were, however, soon overtaken by the establishment of the Derbyshire Constabulary in March 1857. From then on the old, elected Village Constable disappeared from the local scene. He has, in effect, been replaced nowadays by the elected Chairman of the Parish Council, who is responsible to the village for such local functions as are now delegated to 'village government' (Section 3.15).

---

* Of course, in time of war, the lower orders of society are needed to defend the realm and, analagously in our own day, when 'private' medicine cannot provide critical health treatment - there is always the NHS - as Margaret Thatcher pointed out.

3.6 The Justices

Today, as in times past, J.P.s deal with a large number of serious indictable offences (burglary, robbery, offences 'against the person', paternity cases and so on) as well as coping with a plethora of minor offences against the law of the land.

However, over a very long time, for some 500 years, they were not only the authority under whom the village and the Hundred constables sought to keep the King's Peace but, like them, over most of that time, had many other 'administrative' functions at the local level.

The forebears of the 'Justices' were particular knights commissioned in 1195 by Richard I to take, from everyone over the age of sixteen, security to keep the peace.[33] In the next century they became known as 'custodes pacis' - custodians of the King's Peace. The first law recognising their existence was an Act of 1327 which provided that: "in every county there shall be assigned a good and lawful man to keep the peace". Then, in an Act of 1361, the custodians of the peace were formally recognised as justices and given a mixture of 'police', judicial and administrative duties.[34] They were appointed by the Crown and they became the natural supervisors of the local constables who had been established following the Statute of Winchester, some 75 years earlier. Usually the Justice of the Peace was the local Lord of the Manor and at first he, or his Steward, would preside over the village Court Leet. In Crich Parish Sir William de Wakebridge (Section 2.3) was one of the first J.P.s.

In many places, probably too in Crich, the manorial court (or Court Leet) and later, in feudal England, the courts of justice led by the local J.P.s, were held in the Parish Church.[35] The parish was originally an ecclesiastical community, controlled by its vestry: but by the beginning of the reign of Henry VIII it had begun to acquire civil functions and in late Tudor times it had become, in rural districts at least, the important unit of local administration.[36] Many of the functions of the constables came under its control. Eventually the constable was appointed by the Court Leet (and sometimes later by Quarter Sessions) on the nomination of the vestry and the activities of the parish - hitherto mainly the responsibility of the constable - were linked up through him and put under the organised rule of the J.P.s. In this way the advent of the J.P.s downgraded the importance of the constable's office but even so for centuries they were, together, not only the upholders of the principles of the Statute of Winchester in preserving the King's Peace but also the core of local government based on the parish.

In medieval times only six, and later eight, J.P.s were paid in each county (through the Sheriff) to hold Sessions in every Quarter of the year at least. The Justices were mostly resident within the County for which they acted.[37] Other Justices were unpaid and no duke, earl, baron or baronet was allowed to take one of the paid appointments. After Elizabeth some Privy Council members were made J.P.s in counties where they had no property. Since the establishment of the office of Lord Lieutenant it has been usual for J.P.s to be put on the 'Commission of the Peace' by the Crown on the recommendation of the Lord Lieutenant.* As already indicated the Justices of the Peace used the Constables as their executive agents. During the 15th and 16th centuries the Village Constable was still the principal amongst the annually elected (and unpaid) officers of the parish:[38] others were the churchwarden, the surveyor of highways and the overseer of the poor. The Justices, of course, also controlled the functions covered by the surveyors and overseers and together they could initiate county rates to pay for the services provided to the village community. In these administrative activities the J.P.s made particular use of the Chief (or High)

---

* Nowadays J.P.s are appointed by the Lord Chancellor on the recommendation of an Advisory Committee in each county - the Chairman of which is the Lord Lieutenant.

Constables of the Hundred. Early on, when an 'offence' by a village community was presented to the Sessions (for example a failure to repair a bridge or a road) the result of the 'trial' was commonly to fine the parish collectively. It was the job of the Hundred Constable to see that the money was paid over. From then it was only a small step to introduce community rating to pay for essential public works and by the late 18th century when the inadequacy of local government to cope with the problems of new roads and houses and expanding farms was blatant and the imposition of rates was extended to meet the new needs, the Hundred Constable was given new duties as a general factotum of the Justices.[39] He undertook the task of inspecting weights and measures and roads and bridges and he spent much time as a collector of the county rates.

The Justices and the constables working with the churchwarden and other parish officers to carry out the functions of local government operated until well into the 19th century - after the manorial courts and the courts-leet were, by and large, a thing of the past. Thus in 1818 the "Sturgess Bourne's Act" recognised and re-declared the old common custom of notice being given in Church of the date, time and place of "Parish Meetings" - the more modern equivalent of the old freeholders' courts that were usually held in the church[40] (see above). In Victorian times this Act was rescinded but certainly until the 1970s the Clerk of Crich Parish Council posted notices calling Parish Meetings on the Church Notice Boards - an act which, in one form or another, had been carried on for perhaps 600 or 700 years.

3.7 Wage Control

Until the time of the Black Death (1348-49) each Manor tended to be governed by its own custom within the framework laid down by such acts as the Statute of Winchester and under the supervision of the county Sheriff reporting to the King and his Parliament. After the Black Death Parliamentary laws were passed controlling wages (which, because of the shortage of labour, had risen sharply) and society changed from one based on local customs of personal service to one where money was the control on services and goods. It was then (Section 3.6) that special Justices were appointed, like William de Wakebridge, by the Crown to govern the neighbourhood in the King's name and it constituted the first step away from local government by those who had inherited feudal manorial rights to a wider franchise.

The particular measure was the Statute of Labourers of 1349 and it fixed a day wage of 2d for a labourer - and allowed him 3d a day in harvest, for instance.[41] The fixed levels for wages over many occupations held for a time but, in 1389-90 Parliament abandoned the attempt to keep wages down and instructed the Justices of the Peace to regulate them locally "according to the dearth of victuals" (an early attempt to tie incomes to the cost of living !). By 1420 an unskilled labourer could earn 3d a day, the normal skilled wage being 4d or 5d.[42] By 1445 Parliament had again reverted to the policy of a maximum wage. Under Elizabeth I the national control of wages and prices by the J.P.s was more wisely carried on, without attempting to impose everywhere a fixed maximum wage.[43] Nevertheless, the J.P.s decision on wages at Speenhamland in 1795 (Section 3.13) brought great difficulties in its wake and adverse national consequences - as will be seen.

3.8 Tithes

As early as 1066 the Manorial Court in each soke had handled not only misdemeanours, dues to the King and to the local Lord of the Manor - but also the tithes belonging to the local church. A portion of these went to the Lord. The tithe, literally a tenth part of the agricultural produce, was conceived as due to God and hence payable for the support of the priesthood and of religious establishments. Their payment - in various forms - by villagers was a continuing source of friction until the 20th century; they were formally abandoned only in 1936 (Section 10.14).

An early mention of tithes in Crich is the endowment of the vicarage (when Alexander Staverley was Bishop: 1224-1240) with "the tithes of lambs and wool and the usual oblations". In 1278 the then Vicar of Crich - William de Draycote - entered into an agreement with the Abbot of Darley Abbey both about those tithes and also about others on the lands and tenements formerly owned by Peter de Wakebridge.[44] These had been granted to Bricius, the first Vicar of Crich (with the agreement of the Abbey of Darley) together with 40s 0d of rent to be paid annually by the Abbey. By 1550 the endowment of the vicarage included Easter offerings, oblations, tithes of hay, lambs, wool, pigs, geese, flax and hemp as well as the annual pension from Wakebridge in lieu of tithes from that Manor. There were two tithe barns in the parish. The northerly one was on Hindersitch Lane the other on the site of the house now known as 'The Barn' on Chadwick Nick Lane. [355528]

Another charge on the villagers which originated not later than the 14th century was the levy of a parish rate for the maintenance or repair of the church.[45] These ecclesiastical dues, together with those due to the Crown and to the Manor (quite apart from the rents for land paid in substitution for labour) were, for many centuries, the base for charges on the local population to cover local and national governmental expenditure.

3.9 The Relief of the Poor

The main purpose of 'local government' expenditure was the relief of poverty and care for the destitute and aged. For centuries before 1500 there was, in effect, a 'dower-house' system for caring for the old. An aged villein could surrender his holding to his son - perhaps retaining a small cottage or a couple of rooms in the farm, and a few acres, in which he could live out his days. As everywhere until recent times the able-bodied housed and supported the aged of their families. The sick, the poor and the destitute looked for help from the arms of the Church.[46] It was not always adequate and it was not always forthcoming. Well before the Reformation of the Church by Henry VIII the behaviour, particularly of the well-to-do senior clergy, sustained by the regular payment of tithe, was a cause of bitterness towards the Church. Although a rancorous document the mood was well expressed in a pamphlet by Simon Fish called "The Supplication of the Beggars".[47] This was addressed to Henry VIII. It included:

"............In the times of your noble predecessor's past, craftily crept into this your realm another sort, not of impotent but of strong, puisant and counterfeit, holy and idle beggars and vagabonds.... the Bishops, Abbots, Priors, Deacons, Archdeacons, Suffragens, Priest, Monks, Canons, Friars, Pardoners and Sommoners. And who is able to number this idle, ruinous sort which - setting all labour aside - have begged so importantly that they have gotten into their hands more than the third part of all your Realm? The goodliest lordships, manors, lands and territories are theirs. Besides this they have the tenth part of all corn, meadow, pasture, grass, wool, colts, calves, lambs, pigs, geese and chickens. Yea and they look so narrowly upon their profits that the poor wives must be accountable to them of every tenth egg, or else she getteth not her rights at Easter, shall be taken as a heretic.... How much money get the Sommoners by extortion in a year by citing the people to the Commissaries Court and afterwards releasing their appearance for money? Who is she that will set her hands to work to get 3d a day and may have at least 20d a day to sleep an hour with a friar, a monk or a priest"

After the Reformation, Henry - as new Head of the Church of England - decided to overhaul the system of providing relief for the "unfortunate, innocent poor". Earlier legislation had threatened violent beggars with the stocks and floggings "until their bodies should be bloody". In 1517 London had started licensing beggars but the real change came in 1535 - the year of the suppression of 376 lesser monasteries. Parliament enacted that all governors of shires, cities, hundreds, hamlets and parishes should make provision for the poor by receiving charitable alms - so that no person should openly go a-begging.[48] Anyone making an open 'dole' or giving money in alms otherwise than to the poor boxes in each parish were to forfeit ten times the value. This statute took the task of relieving the poor from the church and gave it to the 'civil' power under the control of the local J.P.s. The response, however, was inadequate to meet the need and when the Justices were told to persuade their neighbours to contribute voluntarily they too were ineffective. So - in 1563 - the local J.P.s were empowered to assess their neighbours and to imprison those who did not pay what had become a plain, legal, 'poor rate'. If a parish had more destitute poor than it was able to maintain, the Justices were empowered to license them to beg in the hundreds of their county.

An Act of 1572 provided a definition of the 'vagabond' class and ordained punishment for vagrancy (a vagabond over 18 years of age found guilty of a third act of vagrancy could be punished with death - without benefit of clergy). The same Act also took a positive step to help the deserving poor. A compulsory Poor Rate binding on all parishes was declared - with an assessment to be made on each parishioner. This Act also allowed the unpaid and overworked Justices to appoint, year by year, unpaid Parish Overseers of the Poor to carry out those local assessments.[49]

In 1575-6 the Justices were empowered to spend money on stocks of raw material to "set the poor to work" - for instance on spinning wool and flax. In 1597-8 an Act was passed which put 'Parish Administration' firmly in the hands of the Overseers and the Churchwardens. In 1602, the definitive Elizabethan Poor Law was enacted. This brought together many of the earlier provisions and it endured well into the 19th century. This Act required that the Justices should appoint Overseers in each parish who should assess every property-holder for the relief of the poor. If the assessment was not paid the Justices could seize property of the defaulters or could imprison them. The Act also empowered the Overseers to set the poor to work if they deemed it appropriate. Poor children who came into the hands of the Overseers could be apprenticed by them to a trade - girls until they were 21; boys, like other apprentices, until they were 24. A separate Act dealt with the flogging of vagabonds and the control of "Houses of Correction" - the county provision for the 'undesirable' poor. In these the vagabonds were made to work. (A man in the County Jail for crime was simply detained - he was not made to work).

3.10 Other Duties of the J.P.s

Justices of the Peace, in addition to their duties in administering the Poor Law and in wage control, had numerous other matters to deal with in village government. They were made responsible for the repair of roads and bridges, for local wages and prices, for prisons and houses of correction: they licensed public houses and, when one was levied at all, they levied a county rate. Some of the Statutes defining J.P.s responsibilities illustrate the impact of Parliament on local life. Thus :

   a) The Statute of Bridges of 1531 made counties responsible for bridges outside corporate towns and Justices were empowered to appoint two County Surveyors to ensure that all bridges were adequately maintained. The county funds created for this purpose were sometimes used by J.P.s to help parishes with road repairs.

b) During the period 1555-1586 a series of acts was passed (which were not rescinded until the reforming General Highway Act of 1835) dealing with the repair of roads.[50] Each parish was required to meet annually - under the control of the Justices - and elect two unpaid 'Surveyors of Highways'. The election took place at a Vestry Meeting organised by the local constable (the immediate agent of the Justices) and the churchwardens. The surveyor's job was to supervise and direct the labour of the local villagers in repairing highways - as required by statute. The wealthier villagers (occupying a holding with more than £50 per annum or keeping a draft of horses or a plough team) had to supply a cart with horses and oxen and two men for work on the roads. Others were obliged to supply a man, or go themselves, each year to repair the roads in the parish at a time fixed by the Surveyor and to work under his direction for eight hours on four, and later (after 1562) on six, consecutive days. The Surveyors were supposed to present all defaulters to a J.P. and fines were to be levied at the rate of ten shillings per team and one shilling per man, per day. Many parishioners liable under the law could ill afford to meet their obligations. The loss of several days earnings did not encourage good attendance and by and large the system failed. This was not surprising for many of those required to repair the roads did not use them except to walk from one part of the parish to another whereas many of the heavy users - who caused wear and damage to the village roads - were carriers and tradesmen who came from outside the parish and passed through it on to their destinations. The Surveyors, who were appointed annually and doing only a temporary duty for the community, were in an uneasy position in trying to enforce the law. They were often reluctant (after all they lived in the parish) to resort to the Justices who themselves were often unwilling to enforce penalties. The Surveyors were untrained and could not be expected to know much about road construction and repair. Often they were unable or unwilling to co-ordinate effort in those places that most needed it. Even with minimal through traffic the parish repair system could not have been expected to meet all the demands made on it.

Although the Justices were reluctant to fine individual defaulters from statute labour they willingly 'required' the Parish, at Quarter Sessions, to repair the roadway and would penalise the Parish by the imposition of extra days of statutory labour or by a money fine*. They could then apply the money raised to hire labour to carry out the necessary repairs - not necessarily under the direction of the amateur parish surveyor. Funds were also swelled by the practice which became established (as it had previously with the villeins on manorial estates) of parishioners paying a fixed sum - based on a defaulter's fine - to be relieved of their obligation to perform the statutory duty themselves. Eventually these sources of funds were supplemented by a highway rate. Under a Commonwealth Ordinance of 1654 it became possible for a parish to levy a rate for itself - not to exceed one shilling in the pound. After 1690 highway rates were levied fairly commonly.[51]

It was only later - with the turnpikes - the early ones of which were again put under the control of the local Justices - that through traffic in a village like Crich made a contribution to the upkeep of the roads which, in the 17th and 18th centuries, were so severely damaged by wheeled coaches, carriers wagons, heavy sledges and loads of timber being taken over the poorly designed and maintained road surfaces of the day.

c) In 1562-63 an act was again promoted under the guidance of Cecil, Queen Elizabeth I's chief minister, which returned to the precedent of 1389-90 and required J.P.s to assess wages on the basis of local costs.[52]

d) Additionally, in 1594-1597, the Justices of the Peace were charged with controlling the price of grain in their area.[53]

---

* At the Easter Sessions of 1665 a presentment about faulty roads was made to the Justices (and endorsed by the Grand Jury) by one John Statham - as follows: "Wee present ye Inhabitants of ye parish of Headge for not repayring of ye highway leading betwixt Bull Bridge and Belper Warde"

It can be seen from these examples that the J.P.s had very wide powers locally: their responsibilities held until the creation of elected County Councils in the late 19th century. With all these important judicial, political, economic and administrative duties the Justices became probably the most influential class of men in England. They were Crown servants but were not in the Crown's pay or dependence. They lived on their own estates and off their own rents. What they valued most was the good opinion of their equals, their neighbours and the common people of the Shire. Although nominally appointed by the Crown they were, in practice, selected by their Lord Lieutenant - influenced by the opinion of the gentry of the shire. They had no proper staff - only local amateur officials appointed by a parish or vestry meeting. To have had paid, permanent, 'professional' assistance would have required the imposition of a County Rate which they and their peers were unwilling to pay: inefficient local government was tolerated because it was cheap.[54]

It was legally obligatory to raise a poor rate in every parish to deal with its poor, but the rate payers regarded it as an undue hardship if the J.P.s raised any rate to pay for roads, prisons, sanitation or police - as they were entitled to do. This attitude persisted for generations as was witnessed in Crich when the main argument against the creation of a local School Board was on the grounds of cost to the rate payers (Section 5.4).

Since Sir William de Wakebridge, men who have served the local community as Justices of the Peace and who owned property in the parish include:

- German Pole
- Thos. Lord Cromwell
- Nathaniel Curzon
- John Turton
- Charles Hurt
- Sir Wolston Dixie
- Sir Edward Wilmot
- Sir Robert Meade Wilmot
- Peter Nightingale
- Nicholas Hurt
- Richard Arkwright
- William Turton
- Francis Hurt
- The Duke of Devonshire
- Peter Arkwright
- W. E. Nightingale
- Edward Wass
- George Henry Strutt
- Lord Scarsdale
- Albert Frederick Hurt [55] (see Tables D & E)

A number of other notables connected with Crich Parish affairs have also served as J.P.s. They include :

- Immanuel Halton of South Wingfield
- Sir Joseph Banks of Ashover
- William Jessop
- John Wright
- Gladwyn Turbutt of Ogston

It was by such people - often with members of a family in succeeding generations serving as Justices of the Peace under the Sheriff of the County of Derby - that the local government affecting Crich Parish was carried on until the last decade of the nineteenth century.

3.11 Musters, Militias and Volunteers

In medieval times the Lord of the Manor held his land from the Crown on condition that he provided fighting men (knights) when required - or paid fees which would support a knight (or, there being no conflict, could be used by the Crown for its own purposes - such payments being an early form of national tax).

In Tudor times 'musters' were called by the Crown with the object of establishing that, in the various shires, a Crown agent could check "the armour to be seen and worn upon the back of the persons that shall wear them and made fit for them". In 1558 there was a report that "German Pole of Cryke" had:

"1 corselete
1 cote of plate
1 pyke
1 long bowe
1 sheaf of arrows
1 steele cape
1 haggbute
1 maryon
1 harnisses"

and that he led 20 able men, of whom six were archers.[56]

Queen Elizabeth, in Council in 1574, selected "Honest Captains - having knowledge" to go to the Shires and teach and train people at the Musters.[57]

George, Earl of Shrewsbury, reported back that he had, on 19th and 20th July 1574 held a Muster of Light Horse "with their furniture" in the County of Derby and he recorded that Jerman Pole de Wakebridge had been present (spelling was then somewhat unreliable !)

In 1587 Robert Bunting, Geo Emott and Geo Radford, all of Crich, were called on for active service and in 1595 John Claye (Section 2.4) was required to 'sponsor' a "light horse and its rider". The Muster Roll of 1559 required both John Claye and Anthony Lowe II of Alderwasley (Section 2.6) to subscribe 20 shillings each towards the cost of the campaigns in Ireland.

In such ways were the costs of military activities defrayed in Tudor times (also Section 2.4).

During the Civil War recruitment by either side was not, of course, under 'statutory' control but during the Commonwealth provision was made for the support of soldiers who had been wounded in the War and were no longer able to support themselves. A local example is enshrined in a submission to the Derbyshire Justices of the Peace in 1649.

"The Humble Petition of William Roy of Tansley in the Parish of Crich to the right worshippful Justices for the countye of Derby assembled in Sessions. Humbly Sheweth your worshipps Poore Petitioner that whereas he had a long tyme layne lame of a soore legge wch cme first by a hurt received in the parliament's service, and now not being able to move no further than he is borne and moved by the help of others. And having a wife and a child and being no wayes able to mantayne himssellfe and his family by Reason of the Sorrowes of his Legge which is in great danger to bee cutt offe lest it infect his body. And having received no more from the parish in General but foure shillings and a payinge one Sabboth day by way of Collection from well disposed people never since your poore petitioner began first to bee lame. Therefore your Worships poore petitioner humbly prayeth your good Worships to take his distressed estate into consideration and that you would bee pleased to grant an order that your poore petitioner might have some reliefe from the parish of Crich wherein hee liveth now in his great need and Extremity. As your worships in your good discressions shall think fitting and hee should bee ever bound to pray, etc."[58]

As time went by the Sheriff of the County, formally entrusted with the local business of the Crown, (Section 3.3), had a growing sphere of responsibility and Lord Lieutenants were appointed to lead the local military forces of the County.[59]

After the Restoration in 1660, the Lord Lieutenants of the different counties appointed Deputies and forwarded their names for the approval of the Crown. The Deputy Lieutenants became involved with the militia and jointly with the Lord Lieutenant became responsible for the peace of the County. They had the power to train, exercise and put to readiness and arm the 'soldier-citizens' assigned to military duty.[60] Although the soldiers, when on duty, were paid by the State they were 'found' for service by private individuals whose 'legal' commitment depended on their wealth. Thus, every man with £500 a year - or £6000 in goods and money - was liable to be called on by the Lord Lieutenant and his deputies to provide a horse, a horseman and arms: every man with a yearly income of £50 a year or £600 in goods and monies was required to provide a foot soldier. Each man enrolled was to serve for 3 years, although the general musters of the militia regiments were not to take place more than once a year and the assembly of single companies for training was not to happen more than 4 times a year. Each musketeer was required to take with him ½lb of powder and the same weight of bullets - these to be provided by the citizen who had 'found' or 'persuaded' the soldier reporting for duty. In like fashion, sponsored Pikemen had to be armed with an ashen pike not under 16 ft. long.

Before he could be appointed to the rank of Deputy Lieutenant for the County the candidate had to provide a certificate to the Clerk of the Peace.[61] Initially they had to establish that they had at least £400 a year income - though this was eventually reduced to £200 p.a. Landowners in Crich Parish who were appointed as Deputy Lieutenants[62] were, in:

1711 and 1745	Charles Hurt of Alderwasley
1745	Sir Nathanial Curzon
	Sir Wolstan Dixie
1745 and 1762	John Turton of the Dimple
1760	Nicholas Hurt of Alderwasley
1762	Earl of Thanet
	Lord Scarsdale
	Sir Wolstan Dixie
	Charles Hurt of Alderwasley
1796	Charles Hurt
	Sir Robert Wilmot
1798	Francis Hurt of Alderwasley
1803	Francis Hurt
	George Benson Strutt
	William Strutt
	Joseph Strutt
1832	Francis Hurt
1855	Peter Arkwright

	George Henry Strutt
1869	Albert Frederick Hurt of Alderwasley

In 1757 the local military forces were removed from local, 'feudal', control by Parliament and the Crown was empowered by statute to appoint twenty Deputy Lieutenants in each County.[63] They, and the commissioned officers reporting to them were required to have a landed qualification - part of which had to be in the county in which they served. The requirements were :

Deputy Lieutenant of the County	£400 per annum.
Colonel	400
Lt. Col. or Major	300
Captain	200
Lieutenant	100
Ensign	50 (these levels were reduced in 1769).

The Deputy Lieutenants were required to meet together and then to issue orders to the Chief Constables of the several Hundreds in the County (Section 3.5) to make, and return to them, lists of men in their districts eligible for military service.

Derbyshire was required by the Crown to raise 500 'private' men for service in the Militia and was supposed to pay a fine of £5 in lieu of every man short of that target.

Relatives of men who had been persuaded to join the militia, and who were called for service, were often in need and could appeal to the County for support whilst the soldier was away from home on duty.[64] As an example, the Mayor of Chesterfield made an order of 2s 0d per week on the Overseers of the Poor of the borough for the relief of Mary Graham and her infant - such money to be reimbursed by the County Treasurer; Ronald Graham was on service for 58 weeks. The cost to the County was £5-16s-0d.

During the war with France and with the rebels in North America, in the period 1776-1783, it was estimated that about two out of three able-bodied men between the ages of 16 and 60 were wearing uniform.[65] They were in the militia, the yeomanry and cavalry and in the 'regular' army and navy*.

In the 1790s impressment was used to obtain men for the army and for the navy. At a Special Court of General Sessions in 1795 Derbyshire was required to find 194 'regulars' for the navy and 252 for the army.[66] It was, at that time, left to the County Justices to decide on how many men should be provided by each Hundred and each Parish. The Chief Constables of each Hundred gave notice to the Church Wardens and Overseers of the Poor of each Parish of how many men were required and when they should be available and the Justices set up Petty Sessions to receive the parish returns and to assist and enrol men 'joining up'.

It was the duty of the Parish officers (Constable, Church Wardens, Overseers) to call the principal inhabitants of the parish together to consider the most effectual means of raising the men.[67] One method often adopted was to hold a Parochial Lot (which was frequently held in the Parish Church) to 'select' the military contingent demanded from the parish. The parish officers had the power to grant a bounty to men who would volunteer for the Navy - the bounty to come out

---

* It was difficult to get enough male labour to carry on the work of farming and women took up tasks in every branch of agriculture. Women regularly did the ploughing between 1795 and 1805.

of a rate made on the parishioners on the same basis as the Poor Rate. One third of the bounty could be paid by the Justices when the men enrolled: the remainder was lodged with the County Treasurer until the volunteer enlisted on board one of H.M. Ships. If a parish defaulted in its responsibility to provide its quota of men it was required to pay £10 over and above the average bounty of the district. The number of recruits demanded from each Hundred depended on the number of inhabited houses in it. In 1795 Morleston and Litchurch Hundred, with 2719 inhabited houses was required to provide 39 men. In Crich there were about 350 inhabited houses[68] and so Crich's contribution would be five men for that particular impressment. Actually, in Derbyshire, only about half the appointed quota of men enlisted and the county had to pay £3064 in fines and bounties for the deficiency.[69]

After the French Revolution and with Napoleon beginning his ascent to power there was the possibility of invasion and in 1794 Pitt put a Bill through Parliament to raise 'Volunteer' and 'Yeomanry' forces for the home defence of the country. The Constables were instructed to call parish and township meetings to enable local people "to enter into associations either of cavalry or infantry and of undertaking to provide horses, wagons and cars as the public exigency may require".

By 1798 three infantry corps had been raised and partially equipped in the County - at Derby, Wirksworth and Ashbourne and in 1803 the Derbyshire officers of Volunteers received their first Commissions.[70] In 1803 a Company of Crich Volunteers was established with Thomas Turton as Captain Commandant.[71] His Lieutenant was Jasper Wager and the Ensign George Bownes. The company mustered sixty rank and file. In July 1805 Thomas Turton resigned (Section 9.6) and George Bownes succeeded him as Captain Commandant. By 1808 a 'Wirksworth Regiment' had been formally established [72] - covering the parishes of Wirksworth, Crich and Alderwasley with Charles Hurt as Commandant, holding the rank of Lieutenant-Colonel : Peter Arkwright was also Lt.Col. and the Major was John Blackmore.

To provide a safe firing range at which the men of the Wirksworth Regiment could practice musketry, a wall, about 30 feet high and 20 feet wide was built in Alderwasley Park not far from the Deercote.

Fortunately these forerunners of the present day 'Territorial Army' were not called into action and it was not until the 1940s that their spiritual descendants, the Home Guard, were recruited on a purely local basis.

3.12 Workhouses

Early in the 17th century it was not unusual for communities to establish a regular 'poor house' for the deserving and destitute poor, or to assign a few cottages to them, or to allow them to erect rough huts on the waste. It was easier to feed them or give them a small pension if they had a roof over their heads.

An Act of 1662 formally allowed parishes to move on - within 40 days - any immigrant who seemed likely to become a burden to it. Then in the late 17th century and early 18th a practice began of supplementing wages out of the rates if the labourer was in poverty because of disease or some physical disability - or if he had managed to keep a large family alive (!!) and, as a result, was in need. Some large towns, like Norwich, started to build poorhouses or workhouses in the hope that they would provide training as well as accommodation.[73] In 1722 parishes were authorised by statute to establish similar houses and to apply the 'Workhouse Test'. The idea was that anyone refusing to enter the workhouse could be refused assistance. The 1722 Act recognised that advantage might follow if a group of parishes took joint action.

The poorhouse in Crich on Workhouse Row [350536] was, according to Reynolds writing in 1770, built by the parish authorities in 1734.[74]   It was on the edge of the Nether Common before the Turnpike, the Langley-Mill Road (now "The Common") was made, and before the common was enclosed.

Clapham suggests that there were only 40 poorhouses in the whole country in 1775 - including those set up before the Act of 1722.[75]   The Crich Workhouse was one of a very small group in the County at the time - perhaps a measure of the importance of Crich in the area at the period. That it was under the overall supervision of the Justices is established by a record in the County Treasurer's Accounts for 1782-83 of a payment to "Francis Moor for viewing Crich Workhouse - £1-15s-0d", i.e. carrying out an inspection on behalf of the Justices.[76]

The Crich Workhouse was a so-called 'Subscription Poor House'. It was subscribed to by the parishes of Denby, Melbourne, Mercaston, Pentrich, Wessington, Willington and several others.[77]

The Parish Officers of all local parishes had been invited to 'subscribe' (under certain rules) to send paupers to be lodged, fed and managed according to a circulated list of rules. The subscribing parishes had to pay, quarterly, their quota of the rent, salaries and cost of utensils and repairs of the house. Each month they had to pay, for each pauper sent, their weekly share of all the current expenses of maintaining the paupers in the house.

In 1816 Crich Parish was keeping five of its own paupers there [78] - at a cost for the maintenance of each, per year, of £10 i.e. the cost per week for each individual was 46d at a time when a typical labourer's wage was about 170d a week. (Figure 5).

The subscription poor houses - which were run by professionals working to agreed codes of practice - were reckoned to be better than local parish workhouses under the control, too often, of illiterate and sometimes sordid parish officers who were changed every six months or every year. They were also better than 'Houses of Industry' which worked under Trustees of Directors who were never, or seldom, changed and who were too commonly inattentive and superficially informed.

The parishes who subscribed to the Crich Poorhouse would be required to accept certain rules*. For instance, they would probably have to subscribe for at least a year and give a month's notice in writing if they wished to withdraw. All paupers sent would have to be decently clothed, free of infectious disease and, if an unmarried female, must not be pregnant. Each fourth Monday an Overseer from each subscribing parish had to attend at the Poorhouse to pay dues and inspect the state of the house and the clothing of the inmates. If they didn't attend a fine was due. If they did then a quart of ale and bread and cheese would be provided, but no dinners. There was also, not surprisingly, a set of rules to be obeyed by the paupers. On arrival they were to be stripped and washed down and examined for any infectious diseases: they had to deliver up their clothes to be cleaned and aired. If these were satisfactory they could be worn by the owners: if not they would be ticketed and laid by ready for discharge. Unless they were ill the inmates had to get up when the bell was rung and set about their work. In summer this lasted from 08.00 to 17.00 and in winter from 09.00 to 16.30. They were allowed half an hour for breakfast and an hour for dinner. There was no work on Sundays, Saturday afternoons, Good Friday, Christmas Day and two days afterwards, nor on the Mondays and Tuesdays in Easter and Whit Weeks. Unless sick the paupers couldn't stay in the wards after 07.00 in summer or 08.30 in winter and they had to be in bed at night by 21.00 in summer and 20.30 in winter, and fires and candles were to be put out at these times. They couldn't receive visitors or go out without

---

* The rules sketched here are those adopted by the nearby Ashover Poorhouse - and are likely to be based on the same model as were those of Crich.

permission of the Master of the House and could not be out, under any pretence, after 20.00 in summer or 18.00 in winter. Any pauper allowed out who came back late, was disorderly or drunk could be kept in for two months and fed on bread and water only for the next day. If they missed prayers or divine service on a Sunday (without due cause), if they didn't finish their work on time, if they wasted provisions or were guilty of other offences they forfeited their next meal, and if they repeated the offence they would be fed on bread and water only for two days. If they were absent without leave, refused to work, disobeyed instructions, pretended sickness, made false excuses, should they steal, waste, spoil, curse, swear or lie - then the Master could confine them and feed them on bread and water for so long as he felt fit - not exceeding one day. The Master had to keep a register and report each offence and punishment at the next meeting of the Parish Overseers.

It was, indeed, a strict regime and unlikely to encourage entry to the poorhouse by anyone who could avoid it !

At the same time there were rules controlling the behaviour of the Master and Mistress of the poorhouse. Their aim was, presumably, to ensure that the inmates were not exploited or subjected to unnecessary risk. The Master and Mistress had to live in the 'house' itself and, without written permission from the Directors could not be off the premises after 10.00 p.m.: they could engage in no other business venture: they had to hold communal prayers each day and attend divine service with the paupers each Sunday: they were required to enter all personal details about the poor in their charge in a book to be available for inspection by the Directors at all times and they had to conduct a roll-call every day after breakfast and ensure that discipline was maintained in accordance with the rules laid down for the paupers. There were strict instructions on the keeping of accounts, the ordering, inspection and storing of provisions and other purchases made for the poorhouse. The Mistress had to obey instructions on maintaining hygiene: airing beds, scrubbing floors, washing utensils (detailed differently for different seasons of the year) - frequencies and times for cleaning being prescribed. The premises had to be whitewashed twice a year and everything had to be "kept sweet, clean and decent": thus the dining room table and the seats had to be cleaned immediately after each meal. The Master and Mistress had to supervise the washing and combing of all paupers and themselves deal with the children if necessary. (These had to "be Catechised every Sunday afternoon as soon as they are capable of being instructed"). Preference in apartments was to be given to paupers known to be good housekeepers rather than to those known to be idle or profligate and the sick were to be given separate accommodation. It was the duty of the Master to send for the surgeon or apothecary if he thought it necessary - and to charge the sponsoring parish for the fees involved. At the end, when a pauper died, there were instructions for the Master on what to do with the corpse (and the associated possessions - usually clothing only), and when the funeral was to be held.... "as near Eleven O'clock in the forenoon as possible - unless same happen on Sunday and then it is to be in the afternoon as soon as Divine Service is over".

The bureaucratic detail is perhaps revealing of the possibilities for the abuse of a class of people unable to cope, themselves alone, with the life of the times.

The food provided in workhouses was not very inspiring and it was hardly protein-rich but, presumably it was adequate to sustain existence. In 1815 or thereabouts the bill of fare for the Ashover poorhouse (and presumably it was the same each week !) was:[79]

DAY	BREAKFAST	DINNER	SUPPER
Sunday	Milk Pottage	Butchers Meat & Garden Stuff	Potatoes or Milk Pottage
Monday	"	Suet Dumplings	Milk Pottage
Tuesday	"	Pease Soup	Mashed Potatoes
Wednesday	"	Butchers Meat & Garden Stuff	Broth or Milk Pottage
Thursday	"	Pease Soup	Bread & Cheese
Friday	"	Suet Dumplings	Mashed Potato or Milk Pottage
Saturday	"	Stewed Meat & Garden Stuff	"

3.13 The 1834 Poor Law

At the end of the 18th century the county rates prescribed by the J.P.s brought in, over the whole country, a total of under £300,000 a year. [80] Most of this went on gaols, prisoners, constables and prosecution procedures: a small fraction went on the construction and repair of bridges.

At the level of the parish, in the mid 18th century, the income from rates, over the country as a whole, was under £750,000. The greater part of this went in payments to the poor on an 'outdoor relief' basis. This meant that paupers could, usually, remain in their own homes - though, as seen, some parishes like Crich made some provision for the destitute who could only be sustained in an institution. Then, in May 1795, the J.P.s at Speenhamland in Berkshire failed in their duty to proclaim a minimum wage matched against prices.[81] Prices had risen alarmingly over the previous 50 years (Figure 5). The justices decided, instead, to supplement wages out of the parish rates. A scale was drawn up by which every "poor and industrious person" should receive, from the parish, when the loaf cost a shilling, a certain sum each week in addition to his wages - so much for himself and so much for other members of his family. As the price of the loaf rose the dole was to rise with it. This ruling didn't unduly affect counties like Derbyshire because, at first anyway, alternative employment in mines and factories meant that to retain labour the farmers and other employers had to pay reasonably comparable wages. The 'out-workers' - cotton weavers and framework knitters - however, suffered from low incomes as the years passed (Section 9.7). In the agricultural south the story was different right from the beginning: there the big landlords and farmers had their labour costs subsidised through the rates which were contributed to by the smaller tenant farmers and smallholders in the same parish - who often employed no labour. Once again - and a theme which echoes from biblical times to the present day tax-reliefs in Great Britain - "To him that hath, shall be given; and from him that hath not, even that which he hath shall be taken away". The result, over the country as a whole, was that by 1803 the total of parish rates had risen from £0.75 million to £5.3 million and by 1813 it was £7.0 million - a ten-fold rise in about 50 years.[82] The total parish poor rate stayed at about £7 million until the early 1830s. It became a national scandal.

Parliament eventually met the problem with the Poor Law Amendment Act of 1834 - much of which was based on the ideas of Absolom Barnett (1773-1850) who had been appointed full-time Assistant Overseer of St. Mary's Parish in Nottingham in 1819.[83] Barnett refused applications to make up inadequate wages (amongst the local framework knitters and lace workers) caused either by partial or by underpaid employment. He insisted on the unemployed entering the workhouse as a qualification for relief and he aimed to make the workhouse "so ordered as to be a place irksome and abhorrent to every able-bodied pauper within its walls". The 1834 Poor Law was largely drafted by Edwin Chadwick (1801-90) who was originally an assistant

Poor Law Commissioner and eventually became the secretary of the Poor Law Board. It required that outdoor relief be restricted only to those sick and aged able to sustain an independent life. All others could only receive help in workhouses. In these the conditions were to be such as to discourage unnecessary applications for relief. The Commissioners were obsessed by a pre-occupation with the problems posed by the fit adult workman and overlooked the need for compassionate treatment for old people, children and invalids. The opportunity was taken to re-organise the administration of poor relief. Parishes were grouped into 'Unions' under locally-elected Boards of Guardians. These were responsible directly to the central Poor Law Commission where Chadwick held sway.

In due course paupers from Crich were lodged in Babington House at Belper.[84] This was designed by Sir Giles Scott and built at a cost of £8,700 in 1840 on land sold by George Benson Strutt (Section 3.11). The weekly provisions bill at the time was around £17 for 150 inmates, i.e. about 26d per head a week when a labourer's wage was about 200d a week. (A framework knitter at this time would only be earning about 100d a week (Figure 5)). Thus at a time when the nation's wealth and the wealth of individuals was increasing rapidly the paupers in Belper workhouse were much worse off than those who had lived in the Crich poorhouse many years earlier (Section 3.12).

Babington House was still known as the 'Union' in the early 20th century and a place - even then - to be dreaded by the old and the incapacitated. The building is now a local hospital.

In 1869 Denman Mason, in his diary entry for April 2nd, noted that Mr. Robert Spendlove - the Relieving Officer (whom Denman had helped in October 1867 by making up the Parish Books) had been given an increase in salary by the Belper Poor Law Board of £20 per annum - making a total of £100. This was about twice the rate of pay for a craftsman (Figure 5). Thus does an executive system look after its own !

Following the 1834 Poor Law Act there was a review of the rating system in parishes and in 1839 an assessment of Crich Parish for the rateable values of properties was made. A map was prepared which - with its index - gave details of the owners and occupiers of land, buildings and other property in the parish - and assessed each property for the contribution expected from it to meet the remnant costs of local government. Many interesting aspects of land ownership and tenancy at that time were registered - particularly concerning field names, lime works, etc - which have been used in the present study.

By the 1840s the burden on parishioners for relief of the poor (in mainly agricultural areas) had, as expected, been reduced by almost half.[85]

3.14 The End of Tithes

The other form of local taxation apart from the rates, i.e. the tithes, had been a source of resentment for centuries (Section 3.8) but by the 1840s it had also become less vexatious as the result of new legislation.[86] In 1836 Parliament had passed the "Tithe Commutation Act". This stopped payment in kind and substituted, for payment of tithe, an additional rent-charge on land. In Crich a plan of the township (and of the Manor of Wakebridge which, with the Manor of Crich, had principally provided the support for Crich Parish Church over the centuries) was drawn-up and a report was prepared in 1847-1849 which set-out the charges that property owners were to be required to pay to substitute for their tithe commitment.[87] The associated 1849 Crich Tithe Map gives information on land ownership and tenancy which is even more detailed than the 1839 Crich Rating Map. In particular the field names in use at that time are recorded and make it possible to identify some of the ground mentioned in the medieval Darley

Abbey Cartulary (Section 2.7). Thus the Fridensti, Caluecroft, Waumwell, Le Scotteshaches, Le Lewes and Le Heg mentioned 500 years previously can, respectively, be identified with the Friding down Chase Fields; Calver Croft in Culland; Big and Little Warmwell Fields near the Old Quarry; Scott Ashes between Coast Hill and the Cliff Inn; Le Lewes is probably 'The Lees' between the Hilts and Old Quarrys and Le Heg, or Le Hey, Hays Land in the dip between the Church and Hog Nick by the side of the stream flowing from the high ground to the east of Crich Hill. (Hob Hall Field - the present site of Chase Cliff House - is clearly identified as are a number of other places discussed elsewhere in this volume).

The names of the principal land owners in Crich at the time of the 1849 Tithe Assessment are given in Table E. (As for Table D (Section 2.8) an indication of where their lands were located can be obtained by reference to Figure 7). Comparison with Table D shows that some landowners of importance at the time of the Enclosures in 1786 (Section 2.8 and 6.7) are no longer registered, and that new ones have acquired large holdings in the parish. At this time if a landowner was himself in occupation on his land it was he who was responsible for tithe - otherwise the duty to pay rested with the tenant. The dues which arose from the Tithe Apportionment of 23rd February 1847 - as confirmed by the Tithe Commissioners - were paid on:-

1347 acres of arable land
1689 acres of meadow or pasture
436 acres of woodland
175 acres of roads, waste, canals and railways (Section 6.9)

The "Impropriator" of all the 'Great Tithes' of Crich was Sir Henry Sacheveral Wilmot Bart. of Chaddesden Hall. The Duke of Devonshire, William Spencer, was entitled to all the tithes of lambs and wool and "The Vicar of Crich for the time being" was entitled to all the small tithes other than lambs and wool. These distinctions between different types of tithe originated in the way in which they were instituted. (Section 3.8)

The 'Great Tithes' of Crich had come into the possession of the Wilmot family by purchase (Section 2.8).[88] They had been acquired by Sir Edward Wilmot* (1693-1786) - the famous physician who was doctor to Queen Caroline and also to Frederick, Prince of Wales.[89]

The Duke of Devonshire had inherited the 'Little Tithes' through the Shrewsbury connection: they had, at one time, been in the possession of George Talbot, the husband of Bess of Hardwick - who had inherited 'Crich Manor' through its purchase by the 2nd Earl, John Talbot.

As far back as Bricius, the Crich Vicarage had been endowed with minor tithes (Section 3.8), and even today the Vicar is given the 'Easter Offering', i.e. the collection from the congregations taken at Easter Sunday services in the Church.

---

* He was created a baronet in 1759. Sir Edward became Physician-in-Ordinary to George III and was appointed Physician General to the Army. In 1761 he left London and returned to his family home at Chaddesden near Derby : his mother Joyce was daughter and heir of William Sacheveral of Staunton in Leicestershire. He is named in the 1786 Crich Enclosure Award (Section 6.7) as one of the 'Lords of the Manor of Crich', but he had died by the time the Commissioners made their award and his allotment was inherited by Sir Robert Meade Wilmot - the 2nd Baronet.

3.15 Elected Local Government

The 1834 Poor Law Act marked the beginning of the decline of the role of the Justices of the Peace as the local agents of government. Each 'union' of local parishes, administered by a Board of Guardians of the Poor elected by all the ratepayers, reduced the power of the country gentlemen acting as unpaid 'Justices of the Peace'. They had hitherto been able to decide if a local rate could be raised for any purpose and how it should be spent. Although, apart from relief of the poor, their powers continued for about another 50 years, the Local Government Act[90] in 1888 established elected County Councils as the administrative agents in country life.

Although the J.P.s were retained in the magisterial role in local courts this judicial function was all that remained of the former patriarchal rule exercised by them for some 500 years. Soon after the formation of the County Councils, Urban and Rural District Councils were established and, in 1894, the Parish Council was created in Crich. It took over, as its place of meeting, the old Independent Club Room [350540] which became known as the Parish Room. *(Ed: It still assembles on the evening of the first Monday of the month at the Glebe Centre).*

3.16 Postscript on Local Government

As society has become more sophisticated and individuals have gained in wealth there has been a continuing move away from a sense of community and of collective responsibility, at the local level, for maintaining the Kings Peace and for ensuring the well-being of all the members of the public.

Firstly, when villeins could accumulate enough coin to pay rent and free themselves from labour service to the Lord of the Manor, they did so: secondly, men paid to avoid having to carry out statutory road repairs themselves. Then, intent on their private business, when freeholders could pay for deputies to relieve them of their turn of service as a Parish Officer or for substitutes in the armed forces, they did so.*

Coupled with these avoidances of collective responsibility there has been a reluctance on the part of the wealthier members of the community - the freeholders and ratepayers - to contribute financially to the provision of public services. Reform of the 'police' was delayed because of this - even at a time when it was recognised that the village constable was by no means adequately effective: similarly, in Crich at least, the reluctance to pay a rate to cover the education of the local children (Section 5.4) was an issue that raised local passions.

After about a century of local government growth aimed at improving the lot of the poorer elements in society it looks as though there is to be a reversion, as the wealthy grow wealthier and enjoy tax cuts, to individual self-interest at the expense of the common man and his sense of community.

---

* Perhaps the only 'Official' preserving the spirit of the Statute of Winchester and working voluntarily nowadays is the Justice of the Peace, who has had an honourable record of service over more than six centuries.

[1] Critchley T. (1967) *A History of Police in England & Wales.* London.Constable.p.2
[2] Newsam F. (1954) *The Home Office*
[3] Roffe D. (1986) *The Derbyshire Domesday.*Derby.Derby Museum Service. p.32
[4] Critchley Ibid p.3
[5] Phillimore (1978) *Domesday Book (27) Derbyshire.*Chichester.Phillimore.
[6] Watkins A. (1952) *The Manor of Crich.*Manuscript.p.11
[7] Cox J.C. (1890) *Three Centuries of Derbyshire Annals.*Derby.Bemrose I:p.50
[8] Cox Ibid I pp.55-56
[9] Clapham J. (1949) *A Concise Economic History of Britain.*Cambridge. Camb.U.Press p.72
[10] Clapham Ibid. p.71
[11] Roffe Ibid p.8
[12] Trevelyan G. M. (1942) *English Social History.* London. Longman. p.7
[13] Clapham Ibid. p.97
[14] Roffe Ibid p.9
[15] Trevelyan Ibid p.6
[16] Clapham Ibid p.97
[17] Roffe Ibid p.15
[18] Critchley Ibid p.5
[19] Ibid p.6
[20] Cox Ibid I 110
[21] *Crich Rating Survey* . (1839) Derbyshire Record Office. D.1281/PI
[22] Critchley. Ibid. p.22
[23] Critchley. Ibid p.9
[24] Cox Ibid I p.105
[25] Cox Ibid I p.110
[26] Critchley. Ibid p.10
[27] Ibid p.18
[28] Ibid p.22
[29] Ibid p.27
[30] Ibid p.30
[31] Ibid p.48
[32] Derbyshire Constabulary. *A Short History of the Derbyshire Constabulary.* DC Library 363/D.
[33] Critchley Ibid p.8
[34] Cox. Ibid I p.30
[35] Ibid I p.390
[36] Critchley Ibid p.9
[37] Cox Ibid I p.30
[38] Critchley Ibid p.10
[39] Ibid p.14
[40] Cox Ibid I p.391
[41] Felkin W. (1867) *History of the Machine-Wrought Hosiery and Lace Manufactures.* David & Charles reprint 1967.
[42] Clapham Ibid p.121
[43] Trevelyan Ibid p.190
[44] Cox J. C. (1879) *Notes on the Churches of Derbyshire.* Chesterfield. Edmunds p.34

[45] Clapham Ibid p.296
[46] Clapham Ibid p.294
[47] Trevelyan Ibid p.102
[48] Henson G. (1831) *History of the Framework Knitting and Lace Trades.* David & Charles reprint 1970
[49] Cox J. C. (1890) *Three Centuries of Derbyshire Annals.* Derby. Bemrose. II p.140
[50] Pawson E. (1977) *The Turnpike Roads of Eighteenth Century Britain.* Academic Press pp 67-75
[51] Pawson Ibid pp67-75
[52] Clapham Ibid p.213
[53] Trevelyan Ibid p.171
[54] Trevelyan Ibid p.353
[55] Liber Pacis (1740-1870) : Sheriffs Returns. Derbyshire Record Office
[56] Cox Ibid I p.131
[57] Cox Ibid p.147
[58] Cox Ibid II p.161
[59] Ibid I p.50
[60] Ibid I p.181
[61] Ibid I p.170
[62] Cox Ibid I p.173
[63] Ibid p.184
[64] Cox Ibid I p.190
[65] Ibid p.228
[66] Cox Ibid I p.229
[67] Ibid p.391
[68] Overseer of the Poor Census 1811:1812 Parish of Crich. Derbyshire Record Office D.2365
[69] Cox Ibid I p.231
[70] Cox Ibid I p.198
[71] Ibid I p.404
[72] Ibid I p.207
[73] Clapham Ibid p.302
[74] Cox J. C. (1911) Woolley Manuscripts. Derbyshire Archaeological Journal.Vol33.p.187
[75] Clapham Ibid p.302
[76] Cox J. C. (1890) *Three Centuries of Derbyshire Annals.* Derby. Bemrose. I p.124
[77] Farey J.(1811-16) *General View of the Agriculture and Minerals of Derbyshire* III p.551
[78] Farey Ibid III p.549
[79] Farey Ibid III p.557
[80] Mathias P. (1969) *The First Industrial Nation.*London.Methuen. p.49
[81] Trevelyan G. Ibid p.469-470
[82] Mathias Ibid p.50; p.259
[83] Felkin Ibid p.xvi
[84] Belper News (1987) 13 Aug.1987
[85] Mathias Ibid p.338
[86] Trevelyan Ibid p.514
[87] Crich Tithe Apportionment (1847-9).Derbyshire Record Office.D.2365 A/PI
[88] Glover Ibid p.353
[89] Derbyshire Characters (1977). Derby. Derbyshire Countryside p.16
[90] Trevelyan Ibid p.577

4. TRAVELLING

4.1 Early Tracks

Often places acquire importance because they are on routes established long ago by travellers and traders. Early peoples would avoid wooded and swampy valleys where not only was the going slow but a sense of direction, perhaps following a winding stream, was difficult to sustain. What was wanted by the traveller was firm ground with an ability to see, from time to time, comparatively distant landmarks and with a minimum of largish rivers to cross.

One such route through Crich, the Bronze-Age Ridgeway, came from the south over Heage Firs.[1] It would have crossed the River Amber in the Bullbridge-Sawmills area* Which of two routes was used to ascend to Edge Moor is not now known. Perhaps the favoured one involved a crossing of the Amber near Sawmills which went up by the present-day Wingfield Park Farm [364529] to follow Blackbird Lane on to Mainpieces [365533] near where the ruined windmill now stands. There it would join the packhorse train - Street Lane [362536 to 361546] - a 'green lane' between stone walls, many of which survive, and which leads to Park Head and Edgemoor. Near the Mainpieces there is a branch, Holly Lane, which leads down to Bodencote [372538] and Coalburn Hill [374538] and to a crossing of the Amber at Weir Mill just below the Roman fort on Castle Hill [386541]. This latter could have been the route used by the Romans to take the lead from the ore field on Crich Hill to Ryknild Street.[2] From the junction of Holly Lane and Street Lane a packhorse trail runs west, between stone walls, towards Long Wood [364536] and at one time probably joined-up with a track from Thorphill Farm [362535] to the Dimple Lane near Millgreen [358535] - which is well-marked on the 1786 Enclosure Award Map.

What is possibly a later South-North route, perhaps medieval in origin, would descend from Heage Firs and cross the Amber at Bullbridge, travelling along Drover's Way [359523] and then up through Fritchley and passing the Red Lion Inn (the emblem of John of Gaunt, the Royal Overlord of the surrounding country - an inn which was thatched until the 1890s)[3] - it would go to Crich up the Dimple Valley, either along Mill Green or along Kirkham Lane towards where the Lord of the Manor's mill probably was [358535] (Section 9.5). From the Dimple Green [350541] the route would go up towards the Church, Plaistow, Shuckstone, Dethick Common, Middle Moor, Beeley Moor and further on to East Moor, Big Moor and Hallam Moor into Yorkshire. One can, even now, follow small roads on ridges from Crich to Huddersfield without meeting major towns, valleys or rivers.

In medieval times monks from Darley Abbey travelled north on the ridge to the east of the Derwent[4] - over the Heage Firs route and up to Crich before descending the Fridensti

---

* Such maps as existed before about 1750, when turnpikes were becoming common, were on such a small scale and contained so little reliable detail that discussion of tracks and 'roads' earlier than the turnpikes must be speculative. Exceptions are routes where evidence has existed to within recent times of causeways or packhorse trails defined by walls, banks or hedges.

(Appendix) to cross the Derwent on their way to their property at Wigwell Grange.*[306544]

4.2 Cattle Drovers Routes

Until the early years of the 20th century the Ridgeway routes to the north were certainly used by cattle drovers bringing their herds to the fair held in Crich between the Church and the Cross [349545] - as well as by Crich farmers taking their herds northwards to pasture (Section 10.2). Apart from the drovers road coming up from the south over the Amber crossing at Bullbridge there was another drovers route, also from the south, which was regularly used until the 1920s when the cattle market was discontinued.[5] It was particularly used by the Wilmot family which farmed meadows near the confluence of the Amber and the Derwent at Ambergate. Farmer Wilmot, in order to maintain his droving rights, so long as the Cattle Fair was held, used an old route which went up by Smiths Rough [352523] to Top Hagg Lane [355528] in a 'holloway'. A holloway (also the name of a local village on the edge of the Derwent valley)[6] is formed on a steep slope by rain erosion following break-up of the natural surface by the feet of men and cattle. As the water collects, and then rushes rapidly downhill, most of the top and subsoil is swept away leaving a channel which deepens until it reaches bed rock. Top Hagg Lane is shown as a main route on the 1786 Enclosure Award Map and joins what is now Chadwick Nick Lane near "The Barn" [355528]. From Chadwick Nick Lane a route along the line of the Tors would lead into the centre of the village (Section 4.6) using "Bulling Lane" on the way. This route was undoubtedly used, not only by cattle drovers, but also by packhorses travelling down to the river crossings at Ambergate. Alongside Chadwick Nick Lane there was, within living memory, at the side of the road, a set of drinking troughs for cattle and packhorses.

4.3 Causeways

In the beginning, of course, none of the old routes were surfaced. When possible they followed firm ground and were trodden flat and solid by the feet of animals and men. In some places, sometimes on quite high ground, where even packhorses might have difficulty because of a locally swampy surface, causeways were made.[7] One such - still called Causeway Lane [349558 to 348565] -runs near the ridge from Edge Moor to Shuckstone. Another was built on the track that leaves Crich Town End near the Church and passes near to Fishpond House on its way through Hog Nick near to Edge Farm [354553] and so on to Wessington - the "road to Wessington" of the Darley Abbey Cartulary (besides which the Canons were granted land) and a way travelled by Wessington villagers on their way to services at Crich Church. Again, until destroyed by ploughing in the 20th century by the need for 'wartime' cultivation, there was a well-defined causeway along the parish boundary[8] between Wakebridge and Shuckstone Cross.**

The causeways were quite narrow - usually less than a yard wide - adequate for foot travellers and packhorses but not for wheeled traffic. They were constructed by laying flat blocks of stone in line, rather as the Romans had done in their day. Often only a single row of blocks was used. When the causeways were built quarrying was a matter of crowbar and wedge. Wooden wedges were driven into cracks in the standing rock and were then wetted. As the wedges swelled the local gritstones - with well-defined bedding planes (there were several sources of such rock (Section 9.2)) - separated into largish flat blocks of stone which could be roughly shaped with the

---

* In the 16th century the hall there was owned by the grandfather, and then the uncle, of Anthony Babington of Dethick (Section 2.4).
** Reference will be made later to a number of other causeways in the parish where they lie on what became main routes.

iron tools then available.

In an area like Crich, with plenty of sedimentary rock, with clayey soils but with no supplies of shingle or pebbles to hand, and even though it was expensive, the construction of a causeway was the best means of producing a relatively enduring and stable surface for travelling for a man or for a horse, even if not for a wheeled vehicle.

4.4 Packhorses

In the hilly country around Crich, and in the absence of what we would call roads, it was not easy to use wheeled transport, especially in winter. Packhorses were the usual means for transporting goods and, using the causeways, they were able to move over quite difficult ground. The size of the gangs of packhorses was, even in the mid 17th century, subject to a licensing system and was restricted to reduce the damage done to roads and bridges.[9] The name of the mineral railway from the Warner or Old Quarry in Crich [357542] which passed through Fritchley to Bullbridge (Section 7.4) was, in living memory, still called the 'Gangway' and the name could have been an echo of a route followed by the packhorse gangs, possibly carrying lime from Crich towards the river crossings of the Amber.

Packhorses were faster than horses drawing waggons or carts or sleds over the tracks of those days and, whereas each waggon needed a driver, one or two men could manage a large team of packhorses - so that the saving in wages outweighed the cost of feed. Where the ground was especially difficult packhorse trains had a great advantage, especially since they were more flexible, in that horses could be added to the team or taken away according to demand.

The normal pack load weighed about two hundredweight and was carried in a pair of baskets or panniers about 30 ins deep, 20 ins long and 10 ins wide. The packhorses usually travelled in trains of 12 to 15 horses, though groups of 20 to 40 were recorded on occasion. The horses were often muzzled to prevent them stopping to graze on the roadsides and sometimes the leading horse would have a number of bells attached to his halter and neck-collar to give warning of the approach of a pack-train, especially in the narrow holloways and causeways that abounded in the Derbyshire hills. Most of the packhorses were kept by local farmers when not engaged in transport. Typically such a farmer might keep some 20 or 30 horses available on his land.*

Thomas Bowmer of Barnclose Farm [362532] ran a packhorse service from the parish to Derby in 1661 and acted as messenger to Quakers[10] at Little Eaton to ask them to prepare for the arrival of a party of Friends who had been arrested at Eyam and were on their way to Derby jail. Even as late as 1789 burnt lime was still being transported by packhorse trains.[11]

4.5 Cross Routes

The south-north routes - usually following raised ground - were intersected east-west at Crich Cross, the old focus of communications in the village. In 1857 the cross, listed as a market-cross, was then stated to be ancient.[12] At that time it was described by a local poetess, Ann Perry, as an old blackened wooden cross. That cross was taken down and replaced, in 1871, by the present-day stone cross which was designed and masoned by a local man, Isaac Petts, to whom there is a memorial in Crich Churchyard.[13]

From east to west there was a long-established route coming from Alfreton. Alfreton was once a place of residence of King Alfred, and some remains of his palace were evident in the late 18th

---

* The invention of firstly the steam engine and then the internal combustion engine - both using fossil (and unrenewable) fuels - released much land which had been used to grow crops (hay, oats, etc) to 'fuel' animal transport. One day again, perhaps, it will be necessary to 'grow' fuel for transport !!

century.[14] With the Kings Field - a main centre of lead mining including the Wapentake of Wirksworth[15] - to the west of Crich, and Alfreton to its east, it is not surprising that a route through Crich was established. It came from Alfreton either by way of Oakerthorpe on Ryknild Street (not far from the site of the Roman fort on Castle Hill) and up the hill through South Wingfield to Parkhead, or by the old Weir Mill crossing and along Street Lane to Parkhead. From Parkhead the track went in an almost straight line over what is now the disused Hilts Quarry [352544] to near the Mount Tabor Chapel [350544]. Before the Hilts Quarry destroyed it the 'road' towards the Mount Tabor Chapel was called Gray Lane and is shown on the 1847 Tithe Map (Section 7.4). On the marshy parts of this route, near the stream which comes down from the east flank of Crich Hill, a causeway was built which was still visible until the time of the 1939-45 war. Going west from the Cross the route went over another causeway down the side of what is now the Recreation Ground [349543], through the Sheldon Pingle and then along Bulling Lane at the top of the Chase Fields on the downward slope of which was another causeway. (This route is very near to the Fridensti (Appendix)). It continued on below Crich Carr and down to the River Derwent, where there has been a river crossing at least since medieval times.

In 1390 John de Stepul, who came from what is now Steeple Grange just north of Wirksworth, as an act of piety (another attempt by a rich man to save his soul), agreed with the Abbot of Darley to erect a bridge over the River Derwent near to a house which Walter Stonewell [16] rented from the Canons of Darley. It is possible that Wat Stonewell was the ford keeper for the Abbey, whose members used Wigwell Grange as a summer residence. This was the first Whatstandwell bridge. The present-day bridge replaces an earlier structure which was washed away by a flood: it was built and paid for by the Duke of Devonshire in 1795.[17] The Duke of Devonshire owned much land along the banks of the Derwent - in particular the section towards Robin Hood from Whatstandwell known as 'Wild Common', extending up to Leashaw and encompassing 'Dukes Quarries' [333546].

The route from Wirksworth past Crich Cross to Ryknild Street may or may not have been used in Roman times to take lead from the Wirksworth lead field, but there was another which almost certainly was used in Elizabethan times to get lead from the Kings Field to the Earl of Shrewsbury's smelters in the north of the County.[18] From the river crossing at Whatstandwell this route followed the line of the present road through the 'Wild Common' towards Robin Hood and went up the valley of Oxhay Wood [335550] to Wakebridge and then on up, using the causeway (Section 4.3) to Shuckstone and onwards up the ridgeway towards Chesterfield.

Another route from the Kings Field in Wirksworth into Crich could have used river crossings not far from the confluence of the Amber and the Derwent at Ambergate.[19] The Darley Cartulary identifies a "Fridesseford by the water of Derwent" near to Thurlow Booth. The site of this is uncertain. However, on a map made by Immanuel Halton, the Astronomer of South Wingfield, for the Hurts in 1683* a place on the Derwent down the hill from Thurlow Booth is identified as "Linford" and this may have been where there was a medieval river crossing. On the same map a 'weir' is shown at about the position of Oakhurst [341522] and there is a ford leading into the "Forge Close". From there a path is shown which follows the river bank at least as far as Thurlow Booth and Linford. Between 1683 and 1813 the Hurts built a wooden bridge over the Derwent near to the forge[20] and foot passengers over the bridge had to pay a toll**.

---

* Held at the Derbyshire Records Office at Matlock (D.2535:Add 1986/1/18).
** This bridge should not be confused with the toll bridge below the confluence of the Amber and the Derwent, known as the "Halfpenny Bridge", which carries the road from Heage Firs to Holly Lane.

From the eastern bank of the Derwent a route passes up the hill from the bridge over the Cromford Canal [345520] (at the present day) to what was the site of the "Gamekeepers Cottage" [348524] below Bilberry Wood. The route then - more or less on a level - passes below Bowmer Rough and then on up to the corner at the elbow on the present-day Cowper Lane [346533] - the upper part of which leads to Chadwick Nick. From there the old route passed roughly on the level to a footpath leading into Bulling Lane and then went up past Coast Hill and on to the Townend with ready access both to the lead mines of the Crich Liberty and to the routes to the north over the ridgeway past Shuckstone. This track could have been important commercially not only for bringing lead from the Wirksworth Kings Field (if indeed it did so) but also as a way of transporting iron from Hurt's Forge and timber from Hurt's woods (Section 6.8) to the lead mines on Crich Hill. It is to be expected that there would be a link between this route from the Hurt Forge and the drover's road coming up over the Top Hagg (Section 4.2). It is probable that this was through the 'Sideweie' (i.e. the sunken path on the skyline - mentioned in the Darley Cartulary) which was later deepened to take a metalled road and became known as Chadwick Nick after William Chadwick in about 1734 and indeed the drovers could have followed this way along Bulling Lane to the Fair at Crich Cross.

In the absence of a 'main highway' over the Nether Common between Fritchley and Crich (Section 4.6) there were two paths by which people from Fritchley could reach the route from the Forge to the Liberty. The shorter of these two rose from Fritchley Green, round the Rue Cliff Quarry (Section 9.2), along what is now Fritchley Lane and then up a path (which still exists) to meet Chadwick Nick Lane at a point in front of an old row of cottages in which there was a 'Public House' and which is just south of the old row of drinking troughs.[21]

The other route which headed for the southern end of Crich Township, where it met the northern part of the Nether Common, left the site of the Rue Cliff Quarry (where the Primitive Methodist Chapel was eventually built) and travelled (over the present-day Amber View) northwards along the upper limit of Rue Cliff towards the top of Snowdrop Valley [351537] passing, to the west, a house called the Dumble (now demolished) below Dial Farm [352535].

This footpath is still in use and, about halfway along it, there are the remains of a causeway where it passes over a rill carrying drainage water down from the Tors towards the Dimple. On reaching the position of the present-day main road (The Common) the route passed up to the Wesley Methodist Chapel and along Top Lane to the foot of the Tors Steps and over the Tors to descend to the path leading into Bulling Lane. The Tors Steps provided, of course, an easy access to the Forge to Liberty Route, not only for villagers from Fritchley, but also for those living at the southern end of Crich Township.

There is another route from Hurt's Forge (or possibly from the "Fridesseford") to Crich Townend - the importance of which is uncertain. It left the path along the bank of the Derwent at about the position of the bridge over the Cromford Canal at [339532] and went up past Thurlow Booth, continued above Crich Carr and on to Hindersitch Lane over Coddington towards the Cliff Inn [344548]. At Coddington a footpath left the main route and went straight across to Cliffside [341552] and Wakebridge.

4.6 Metalled Roads

By the beginning of the 17th century (the Gunpowder Plot of 1605 is a useful pointer) gunpowder was becoming generally available and was brought into quarrying and, together with rudimentary crushing machinery, this meant that comparatively small-grade stone became available for road building. Although the refinements devised by Macadam in about 1815* were yet to come, the availability of crushed stone in the Crich area made it possible to provide a much wider stable surface than could be achieved economically with the massive blocks typical of the causeways. With wider, firm surfaces (at least in summer) the use of wheeled transport became easier and the use of packhorses and that of the sleds used for heavy loads of stone or timber - at least for local transport - declined.

In favourable parts of the country oxen-wains had been used for centuries. In the middle of the 15th century it had been possible to undertake, using oxen-wains, journeys as far from Derbyshire as Southampton[22] - carrying lead there and bringing back foreign dyes for local clothiers. On the new roads, however, with a surface of smallish sharp stones, oxen were used less and less for, with their cloven hoofs, they suffered appreciably - even though they could be worked every day for longer hours than horses.[23] By the end of the 18th century although the use of wains drawn by oxen had taken over from the packhorses in hilly districts, on the rudimentary roads of the time they had almost given way entirely to carts and waggons.[24]

In Crich, at the beginning of the 18th century a primitive network of roads had been established. The 'main' road within the village was probably one that went down from the Church, past the Cross and down to the Market Place. The painting of 1728, formerly in Wheeldon House (Section 2.7) shows what appears to be a stone-surfaced road down Bown's Hill.

It has been suggested[25] that a principal route from the Market Place to the southern part of Crich Township was up Sandy Lane to where the "Jubilee" now is [349539] (Section 5.8) and along Top Lane - having met Bennets Lane where it levelled out - to follow the line of the Tors to the position of the Wesley Methodist Chapel [350537] which, when built in 1765, was on and facing what was then the 'main road' at the south end of the village and abutting the main area of common land in the parish. A spur to this road reached along behind a row of cottages on "Workhouse Row". There is no evidence of an extension of this route towards Chadwick Nick either on the 1839 Rating Map,[26] on the 1786 Enclosure Award[27] or on the detailed 1847 Tithe Map.[28] The steep ground under the eastern edge of the Tors (on the western edge of the Nether Common) would probably be uncultivated and there may have been a track along it. There is a track on the Upper Common - in use as a path to this day and accessible from the Tors steps - shown on the 1839 Rating Map, drawn before Stephenson built his mineral railway, which runs along the top of the Tors ridge. Either this, or a lost track along the foot of the Tors, would tally with the description given (possibly fictionalised but equally possibly a transmission of an oral tradition) of the route along which the Eyam Friends were conducted from the Market Place to the Top Hagg and down to cross the Amber on their way to Belper, Little Eaton and Derby[29]. Davidson uses the phrase "Down the track on the Common among the gorse and heather". The implication is that there was then (1661) no 'road' down the centre of the land on the Nether Common (known today as The Common): this would, of course, be carefully cultivated by those parishioners with appropriate rights. (The Friends transportation to Derby jail was before the final enclosures of common land in the parish which took place in 1786). The supposition is given support by a study undertaken by Alban Bower who once lived in Grove House. He studied the layout of the buildings around the rather unusual area south of the present Kings Arms Inn and towards the top of Snowdrop Valley [351537]. He speculated that the rows of cottages are set back for the reason that they were built around a 'green' or assembly area where the township met the Nether Common Land. In the Tithe Apportionment the area is

---

* Whereby a surface of smaller crushed stone was placed on lower, slightly convex beds of increasing stone size and provided a well-drained and stable surface.

called the "First Common Piece" and could have been the point of access to the common land from the Township.

Whether meaningful or not it is certainly true that even as late as the 1930s the area at the head of Snowdrop Valley, where there was a common water pump, was a place of assembly. There, on Whit Mondays, the congregations of the church and the chapels gathered together to sing hymns on their tour of the village.

If there had been a road down the Nether Common along the track of the present highway leading towards Fritchley and the top of Bullbridge Hill it is not unlikely that it would have been called the "Fritchley Road" or something similar. Actually there are, on the map accompanying the 1786 Enclosure Award, two roads running roughly along the boundaries of the common land which incorporate the name 'Fritchley' in their title. The Dimple Lane leading from near Crich Market Place to Mill Green and on to Fritchley Green is called 'Fritchley Mill Road' (Figure 8). The other road now known as Chadwick Nick Lane is identified as "Fritchley Road".

It is reasonable to suppose, therefore, that the first proper road down over the common land - the road now called The Common - was the turnpike Langley Mill Road (Section 4.7), the name it is given in the Enclosure Award.

4.7 Turnpikes

After being relatively stable for hundreds of years, the population of England - and the population of Crich - began to increase in the 17th century, and after about 1700 the increase was rapid (Figure 9). Alongside the population growth there was in increase of commercial activity and the harmful effects of through-traffic on local roads grew (Section 3.10). To try to control the situation a series of traffic regulations was enacted.[30] Thus in:-

- 1621 - and reissued in 1629 - a proclamation of James I required that no four-wheeled waggon or carriage should carry more than a one-ton load.

- 1654 Cromwell's ordinance limited the number of horses to be used on a vehicle to five

- 1741 turnpike trustees were empowered to erect weighing engines and charge 20s 0d per cwt for all carriage and waggons with loads exceeding three tons

- 1753 the first "Broad Wheels Act" regulated the widths of wheels.

- 1773 The General Highway and Turnpike Acts laid down complex schedules of maximum loads and by offering turnpike toll reductions and surcharges encouraged broad wheels and rollers and flat 'tyres' without protruding nails.

The capacity of a waggon hauled by six horses was, legally by 1765, anything up to six tons. Six packhorses on the other hand could, at most, only carry a ton between them and with even poorly constructed metalled roads the packhorse gangs could not compete commercially.[31] The regulatory system never worked very well but fortunately road construction improved and this was a better way forward than the restriction of loads artificially to what the road surfaces could bear. This is why Macadam's innovations were so welcome.

The tolls exacted by the early turnpike authorities were intended to ensure that the costs of road maintenance were met largely by the users of the roads, rather than by the local ratepayers (Section 3.10) much to their relief and to that of the local 'amateur' overseers of highways.

In Crich Parish, a 'transit area' if ever there was one, with a heavy local burden of road maintenance, the main demands for wheeled transport and good roads came from the lead industry, the coal mine owners and especially from the lime-burners. (Cheap lime was in great demand for agricultural improvement in the middle part of the 18th century (Sections 6.8 & 9.1). The demands were met, in the first instance, by the creation of local turnpikes.

To establish turnpikes it was necessary at first to get an Act of Parliament to establish a 'Trust'. The petition to Parliament was often submitted by the local Justices of the Peace, who would satisfy themselves that existing provisions were inadequate.[32] An Act was necessary for the Trustees (often local landowners and farmers but, in the early days, the local J.P.s) to obtain the right to take a toll for passage along a public highway, to have a monopoly for the toll and to provide adequate protection for all parties affected by the working of the Trust. Usually Parliament required that salaried officials be appointed, that there be an adequate number of trustees and that there was a specified quorum for meetings of the Trust. By 1707 the amount of work thrust on to the J.P.s by the growth of turnpiking meant they couldn't cope with the workload and independent 'Commissioners' were appointed (a property qualification being a common requirement). The salaried surveyors were no longer required to act as Clerk and Treasurer and were able to develop a more professional approach to the tasks of road building and maintenance. The Justices still retained some powers to examine Turnpike Trust affairs and they would carry out legal functions of arbitration in such disputes as :

- the amount of statute work due to a trust
- the level of compensation to be paid to landowners

They would punish those who attempted to deceive a trust or destroy its property. After the 1740s Turnpike Acts usually conferred powers to:

- compound for statute duty and tolls
- control the value and lease of the tolls
- set-up side gates
- purchase land compulsorily
- contract out for road repairs

To supplement income from tolls, Trusts began to borrow money to carry-out development and improvement of their roads. By the late 1700s, with rising industrial production creating wealth and with the increased rent to landlords following enclosure and especially with the farmers able to sell their produce at rising prices (Figure 5), there was a significant increase in wealth and capital available for investment. Loans to turnpike trusts became a reasonably safe and attractive proposition, paying between four and five per cent interest. Such investments by local worthies, moreover, also improved the local 'infra-structure' very much to their own overall benefit.

In Derbyshire, in the 1750s, 22 Turnpike Acts were passed due, at least in part, to the increased traffic in minerals, particularly lead and iron, brought about by the Seven Years War which started in 1756.[33] Clive was victorious at Plassey in 1757 and Wolf was killed at Quebec in 1759. With the demand, particularly, for lead it became necessary to improve transport out of the Kings Field and out of the White Peak. As a consequence the Nottingham to Newhaven Turnpike Trust was created in 1759. Its objective was to facilitate the transport of lead towards the Trent Navigation and so to the sea and arsenals of London, the route once used by the Romans. An additional advantage would be that lead ore could be carried to the source of fuel for smelting; in the reserves of Sherwood Forest there was timber available not only for making charcoal but also for the 'white coal' used for smelting lead ores (Section 8.2).

The Nottingham-Newhaven Act established that the new Trust would be responsible for the roads in four districts.[34] The 2nd District covered the roads from Oakerthorpe, on the old Ryknild Street, to Ashbourne. This turnpike started at Four Lane Ends [389558] and there was a tollbar at Wingfield Gate. The road climbed to South Wingfield where, in 1825, the gradient was eased by blasting a cutting through the rock. The Manor Hotel at South Wingfield was then a coaching inn called the Horse and Groom.[35]

From South Wingfield the road ascended to Parkhead, where there was another tollbar. This was destroyed when the roadway was later widened at the Reservoir Corner [361545]. The gate posts were moved to become part of the wall dividing the "Top Side" and the "Bottom Side" on The Common at the top of the Dimple[36]. Watkins reported that the Ludlams of Thorpehill recalled wheeled transport using Street Lane (Section 4.1) to avoid having to use the Parkhead tollgate and pay.[37] From Parkhead the turnpike went under the western edge of the millstone outcrop towards Lane Ends [358548] thus avoiding the marshy ground over which the old causeway passed. At Lane Ends it turned sharply south-west, crossed a small stream using a bridge at Brook Bottom [354547] and went up Roe's Lane to Crich Cross. At the Cross the turnpike turned south to descend Bowns Hill to the Market Place passing the Black Swan (Section 5.6) and then the old troughs, used by cattle and packhorses for generations. Leaving the Market Place the turnpike ascended Sandy Lane and followed the line of the Tors over the Upper Common until, where the road now meets Cowper Lane from Chadwick Nick, it turns west and runs down the hill past Chase Cliff, leaving Thurlow Booth to the south and then down to the bridge at Whatstandwell. From there the turnpike climbed steadily to Wirksworth Moor and then turned north-west to Steeple Grange and on, eventually through Middleton Cross to join the present Wirksworth to Ashbourne Road (B5035) at Gedney Hole. An advertisement in the Derby Mercury in February 1777 gave notice of an auction to be held of the tolls for the Whatstandwell Bridge Gate, the Parkhead Gate and the Wingfield Side Gate and noted that in the previous year the tolls had produced £183 more than the expenses of collecting them.[38]

In 1776 the Cromford Bridge to Langley Mill Turnpike was authorised.[39] This came from Cromford alongside the Derwent to Lea Bridge and then up to Holloway, along Leashaw to Windy Gap [337556] and then from Wakebridge up Cliffside to Crich Town End and then down to Crich Cross where it joined the Oakerthorpe to Ashbourne Turnpike as far as the Market Place. From the Market Place the road headed just east of south across the Nether Common to the top of Bullbridge Hill. On the 1786 Enclosure Map this road, now known as The Common, is identified as the 'Langley Mill Road'. As the road descended Bullbridge Hill it passed through a tollgate at the cottage which stands at the end of the Hagg Lane [356527] and opposite Allen Lane, which leads down to the 'Green' at Fritchley.[40] The posts from this toll bar are now mounted in a field between Bowmer Lane and Bullbridge Hill.

It is probable that it was at the time that the two turnpikes were built through Crich that the other 'main roads' in the village were made. Perhaps the first was from the Ashbourne Turnpike to Chadwick Nick, along what is now called Cowper Lane (the line of the old route from the 'Forge' to join Bulling Lane (Section 4.5)), and beyond Chadwick Nick to the top of Bullbridge Hill on what was then called Fritchley Road and is now Chadwick Nick Lane. Another candidate for a good surface would be the Fritchley Mill Road, now Dimple Lane. Eventually the road system as it is now established would be surfaced with crushed stone.

With the coming of 'macadam' roads which could be built economically in valleys and with increased wheeled traffic, Jedediah Strutt of Belper, Richard Arkwright of Cromford and Francis

Hurt of Alderwasley got together in 1817 to finance the turnpike from Belper to Cromford, for the benefit of their businesses. This road is now the A6. The Enabling Act also provided for making a "branch of road from and out of the Belper to Cromford turnpike near the River Amber to join the Turnpike Road at Bullbridge".[41] This, of course, was the 1776 Cromford to Langley Mill turnpike.

There were three toll booths at Ambergate in front of the Hurt Arms Hotel and, on the Ambergate to Ripley road, one at Buckland Hollow[42], which was demolished about 1980.

With these new roads crossing Crich Parish from east to west and from the Town End south to Bullbridge and with the connections made with the valley turnpikes, and before the railways were established, a regular horse-drawn courier service for light goods was developed. By 1835 Joseph Leam - who lived on Mill Green - ran a service to Derby every Friday.[43] The Crich carrier Topham went to Nottingham every Wednesday and Saturday and to Wirksworth every Monday and Thursday. In 1846 it was recorded[44] that coaches (presumably, from the timing [see below] they were mail coaches) were running regular passenger services into and out of Crich. The most important 'pick-up' point seems to have been the Bulls Head Inn which used to be opposite the Church. There were three main coach services. "The Mail" ran to Manchester leaving the Bulls Head at 10.00 a.m. and to Derby, on the return journey perhaps, leaving at 5.00 p.m. "The Champion" left for Manchester at 10.30 a.m. and for Nottingham at 4.30 p.m. The "Peak Guide" left at 12.00 for Ambergate and at 4.30 p.m. for Buxton. In addition there was an 'Omnibus' which went to Ambergate and to Matlock four times a day.

So, before the middle of the 19th century, using the turnpike roads and horses, there was a well-developed 'public transport' system serving the parish.

By 1857 a postal service from Mary Leam's at Fritchley despatched letters at 7.00 p.m. and received them from Belper at 8.00 a.m.[45] Joseph Witham ran a similar service from Crich (Section 9.1).

The materials for road building and repair within Crich Parish were free to the surveyors concerned. There was a provision in the 1786 Enclosure Award which granted such a right in perpetuity. It referred to the Tors Quarry, the Edge Moor Quarry and the Rue Cliffe Quarry and stated:

> "And we the said Commissioners .... do hereby set out and appoint such part or parts of the said Commons and waste grounds as we think proper not exceeding in the whole Six Acres to be used and enjoyed for ever here after in common by the Lords of the said Manor of Crich and proprietors of Estates within the same for the purposes of getting stone and other materials for building, rebuilding or repairing of bridges, walls, fences and other works within the said Manor and for reparation of the highways and private roads which now are or shall be within the same".

4.8 Canals

The Cromford Canal which runs inside, but near to, the southern and western limits of the parish was planned by William Jessop in 1788 and the money for it was raised in a very short time.[46] It has often been described in detail - for example by Nixon - and its usefulness to Crich as a means of exporting bulky and heavy loads, in particular of masonry and of lime, will be illustrated in Part II (Section 7.4 and 9.2). Suffice it here to say that its existence supplemented, for heavy loads, the work of the carriers on the turnpikes (before the advent of railways) who could deal adequately with lighter goods.

In 1835 Pigot's Directory claimed that goods could be despatched "To all parts of the Kingdom by G. Wheatcroft and Sons* "Fly Boats" operating from the Bullbridge Wharf".

4.9 Railways

On July 16th 1836 George and Robert Stephenson were appointed engineers-in-chief for the construction of the North Midland Railway and, in particular, for the stretch between Derby and Leeds.[47] The line ran through part of Crich parish and in July 1839 the Bullbridge contract employed 200 horses and 1400 men on its three and a half mile stretch. Because of the scarcity of houses the navvies who could not secure rented accommodation erected their own homes. The huts and shanties they built were usually made of wood, turf, mud, stone, bricks or anything else they could get hold of. Tarpaulins were frequently used to cover their shanty roofs. 96 square yards of calico used as cover for a stack in Crich, it was reported, was stolen by the navvies for this purpose. The line was officially opened on July 30th 1840. When it was completed the railway, the canal, the river and the Langley Mill Turnpike were so close together at the point where Stephenson had sunk a 'barge' to carry the canal over the railway that a good out-field cricketer could, it was said, throw a ball over all possible forms of transport.

By the time that Denman Mason was writing his diary in 1867 rail travel had become commonplace and a branch line from Ambergate, with stations at Whatstandwell, Cromford and Matlock Bath had been established at least as far as Matlock Bridge. Although Denman did much local travelling by pony and trap - including one journey he records on 10th January 1868 to Church Broughton (to collect a tithe due to his grandmother Mary Marshall) - of which he comments "a very cold drive of nearly 30 miles through deep snow", he and his circle moved about a lot by train. Records of visits to friends at Matlock, Smalley and Derby, by train from Ambergate or Whatstandwell occur frequently in his diary. On one trip to Derby he mentions watching a competitive balloon ascent in the Arboretum, the winner being Jackson of Derby. He mentions one trip to Sheffield on 8th August 1867 when he and a friend took train from Ambergate at 6.30 a.m.. He notes that they "walked down the new railway to Chesterfield, 12 miles, called at Dronfield on our way - arrived at Chesterfield at 1 p.m., stayed to see the races which was very good, about 10,000 people on the course. Horses ran well and appeared in good condition - took tea in Chesterfield and left for home by the 8.30 train - feeling considerably tired after the day's pleasure". The railways had, truly, opened-up new opportunities for 'ordinary' people. In his entry for April 10th 1868: Good Friday, Denman records that "J. Holden, J. Dawes and self went by first train to Matlock Bath. The place was quite busy. No less than 9 special trains came in and upwards of 10,000 people. The day was fine and all persons appeared to enjoy themselves .... returned home by last train at 8.30 p.m....." On the following Good Friday, 26th March 1869, the diary notes: "Pleasant weather. 7 excursion trains to Matlock Bath. Many visitors attended at Crich - the Stand on the Cliff being the principal point of attraction". This, of course, was the Stand rebuilt by Francis Hurt in 1851 (Section 2.6)

4.10 Changing Times

From about 1820 - when the new valley turnpike roads were opened - travel and trade began to leave Crich. The trend was accelerated when the North Midland Railway also pushed up the Amber and then the Derwent Valley. With the decline of the lead trade from the mid-nineteenth

---

* The Wheatcrofts were corn millers and boat builders, as well as transport operators.

century onwards the end of Crich as a commercial centre began to be spelled out. When, eventually, the textile traders were concentrated into the valley factories and, temporarily at least, the economical working of limestone became more difficult, the parish of Crich entered a post-industrial phase of relative peace. It lost its industry and its importance as a high-ground 'transit' area had vanished - for who would climb 'the Hill' unnecessarily ? Except, of course, for tourists looking for novelty or a pleasing view. As Denman Mason indicated over 100 years ago Crich was, early on, a popular tourist attraction for those who could now travel easily and had the leisure to do so.

[1] Tudor T. L. (1926) *The High Peak to Sherwood.* London. Scott. p.236
[2] Watkins A. (1952) *The Manor of Crich.* Manuscript. pp.9-10
[3] Watkins. Ibid. p.43
[4] Tudor. Ibid. p.241
[5] Watkins. Ibid. p.47
[6] Hey D. (1980) *Packmen, Carriers and Packhorse Roads.*Leicester.Leics. University Press p.60
[7] Hey. Ibid. pp.64-70
[8] Watkins. Ibid. p.49
[9] Hey. Ibid. pp.86 et seq
[10] Davidson T. (1901) *Margaret Lynam : Quaker.*Derby.Sainty.p.1
[11] Pilkington J. (1789) *View of the Present State of Derbyshire.*Derby.James Pilkington II.p.312
[12] White (1857) *History, Gazeteer and Directory of Derbyshire.*Sheffield. White p.255
[13] Wragg J. (1983) : Private Written Communication
[14] Universal British Directory (1791) - Derby Local Studies Library p.29
[15] Ford T. D. and Rieuwerts J. H. (1981) *Lead Mining in the Peak District.*Bakewell. Peak Park Joint Planning Board. p.9
[16] Cameron K. (1959) *The Place Names of Derbyshire.* Cambridge. Camb.Univ.Press p.437
[17] Farey J. (1811-16) *General View of the Agriculture & Minerals of Derbyshire* II p.22
[18] Hey Ibid. p.109; p.122
[19] Darlington R. A. (1945) *The Cartulary of Darley Abbey.* Kendall. p.539
[20] Farey Ibid.II p.24
[21] Watkins. Ibid. p.48
[22] Hey. Ibid. p.91
[23] Ibid. p.97
[24] Farey. Ibid. II p.59
[25] Wragg (1983) Ibid.
[26] Crich Rating Survey (1839) Derbyshire Record Office:D 1281/PI
[27] Crich Enclosure Award (1786) Derbyshire Record Office:Q/RI2
[28] Crich Tithe Apportionment (1847-9) Derbyshire Record Office:D 2365 A/PI
[29] Davidson. Ibid. p.4
[30] Pawson E. (1977) *The Turnpike Roads of Eighteenth Century Britain.* Academic Press. pp 67-75
[31] Pawson. Ibid. p.293
[32] Pawson. Ibid. p.82
[33] Pawson. Ibid. p.152
[34] Dodd A. E. & Dodd E. M. (1980) *Peakland Roads and Trackways.* Ashbourne Moorland Publishing Co. p.152

[35] Dodd & Dodd. Ibid. p.155
[36] Watkins. Ibid. p.42
[37] Ibid. p.43
[38] Derby Mercury Newspaper. Derby Local Studies Library. 21st Feb 1777
[39] Albert W. I. (1972).*The Turnpike Road System in England 1663-1840*. p.212
[40] Watkins. Ibid. p.44
[41] Dodd & Dodd. Ibid. p.145
[42] Watkins. Ibid. p.47
[43] Pigot & Co.(1835) *Commercial Directory for Derbyshire*. Matlock. Derbyshire County Library. 1976. p.37
[44] Bagshaw S.(1846) *History and Gazetteer of Derby and Derbyshire*.Derby Local Studies Library. p.167
[45] White. Ibid. p257
[46] Nixon F.(1969) *The Industrial Archaeology of Derbyshire*. Newton Abbot. David & Charles. p.147
[47] Williams C. (1984) *Driving the Clay Cross Tunnel*. Cromford. Scarthin. p.49;p.52

3. Crich Fair
The annual fair in 1908 on the Market Place; always held in the second week of October. Sheep, cattle and pigs were sold at Crich Fair in the nineteenth century but the train and the cattle lorry took the trade to Derby Market and the fair survived for entertainment

4. Whitsuntide 1950
Headed by the Crich Silver Prize Band a contingent from the Wesleyan Chapel parades via Bulling Lane to the Church

5. MEETINGS

5.1 Introduction

The earliest public meetings in the parish, in pre-Norman Conquest times, were probably those of the tythings (Section 3.1). After the Conquest the Lord of the Manor with his baronial court, and then with the Court Leet (Section 3.4), would provide the focus for public meetings - which would often be held in the Church. In successive generations local administration was based on vestry meetings and eventually on parish meetings (Sections 3.6 & 3.15) and in due course the 'administrative' meetings of the village moved from the Church to the Parish Room (Section 5.6). The Church also provided a public place for an early school (Section 5.4) - well before purpose-built school buildings were erected. These also became a venue for public assemblies; as indeed did the chapels and their associated schoolrooms. Of course, 'ale houses' and public houses, meeting the needs of travellers and local roisterers, have for long provided an opportunity for people to foregather. This chapter gives some detail on such activities in Crich.

5.2 The Church of St. Mary

The foothill of Crich Hill, probably once called St. Thomas' Mount, where the Church now stands, was obviously always a desirable place for people to gather together. Without being too exposed they could see around. One local romantic once suggested,[1] since so often sacred buildings follow one another on the same site, that there may have been places of worship there in times earlier than the building of the present church. He even postulated that the name of the inn on the site (open until the 1950s) the "Bulls Head", may indicate use of the site in Roman times as a place for a Mithraic Temple. Whether or not this was so, the place could well have been used as a meeting place in Roman times and in the Dark Ages. What is certain is that the building of the present Norman Church was started in the 12th century. In every sense it is a 'Guide Book' church. There are not only some often-mentioned[2] features like the rare stone lectern and the Norman font with its heavy cable moulding but many memorials from that of William de Wakebridge (who died in 1372) to the present day - all of which contribute something to the story of the village.

A wall plaque lists the 44 Vicars of Crich since W. de Draycote in 1278, and the name of Bricius who was vicar before then. The original building, erected by Ralph FitzRalph in the reign of Stephen (1135-54), consisted of the north and south arcades of the nave;[3] then in the 14th century the church appears to have been thoroughly renovated and rebuilt. To the Norman nave was added, about 1320, the south aisle and then in about 1350 the chancel, tower, spire and north aisle - all in the Decorated style. The nave was raised in the Perpendicular period[4] - the roof and the clerestory windows (and the porch on the south wall) belong to that period - the probable date being about 1400. The first chantry endowed by Sir William de Wakebridge dedicated to St. Katherine, and others, in 1356 was probably at the east end of the north aisle; the second, of 1368, in the south aisle. The niche in the wall of the north aisle contains a tomb and an effigy, thought to be Sir William, on which a figure (now broken) is seen holding a Katherine wheel to the ear of the recumbent knight.*

A major memorial of interest is the alabaster tomb of John Claye who died in 1632 (Section 2.4). It is now in the sanctuary and commemorates not only John and his two wives, Mary and Margaret, but also shows five kneeling figures representing John's children. A name is given over each, but the inscriptions are now almost obliterated. This occurred during the early 1700s when Joseph Mather, who was permitted by the Churchwardens to hold school in the chancel, allowed his scholars to climb on the tomb - "which infamous practice was continued till about 1732" in Reynold's phrase.[5]

> Reynold's (the antiquarian of Plaistow) transcribed the text on Claye's tomb as follows:
>
> "Here lyeth John Claye, Gentlemen and Mary whom he first did wive,
> With her he lived near eight years space, in which God gave them children five.
>
> Daughter of William Caulton Esq. who was unto that King of Fame,
> Henry 8th, Chief Cock Matcher and servant of his Hawkes by name.
>
> And as she had a former match, Charnell of Swarkestone in Leicestershire,
> So she deceast, this Claye did take the widow of German Pole Esq.
>
> Daughter of Edward who was son to Sir J. Ferrers of Tamworth, Kt.
> She lies entombed in this Church with her by whom he first was plight.
>
> So now this Claye is closed in Claye, the fairest flesh doth fade like grass:
> He had one sister who unto Stuffyn of Shirebrook married was.
>
> For death doth give an end to all, and now this Claye shall rest there in.
> All claye to claye shall come at last, by death the due reward of sinne.
>
> Thou death, his death, Thy death is he whose soul doth rest with Christ for aye.
> The sting of death can no one flee, the greatest Monarchs are but claye".
>
> Perhaps it is as well that the clambering schoolboys 'rubbed it out'.

There is, attached to the north wall of the chancel, another memorial to the Claye family which wryly records:
> "Truies doth teach, experience tryes,
> That claye to dust the wind up dryes.
> Then this is a wonder, count we must,
> That want of winde should make Claye dust".

---

* At one time the church porches were the places where village inquests were held when there had been a case of violent, "sudden or unexpected or unexplained" death in the village. The corpse was not taken into church but was viewed by the jury seated on the (permanent) stone benches in the porch. The inquests were often held on a Sunday and the jurors would be brought in from neighbouring parishes. (As late as 1872 an inquest was held on a corpse on the parish bier in the porch of the Church at Breadsall).[6]

An unusual 'memorial' in the north aisle of the Church is an oak beam dated 1640 and carved with the name of the Reverend Thomas Shelmardine, who held the Crich living from 1629 to 1660. The beam came from the old chancel roof and also had the names of the two Churchwardens, John Haslam and John Smith, carved on it. Shelmardine, a diligent man "very cheerful in converse. A kind husband to an Holy but very melancholy wife"[7] was a Presbyterian who against all the odds held the living during the Commonwealth and was ejected from the living at Matlock (where he went on leaving Crich) when the Bishops returned to power after the Restoration. A touching brass plate commemorating Shelmardine's infant son Ephraim, dated, 1637, is fixed to the chancel wall near the vestry door. It says "Noe sooner bloomed but blasted. Yet to revive at the refreshing".

During the Commonwealth a Parliamentary Commission enquired into the condition of ecclesiastical benefices around the country and there is a record of evidence of seditious language, probably about 1650, brought against one Smerwick Clarke who, though not on the list of Vicars of Crich, was either holding the Crich Benefice or officiating for Shelmardine.[8] It runs as follows:

Crich	Articles Concerninge Smerwick Clarke
<u>Witnesses</u>	
Patrick Moris	"Hee usually speakes against the Army saying that they goe on in there one strength and in the pryde of there one harte and that God will not deliver them"
Mary Moris	"Hee spooke in justification of Hamleton* sainge that he was wrongfully put to death and when the Generalles declaration which he sent to the good people in Scotland came forth hee said it was lyes and said that England was the first that brooke Covenant and that the Scotes was the first that selled Reformation (sic) in England".
Mary Moris	"Upon a victory in Ireland against the Rebelles there and a day of Thanksgivinge beinge apoynted by the Parliament and a booke coming to hand concerning the same, he said it was lyes and trudd it under his feete and said: would he reed lyes in the Church?"
Gorge Browne	"And when the Lorde Generalle went into Scotland he said to the Clark I warant thee Clarke, Crumwell will come back with a Bluddy Nose".
Milesent Browne	"And concerning Richard Varden hae said that hee would make him stand upon a Tube bottome with a

* The Duke of Hamilton - sent by the King to Scotland to suppress the Covenant. Adjudged guilty by Parliament of High Treason against the State and put to death on 9 March 1649

Milesent Browne	"He usually carrieth about with him the King's picture uppon a books liefe and usually sheweth it to such as have been enermy to the State".
John Wyld	"And concerning John Wylde hee said that none was against him but such as wear malicious envyous persons and such as weare in a Consperasi against him and that they wear of the devell and to the devell they will go".
Richard Varden	"Hee is knowne to be a Comone lyer and a frequenter of leude Company and is only sosyety is the basest of men and wee for our partes cannot say that ever wee heard him pray for the good successe of parliament".
Charity Littlewood	"And upon his present aposinge of him hee said that hee cared neither for the parish nor Benit (?Benefice) but he would have it from above that he would breake open the Church doore upon the Saboth day morning and hat broken the loocke of the lych gates. And when the Parliament hath appointed dayes of Thanksgivinge for any victoryes he hath changed them to other days of his one devisinge and in his preaching hath caled them Rotten parliamentires".

Some of those indictments are such as buttress the prejudices of the present day when chauvinism reveals itself in the Western World and which, in three hundred years time, will appear equally pathetic to what one hopes will be a less bellicose world.

During the Commonwealth an important centre of Presbyterian activity was the Wirksworth Classis - or Classical Assembly.[9] The Minute Book covering 1651-58 is extant. In the Church of England it was the bishops who appointed priests, but the Presbytery could appoint its own ministers. A set of rules for appointment required candidates to be over 24 years of age and to have taken the 'Covenant'. There was a set of rules for the examination of applicants to be appointed to the ministry - covering their education, their way of life and their ability at discourse. The Wirksworth Classis met once a month, usually at Wirksworth - but certainly once at Crich - and the prescribed monthly fasts were held on six occasions in Crich. There was obviously a close link between the Wirksworth Presbytery and Crich, for it was resolved on 16th November 1658 to hold the "Classical Meeting for the next 3 months to be kept at Crich next day after the ordinary Classical day in each month".[10]

After the Civil War, and especially after about 1750 as the Industrial Revolution was getting under way, there was an increase of population (Figure 9) and there began a radical change in British life - not only in the way things were made but in agriculture, in transport and eventually in social organisation and the way in which local affairs were administered. Most of these things had been fairly unchanged for many many centuries: now everything was about to change.

To the benefit of local landowners increase in population was accompanied by a fairly rapid increase in agricultural prices (Figure 5). The increased wealth of the local land-owning class -

who had 'bought-in' to the parish by purchase of land and manorial rights from the Shrewsburys - began to show in the Church. There had been brass plates displayed to the memory of parishioners for some time. For instance, there was a plate dated 1652 to John Kirkland, yeoman, whose family had farmed at Wheatcroft, it was said, for 500 years.[11] An earlier Kirkland had endowed a still existent charity (Section 10.8).

The later monuments celebrating local worthies were probably less "for the safety of their souls", as had been the medieval hope, but perhaps rather more to establish and demonstrate the place of their families in the local community. In the chancel there are brasses to the Marshalls (1757 and 1758), Smiths (1837) and the Towndrow Harrison children (1837); in the nave there are brasses from the Cooper family (1829) and the Redferns (1803 and 1835). On the walls of the chancel there are plaques to Samuel Travis (1866), David Woodhouse (1804), Jane Woodhouse (1823); near the font plaques to Ralph Wheeldon Allen (1788) and Samuel Allen (1805). John Saxton (1847), whose family lived at the Mansion House at the foot of Bown's Hill, is commemorated on a memorial on the wall of the south aisle. Outside, on the south wall of the porch, is a tablet which has appeared on nearly all wedding photographs taken outside the church for generations. It is in memory of Sarah Towndrow, the daughter of Richard and Ann Towndrow, who died in 1819. Its motto - perhaps not always noted by the bridal party being photographed - is "Be ye also ready".

On the outside wall of the south aisle is a large plaque commemorating the Cooper family, covering the period 1772 to 1842. The Coopers, it would seem, employed an ignorant mason and didn't check his work for, according to the inscription, a son Robert was born two years after his mother Ann had died.[12] On the east wall of the chancel, outside, is a detailed family plaque to the Wright family which dates the death of John Wright as 1777, when he was 59. The Wright family bought into the manorial rights of Crich through the sale by the Hon. Henry Howard (Section 2.5) in 1660 and, at the time of the 1786 Enclosure Award, not only received allotments on Plaistow Green and Coddington Bank, but also at the time of that award shared ownership of a number of plots of ground between the Cliff and Edge Moor (they had been enclosed at earlier times) with the Hon. Nathaniel Curzon.

On the inside of the north wall of the chancel there is a tablet of a later time to which a story of interest is attached. It is to the memory of German Wheatcroft. (There is a family tomb of the Wheatcrofts under the yew trees to the south of the church, and a monumental tablet to an earlier German Wheatcroft above William de Wakebridge's tomb).[13] The story was revealed in the Crich parish magazine of the time. Captain Wheatcroft was serving in India in November 1857; he had earlier fought in the Crimea. His wife had a dream one night in which her husband showed great anguish. She told her family of this the next morning and was so apprehensive that she refused a series of tempting social invitations - which was remarked on by all her acquaintances. Eventually she had a telegram telling her that her husband had been killed before Lucknow on the day after her dream. After considering the effects of longitude on time she could not accept the accuracy of the date of Wheatcroft's death given in the War Office notification. Eventually the Wheatcroft's solicitor contested the matter with the authorities and when, in March 1858, a fellow officer who had been with the Captain when he had been killed affirmed that the War Office had their date wrong and that Mrs. Wheatcroft's premonition had, indeed, occurred on the actual day and time of his death, the War Office finally made a correction to the official record and acknowledged that they had done so.

These various monuments fixed to the church fabric have endured down the years. At one time less permanent ones were also displayed. Many years ago it was the custom to place a memorial garland on one of the pillars in the church in honour of any maiden who died unmarried. Reynolds recorded that this was still happening in the 1770s.[14]

Reynolds wrote at length about Crich Church and its history and seemed especially interested in the bells. He recorded that before 1721 there had only been four bells in the Tower. When he was writing in 1770-71 the fourth bell had been broken and had been sent to Rotherham to be recast. On its return there were, in the Tower, "The Great Bell" (what today would be called the Tenor) which had been made in 1626; the fourth (recast in 1771) had originally been cast, or perhaps recast) in 1616 (since according to Reynold's observation it had the date 1583 circumscribed on the rim); the third bell was made in 1580 and the second in the 1670s; the smallest - the new 'treble' - being made in 1721. There were other bells in the tower too. An old custom in Crich was to ring the Sermon Bell after chiming all the main bells together: this persisted until 1769. After that time the Sermon Bell was rung on its own at first and then all the main bells were chimed. (It would seem that the art of change-ringing developed by Fabian Stedman in about 1668 had not yet been adopted or learned in Crich.) When the chiming ended a small bell called the Ting-Tang was then sounded.[15] This bell had been in the tower for over 70 years without a clapper before the custom changed. (Bellringers today have different customs - as will be seen (Section 10.13)).

Reynolds also noted some facts about the 'housekeeping' of the church. In 1692 a weathercock was installed on the church spire. It was bought from Birds of Mansfield by the Churchwardens Thomas Bowmer and John Beardah at a cost of 28s 0d. The gilding cost 12s 0d. In 1769 the weathercock was taken down and regilded at the behest of David Waterhouse and George Bacon who were then the Churchwardens and who, of course, had many duties to perform in the government of the village (Section 3.6). The tower and the spire were repointed at the same time. In the 18th century the inside of the church was whitewashed - a legacy, perhaps, of the Puritans. It was certainly whitewashed in 1739 and again in 1769. The whitewash coating was removed at the time of the 1861 restoration.[16]

It was a custom hallowed by time that parishioners would be buried in the churchyard. Over time as the available ground was used up, a return was made to the area first used where the bodies (and usually the skeletons) had decayed beyond recognition as human remains and the cycle began again. This seems to have worked well over the centuries. However, when the 'aristocratic' families who had usually been buried in tombs inside the church were no longer powerful and when the yeomen, farmers and landlords who became affluent towards the end of the 18th century became the leading figures in the local community and families could afford to do so, many tombs and family vaults were built in the churchyard. There are a number of Bowmer family tombs and copestones near the church door, and some 20th century graves, and in the area just south of the porch there are tombs for the Smith family - Joshua aged 73 in 1773; William 92 in 1790; William 70 in 1822 and Ralph Wheeldon Smith 69 in 1861; his wife Ann was buried in 1866 aged 78*: for Henry Turton 1800, William Marshall 1856 and a Towndrow of 1890.

The erection of such tombs prevented the easy recycling of the graveyard for burial places, and over the years it has been considerably extended quite a distance away from the church down "Ralphs Furlong" (Section 2.7).

Nevertheless, even in the mid 19th century, Crich and its church had a time of notoriety because of its graveyard. In an issue of "Chambers Magazine" of the 1850s is a report of the scandalous condition of the churchyard where the older graves were being used again and the

---

* Ann Smith was Denman Mason's mother's mother.

bones of the former occupants lay uncollected on the open ground.[17] With the rapidly increasing population, it would seem, there was insufficient time between successive burials on a particular site for nature to bring ashes to ashes and dust to dust.

Deep graves in Crich churchyard and its environs have always been difficult to make for the solid limestone of St. Thomas' Mount is very near to the surface of the ground; the old Church Quarry [349546] borders the churchyard. Within living memory a quarryman Sexton used to obtain, improperly, blasting cartridges from the Cliff Quarry to help him in his task of excavating a deep grave.

The concern of the Church to control its 'flocks' has been evident over the centuries. In the Crich Cartulary (of which there is a copy in the Harleyan manuscripts) there is a copy of an encyclical letter of Simon Islip, Archbishop of Canterbury,[18] of the year 1362 drawing attention to the 'shocking' neglect in the observation of Holy Days - when no work of any kind was allowable. The Archbishop sent a solemn warning that the Holy Days were not to be deemed holidays. In Crich this warning was strongly backed-up by Sir William de Wakebridge,[19] but it had little or no effect. Many who should have gone to the church services spent Holy Days in sport and drink - perhaps coursing near the "Greyhound Inn" on Roe's Lane or in bull baiting near the church at the "Bulls Head" - a more likely origin for the name than Mithras.

Again in the 17th century religion and attendance at church was a matter of great 'State' interest. At this time non-Anglicans were systematically harassed. Thus, although there is no record of heavy penalties, in 1634 six people in Crich were arrested for the 'crime' of being absent from church "these three Sabbath Days last past"[20] - they could well have been Roman Catholics (Section 3.5).

It is not likely that there were, even in the mid 17th century, many declared Roman Catholics in Crich. Certainly in 1677 when the Archbishop of Canterbury ordered a religious census the figures for Crich Parish (not including youngsters under 16) showed that, of the people listed,

      404 were church attenders
      2 were 'Papists'
      3 were 'Non-Conformists'.[21]

In the surveys carried out in 1705-6 the Crich Vicar Thomas England (and the churchwardens William Nightingale and Christopher Silvester) certified that there were no papists resident in the parish.

Although it seems that at the time of his visit to England Denman Mason's family chiefly attended the Wesley Methodist Chapel he recorded many attendances at services in Crich Church - including those to hear the Banns read for his sister Millicent. He made two comments full of 'intimations of mortality'. On January 1st 1868 he wrote: "Very pleasant day for the opening of the New Year. The old Church gave forth a merry peel to welcome its arrival and many persons who give 1868 a hearty welcome will never see it close". At the end of January 1869 Denman recorded the accidental death of his Uncle Thomas in Australia when, drunk, he lost command of his horse which turned off the road and capsized the cart down a creek; it fell on his neck and broke it in two places. Denman then used the penetrating phrase: "- thus without a moment's warning removing him from time into eternity". The next entry in the diary reports: "There is considerable sickness going the rounds of the country this month caused, it is believed, by the unseasonable weather. On Saturday night last the 6th inst. (*February*) there was no less than 12 persons ready for burial (in Crich Churchyard) on the following day. Crich, however, appears pretty clear of fevers etc at present". An epidemic like that nowadays would cause a scandal - so perhaps there has been some progress in the last 100 years.

5.3 Chapels and Assemblies

In the 17th century, the Quaker John Lynam lived at Dingle Farm [371535] just outside the Crich parish boundary, but he farmed land on the Mainpieces and elsewhere in the parish, and Crich and Fritchley were the centres of his community. The Vicar of South Wingfield, Peter Coates, who deemed that Lynam owed him dues and who detested Quakers, took him to court and the Justices (who, as a group, were then not averse to persecuting Quakers and other Non-Conformists)[22] threw him into Derby Jail in 1661. It was while he was there that his wife Margaret arranged for the succour of a party of 'Friends' being taken by four constables from Eyam to Derby Jail. The Quakers, 41 of them including 10 women, were holding a meeting at Eyam when they were raided by a constable and a troop of soldiers.[23] They refused to give sureties for good behaviour and were committed to prison for a month. Margaret Lynam and two farmhands carried bread, cheese and oatcakes and milk to the party "in Farmer Claye's barn" where they were shut up in one room with no provision at all for their comfort or sustenance.[24] (Their way from Dingle Farm went up through Thorpehill Wood (on the old bridle or 'packhorse' way), down 'Nun Field' and then along up Dimple Lane). Margaret also arranged for the Friends to be given food at Little Eaton on their way to Derby - where Thomas Bowmer had been able to warn Friends in Little Eaton of their expected arrival. About a month later, the Eyam Friends were released from jail - as was John Lynam. About two years later John Lynam was again prosecuted by the Vicar of South Wingfield. Eventually, after steadily maintaining their testimony for nearly 30 years, John and his wife wearied of the continued persecution and felt able to leave. They went to Pennsylvania with many other 'brethren' and 'sisters' from Derbyshire and founded a township called Darby, seven miles south-west of Philadelphia where, free of clergy and informers, they were able to spend the evening of life in peace and quietness.

Just after the Restoration of Charles II in 1660 the Act of Uniformity was passed by Parliament - in 1662. Over the country as a whole two thousand Puritan Ministers gave up their livings and went on to endure persecution for conscience sake.[25] In this they were following the example of their 'enemies' the Anglican clergy, who had suffered like things for the previous twenty years rather than desert the church in her extremity. It was under these circumstances that the Rev. Thomas Shelmardine, Vicar of Crich during the Commonwealth, was hounded out of the church. Thomas had a surviving son Daniel who was born in Crich in 1637 and was educated at Repton and at Christ's College, Cambridge, where he took a degree as Bachelor of Arts.[26] In 1657, at the age of 20, Daniel was ordained minister by the Presbyterian Assembly of Elders for the Wirksworth district - which included Crich - and went to Barrow on Trent. He too was ejected in 1662. However, after the 1689 Toleration Act he became licensed as a preacher again and became one of the first legally qualified non-conformist preachers in Derbyshire.

Non-conformism then, though not recognised in the Establishment Census of 1677 (Section 5.2), had some strong roots in Crich Parish. Certainly by the end of the 19th century it held an important place in the life of the village. The first chapel built in the village, the Wesleyan Methodist Chapel, was opened in 1765 and was twice visited by John Wesley - in 1766 and 1770.[27] A "meeting-house for dissenters" (probably the Wesleyan Methodist Chapel) in Crich was finally given a license in 1770.[28]

Denman Mason noted in his diary on 30th December 1866 that exactly 100 years previously, when John Wesley had first preached at the Chapel, Wesley had been "entertained at the common house by Aunt Smith"*. The pulpit used by Wesley is still in regular use.

---

* In the same entry, of 30th December 1866, Mason also states that the chapel "was lighted-up with gas". This was well before gas mains were laid in the village. (Section 10.4). The chapel must have had its own gas generator - possibly using coal and of the type made by Boulton and Watt as early as 1805; a model is on show in the Science Museum at South Kensington.

The Primitive Methodists opened a chapel on Sun Lane in 1855: previously they had met in a room erected by the Independent Friendly Society (Section 5.6) in 1835[29] - the Parish Room. They had already built a chapel at Fritchley in 1829, which was rebuilt in 1852, and they opened another at Crich Carr in 1877. The Fritchley Chapel has now been made into a dwelling. The one on Sun Lane is a motor-cycle workshop.

The Baptists opened their first chapel in Crich in 1839 on Roe's Lane but, by 1875, it was in a dilapidated state and they made a bid for the present site on the Market Place. This was then occupied by the 14th century Manor House of Sir Roger Beler and some cottages which had been owned by Ralph Wheeldon Smith - a descendent of the Ralph Smith of the 1660 deal with the Shrewsbury's executors. His son, Ralph W. Smith the butcher (Denman Mason's uncle (Section 2.9), got into some financial difficulty in the mid 1870s and had to part with some of his property, but never intended to sell his house, then called Wheeldon House. Smith claimed that the Baptists wanted the site, the auctioneer for the cottages was a Baptist, and Smith lost his house before he knew what was happening. To the end of his life he insisted that he had been the victim of sharp practice. There was much bad feeling in the village about the incident and it was still talked about by older people in the 1950s.[30] Watkins claims that people supporting Ralph Wheeldon Smith were so incensed at what they regarded as a swindle that, as one of them told him with great bitterness, many thought that: "All the Baptists ought to dangle like tassels at the end of ropes!!"

In 1970 when repairs were being carried out to the floor of the Sunday School in the Baptist Chapel, the well of the Manor House was re-discovered: it was 18ft deep to water level and had 13 ft of water.[31]

The United Methodists opened the Mount Tabor Chapel in 1864. This was largely built by quarrymen in their spare time. The lower part of the building, entered directly from Bown's Hill, was used as a schoolroom for children of non-conformists who preferred not to send their children to the Church School further up the hill towards the Cross. (Each child paid 5d a week to attend). The chapel was closed (there were only four members of the congregation left) in 1983 and in 1986-7 was converted into two dwellings.[32]

The Congregational Chapel at Fritchley was opened in 1841 - the members had previously assembled in a room over the Fritchley Stores. It, too, had a schoolroom which is still in regular use as a social centre.

In January 1870 the Fritchley (National) School (Section 5.4) was opened under the benefaction of Miss Annie Hurt. This Anglican school also served as a church - a 'Mission Church' - for local members of the Church of England, being served either by a curate or by the Vicar of Crich. In the 1870s schooling was cheaper at the Fritchley School than at the Mount Tabor. It was but 4d per week!

Other chapels in the parish were built at Wheatcroft and at Whatstandwell. Altogether, at the end of the 19th century, there were some twelve places of worship in the parish if the Friends Meeting House at Fritchley is included in the list.

The Society of Friends became publicly prominent in Fritchley in 1863. They had been named "The Quakers" after Judge Bennet in Derby in 1656 told George Fox, the apprentice shoemaker from Nottingham,[33] that he would make him quake before the law - an allusion to the religious fervour which shook the preacher from head to foot as he addressed his Friends.

It was in 1863 that John Grant Sargent, born in London in 1813, purchased Wightman's Bobbin Factory (Section 9.5). Sargent was a dissenting Quaker from Cockermouth who resisted changes to the original doctrine, practices and disciplines of the Quakers.[34] He proposed a 'meeting' for worship in a form to encourage members to adhere to the "ancient path".

Fritchley became the centre of the dissenting Friends and became known as the 'Smaller Body' of Friends in England. The Fritchley Meeting, for some time held at Fernside on Bobbin-Mill Hill, had the benefit of a trust fund established in 1885 by Matilda Rickman.

In 1897 the present Friends Meeting House was opened on Chapel Street in Fritchley. A detailed history of the Quakers of Fritchley was prepared in 1980 by Walter Lowndes, then a member.

In his diary Denman Mason records many chapel events. For instance he notes, on 6th May 1867, that the Wesleyan Anniversary Tea Meeting had been held with Mr. Smedley's Holloway Choir in attendance and they sang several beautiful anthems. The collections amounted in all to £12. On 25th August 1867 he went to the Fritchley Chapel Anniversary Services and on 10th November 1867 he not only went to Alderwasley Church in the afternoon but also to Crich Chapel (the Wesleyan) at night. On 17th November 1867 he went to Crich Church in the afternoon - his 'shipmate' Sam Turton had arrived by train from Smalley by the 10 o'clock train - and in the evening to the Wesleyan Chapel again. On 2nd February 1868 Denman and Jas. Holden and J. Dawes went to Alderwasley Church in the afternoon and to the Wesleyan Chapel at night when his sister Millicent, who was to marry Sam Turton and move to Smalley, was presented with a very beautiful Bible by the teachers of the school - on her leaving Crich.

Millicent was married on 5th February 1868: "At half past ten we were on our way to Church, the first carriage containing Mr. and Miss Turton, Mr. Walters of Belper and Miss Wheatcroft, the second carriage being occupied by Millicent, Miss Grundy, Henry and myself. On arriving at the Church the road was filled by about 500 persons: also inside the Church there was a very large company, in fact persons came from Matlock, Belper, Alderwasley, Holloway and Mayfield, showing good respect. On our return home they were met by Mr. and Mrs. Lee of Dimple House, Mr. and Mrs. Dawes, Mr. and Mrs. Brown, Mr. and Mrs. Wheatcroft, Uncle Ralph and cousin Susannah Smith, cousin Charles from Belper, Ann and Isaac Bowmer of Ridgeway, Mr. Piggin, Mr. Holden, Mr. J. Dawes, Mr. Baker, Miss Boag, Mrs. Hollis (from Ireland), Aunt Mary Ann and others.

The Breakfast Table was filled three times. Mr. Holbeck the Church Minister who married them came from Church in the last carriage and very kindly presided at the head of the table, after which he made a very nice speech and was happy to say that he had never seen so large a company at a wedding in Crich Church before. The bridesmaids, Miss Turton, Miss Wheatcroft and Miss Grundy were dressed in white (book) muslin with long trains, wreaths of flowers and hair in curls, with pink sash ribbon and tool falls. Sister Millicent was altogether white with a wreath of orange blossoms on her brow. The party was well managed and all persons appeared to enjoy themselves and at 6 o'clock pm Mr. and Mrs. Turton took their departure for Buxton in Farnsworth's carriage, the company singing "God Save the Queen" as they drove away. The company broke up about 12 o'clock but several persons, with Charles Smith and myself, did not see bed until about 3 o'clock on Thursday morning.

<u>Thursday Feby 6/68</u>   Drove Charles Smith home to Belper this morning. Called at Uncle Johns and left them some brides' cake. Went to Mrs. Grundies for tea - returned home with J. Holden not very well from the effects of indulging the day before".

On Sunday March 1st the rain was intense and but few people attended the Wesleyan Chapel. "Old blind John Storer preached morning and evening". On Wednesday 11th March 1868 Denman, his brother John and Miss Boag travelled "to Heanor to hear the great Wesleyan preacher 'Punchon' at the Wesleyan Chapel Service at 6.30 pm. Place crowded with people from all parts. The text was taken from the 4th Chapter Isaiah 3, 4 and 5 verses. This great man is about to leave England for America for the purpose of marrying his wife's sister, which the laws of England will not allow, after which he will return home again. He is thought to be quite equal to Spurgeon".

On Sunday 28th March 1869 Denman reported that it was a "cold winterley day with heavy fall of snow and in consequence of the inclemency of the weather there was no preaching at the Wesleyan Chapel in the morning. The evening, however, was very fine with a clear moon. Self, Mother and Brothers went to Chapel. Old John Storer preached. It is now nearly 40 years since he stood in the Wesleyan pulpit to preach for the first time". John Storer preached morning and evening again at the Wesleyan Chapel on 25th April 1869.

Obviously John Storer served his chapel well - and he had a regular and appreciative congregation. Attendance at chapel and church was an important phase of people's lives in the 1860s.

5.4 Schools

Before the non-conformist congregations established their own schools at the Chapels there was the school started in the Church Chancel by Joseph Mather.[35] Reynolds, in 1758, called Mather "a lame ignorant person" - but his school ran on until the early years of the 19th century.[36] In 1799 a 'private' school was established in a newly-erected dwelling house and school on Crich Common (now a private property called the "Bower"). The schoolmaster was John Walker. He advertised his fees in the "Derby Mercury" of 17th June 1799. They were:

Entrance	10s 6d
Washing and Mending	£1 1s 0d per annum
Board for young gentlemen under 10 years of age	£9 9s 0d per annum
Board for young gentlemen of 10 years and upwards	£10 10s 0d per annum

His charge for education - including "English grammatically, writing and arithmetic, Merchants Accounts, Mensuration and Algebra" was £2 2s 0d pa. He declared that new pupils would be admitted on 22nd July 1799 but that those already at school would have no summer vacation in 1799. In this way did the parents of those times, who could afford it, dispose of their children. To set the scale of charges in context: at that time a framework knitter - working long hours - would earn about £25 a year (see Figure 5) on which to keep himself and his family.

In 1847 this school, then called "Crich School" and the property of Robert Lee of Dimple House - which had been run by John Walker for nearly 50 years - was occupied by W. Walker B.A.

A report of 1833 recorded that there were then, in Crich, ten 'day' schools which dealt with 115 boys and 112 girls and three Sunday Schools with 157 boys and 140 girls.[37] Crich Sunday School had a lending library attached to it. In addition, in other schools in outlying parts of the parish, there were day schools with 36 boys and two Sunday Schools with 137 boys and 92 girls - this at a time when the local population was of the order of 2000 (Figure 9). Many of the above 'dames' schools had a short life - depending on the energies and abilities of a few impecunious or charitable teachers who worked in their own homes and charged a small fee to their pupils. One such was Mary Cawood - with her house just above the Cross on the Langley Mill-Cromford Turnpike.[38]

Later, in 1885, the Society of Friends allocated money from the Trust Fund established by Matilda

Rickman to start a 'private' school in a room at the large house "Chestnut Bank" on Bobbin-Mill Hill at Fritchley. This "Quakers School" closed in the later 1920s. The later, more formal, system of education in Crich began in the middle years of the 19th century. It was built on the creation of two voluntary societies. The first was the non-conformist "British and Foreign Schools Society" founded in 1808.[39] This was followed by the formation of the Anglican "National Society for Promoting the Education of the Poor in the Principles of the Church of England" (!!) in 1811.

Parliament gave grants to both societies; in 1833 it was £20,000 and divided equally. Each society gave grants for buildings to local groups of their own persuasion provided that such groups raised at least half the cost themselves: the running costs were met by the children's weekly pence and by local subscriptions. This applied not only to new foundations. Some of the charity schools connected with the Established Church were rescued "for the communion" by a Vicar taking over and providing support by collecting local subscriptions and with the help, so earned, of a 'National Society' grant. The "Parochial School" (Church of England Parochial School - or Church School - or 'National' School; what is nowadays the 'Top' School near the Cross) which was established in 1848 is included in a Grant List of 1860-61. This list was published in the 1861 "Newcastle Report" - which was a report of Commissioners appointed to enquire into the state of 'Popular Education' in England. Following this Government Enquiry the first English Education Act was passed in 1870 - put through Parliament by W. F. Forster. For the previous 37 years Parliament had been voting increasing sums of money annually to aid the provision of schools by voluntary bodies - but it was finally recognised that voluntary effort could never be sufficient to meet the needs of elementary schooling. The basic principle of national responsibility for education was accepted at last. The reform came late (compared with other European countries) possibly for two reasons. There was strife between the different denominational voluntary bodies providing schools and there was widespread unwillingness to pay rates to support denominational schools - indeed a very general unwillingness to pay rates ! As will be seen - both these factors are strikingly illustrated by events in Crich in the 1880s.

The 1870 Education Act required a survey of school places in every parish and town and voluntary bodies were allowed six months to fill deficiencies. If then provision was still inadequate School Boards were to be elected. The duties of School Boards were to build and run the new schools. They had power :-

- a) to levy a rate for the building and maintenance of schools
- b) to meet the fees of children whose parents could not pay (whether those children were attending a Board or a Voluntary School)
- c) to make attendance compulsory within their own areas (few Boards exercised this power)
- d) to decide whether or not religious instruction should be given - with the proviso that if it were it had to be undenominational

By the 1880s the two 'voluntary' schools, the Parochial School of 1848 and the 'British' School based on the Mount Tabor Chapel in Crich were well established [40] - as was the 1877 Crich Carr School (with 65 boys and girls) and the Fritchley 'National' School, built with the Hurt money (Section 2.6). It was stoutly maintained by the local people that there was no need for a School Board to be established in Crich. (By 1875 South Wingfield, and by 1882 Belper, Ripley and Heage, had all elected School Boards).

Indeed, as an insurance against a School Board whose first action would be to levy a rate, it was not unusual for the organisers of voluntary schools to receive more liberal subscriptions than formerly from local people. In 1883 the Rev. J. J. Blandford - one of Her Majesty's Inspectors of Education - noted that the Vicar of Crich was "unpopular with a large proportion of the Parish - but the idea of a School Board at Crich is even more so".[41] The Vicar may have been unpopular with the non-conformists - the supporters of the British' School - but the Anglicans provided him with generous subscriptions for the Parochial - or 'National' School. The British and the National voluntary societies may have co-operated at national level but in Crich there was tension between the two sets of schoolmasters and school children.

In April 1883 posters were put up around Crich inviting local people to a meeting to consider the 'School Question'. The promoters of the meeting suggested that unless some action was taken a School Board to cover Crich might be instituted. The need for action was that a new building was required for the British School - the building being used (at the Mount Tabor Chapel) being such that it was not up to the standard required to earn a Government Grant. The proposal to be considered at the Meeting was that a Board of Managers should be convened and that subscriptions should be solicited for starting a new school to be run by Mr. Scott and his family who, at the time, were running the school at the Mount Tabor Chapel and who were very popular with the non-conformists in the village. Should their proposal be adopted, the promoters of the meeting claimed, it would be the best and most economical way of meeting the acknowledged local need, of retaining the services of Mr. Scott and his family and it would provide parishioners with a means of controlling their own school.

Within days of the posters appearing the National School (Parochial School) Managers had posted another bill up and down the village. This claimed that the Education Department had informed them that its architect agreed with HMI in thinking that the 'British' Schoolroom at the Mount Tabor Chapel was wholly unsuitable for school purposes: the Education Department declined to accept the building or make a conditional promise of an Annual Grant: the children would not be examined by HMI and would not, therefore, be able to obtain the certificate of proficiency award required (under the Byelaws of the local Attendance Committee) to be exempted from the obligation to attend school. The 'National' Managers claimed that the acknowledged Government Schools in the parish were the Crich Parochial and the Fritchley 'National' Schools: "at both of which the interests of the parents with regard to the education of their children will always be carefully guarded and considered by:

> W. T. Sumner - Master of the Crich Parochial School
> J. H. Barnes - Master of Fritchley National School".

Clearly the Anglicans wanted a monopoly for their school - where Church of England doctrine would form the basis of religious instruction. But, of course, this would not be accepted by the non-conformists: it would have been a betrayal of their belief - and then that mattered.

Mr. Scott responded - again by bill posting - announcing the opening of his school on April 30th. His notice is worthy of reproduction:

> "The fees will be less than those of the Parochial School. It is placed under the Government for Inspection so that parents need not be afraid of 'summonses' as reported by the Vicar and his party.
> The parents can rely on the full support of the British School Committee who will protect them in all things connected with the education of their children. Parents are invited to consult any of the above gentlemen (*The British School*

Committee) who will be glad to furnish information and who will certainly not mislead them and in whose hands they will be perfectly safe.

Thursday, May 1st : Public Tea and Entertainment"

The Public Tea took place and was a great success. The "Derby Mercury" reported a good response to the appeal for funds and that 240 children attended the school on its first day. This was about 80% of the numbers attending the Parochial School. The antagonism between the National and the British contingents was obviously strong and the Education Department - which had pointed out earlier that the National School Managers poster included inaccurate and misleading statements (how very un-Anglican !) - demanded that all the posters, from both sides, be taken down.

That the antagonism was very real is revealed in a letter which the Master of the Parochial School wrote to the Vicar. He complained that :

"............on our way to and from school, Mrs. Sumner and I are very much intimidated by Mr. Scott and his scholars attending the British School. The children are so rowdy and boisterous to our teachers and scholars that I need hardly tell you it interferes very much with us in teaching good manners as per the Education Code. I have spoken to Mr. Scott regarding it but since then they have been much worse.......at 10 minutes past 4 (on May 1st) the scholars attending the Scott's School rushed into our classroom and commenced ringing the school bell, throwing down the blackboard and stamping on the floor. I at once went out and the children started to throw stones, etc. On my going home they followed me and I had to hasten my steps or I should have been hurt....Many children complain (on May 14) of Scott's scholars throwing stones and shouting names and (on May 29) many children were crying because Scott's scholars had been hitting their faces with nettles. ..... When going to school, the boys stood in a line to oppose us. A stone hit Mrs. Sumner in the face and caused much pain (June 19). ......June 20 Mr. and Mrs. Sumner going home when 50 of Scott's scholars with Mr. Scott stood in the midst of them and shouted approbrious epithets. Mr. Scott laughed and said: "That's it, boys".

Feelings were certainly high and Sumner ended his letter to the Vicar by commenting: "I rarely go out alone whilst it is light, afraid of intimidation".

When the Education Department would no longer formally accept the Mount Tabor Chapel as a suitable building, Scott and his British supporters found another, acceptable to the Department, and the non-conformist school continued to flourish.

The continuation of Scott's School, and its support by the Education Department, again raised the ire of the Parochial School Managers. They pointed out, in a protest to the department, that the Church School had been enlarged as a result of very generous voluntary effort and that all the educational needs of the village could be met by the Church. A total of £611 had been raised in one year, including £110 from the Duke of Devonshire, £50 from the Vicar, £10 from Florence Nightingale and £10 each from T. W. Evans (the Squire and Cotton Magnate of Darley Abbey - a place with a centuries-old close connection with Crich Church), the Clay Cross Company and the Butterley Company. Over £400 had been collected in a year by National supporters - many of them humble villagers - in Crich itself. After this effort, the Church School Managers claimed, Scott's School (it was always so referred to) was unnecessary, it was conducted for private profit and it would close in no time.

In fact the foundation stone of a new building for the British School (nowadays known as the

'Bottom School') was laid in 1884 and on 5th January 1885 Scott opened his school in the new building. On 11th May 1885 one Dyson (who lived at the 'Bower' where Walker had run a school in the 1790s) was appointed Headmaster of the new school.

By 1899 both the Parochial and the British Schools were putting up a united front to the local School Board. Crich was in the jurisdiction of the Dethick, Lea and Holloway School Board (formed after 1882) and the managers of all the schools in Crich Parish and the ratepayers petitioned the Education Department against the "call on the ratepayers to contribute to schools at Lea. Voluntary Schools in Crich Parish were: The Crich National School with 329 pupils, Crich British 260, Crich Carr National 89 and Fritchley National 141. It was unjust to make poor Crich, with four voluntary schools, contribute to Lea with only one. If Lea School was too small then its managers should refuse to take any Crich children - or raise the fees".

It seemed that by the end of the century educational peace had returned to the village though, as is recounted in "The Crich Tales", rivalry between the Top and Bottom Schools (almost amounting to guerilla warfare) was still very keen, even in the 1930s.[42]

In 1902 the School Boards established under the Fisher Act were abolished and all publicly funded education was placed under elected County Councils. It remains there to this day. For how much longer may be in question ! (Section 3.16).

Schoolrooms were used not only for teaching pupils but also as places of assembly for village functions. Denman Mason noted that on 7th August 1867 "Crich Flower Show was held this day in the Parochial Schoolroom when some first-class flowers and garden produce was shown. The following prizes were awarded to Edwin Mason. Spring onions - bunch of six - first prize: radishes - first prize: kidney beans - first prize: apples - 2nd prize: white potatoes - first prize: red potatoes - 2nd prize: carrots - 2nd prize being 4 first prizes and 3 second prizes. The day was very fine". This was his only note of approval of anything his father did: the list of prizes was very like what would be given today.

Another public gathering in 1868 was organised by Jim Holden, J. Dawes and Denman Mason. It was the Annual New Year's party - actually held on 14th January 1868 - "when upwards of 60 persons took tea. Doctor Hall occupied the Chair during the evening. Miss Miers of Bakewell presided at the piano and J. W. Lee on the Harmonium, self taking the part of M.C. Several songs were well encored especially the "Worn Out Tile" sung by myself and the "British Lion" by J. W. Lee. The company enjoyed themselves and the affair ended at 2 am Wednesday morning".

Obviously quite a party - and possibly the forerunner of the New Years Eve Whist Drive and Dance (Section 10.11) later organised for over 50 years by the Crich Cricket Club - usually in the Bottom School.

5.5 A Celebration on the "Hill"

Another mid-19th century gathering in Crich about which there is a record was the celebration of the end of the Crimean War in 1856.[43] The Treaty of Paris had been signed at the end of March and on a Tuesday in mid June Crich was decorated with flags, floral arches, garlands and mottos. Squire Hurt of Alderwasley gave support and provided a dinner for 500 inhabitants. Bands were engaged from Derby and Sutton-in-Ashfield to add music to the merriment.

In the afternoon a grand procession, led by members of the Druid's Lodge set out from the Market Place and marched up the hill to the Cliff. It was headed by banners and two mottos bearing the words "God Save the Queen" and "Peace to all the World". The hero of the day was Sergeant Wetton of the 95th Derbyshire Regiment - a local man who had lost a leg at the storming of the Heights of Alma. He sat on the top of a triumphal car designed and decorated by a member of an old Crich family - Mr. R. L. Saxton.

The final gathering was in the evening and people came from far and wide in the county - in flats, carts, gigs and phaetons - and assembled around the foot of the Stand at the top of Crich Hill. As darkness fell the crowd grew to about 4000 and two beacons - one by the Stand, the other on the south side of the Cliff - threw out a smoking flame. There were blazing tar barrels, rockets and fireworks and the sound of cheering, the strains of music and the firing of cannons went on till well past midnight.

Crich was not alone in celebrating on this day for at night, from the Stand, could be seen the beacons of the Peak, of Nottingham and of Leicestershire as well as the Furnaces of the Erewash Valley.

5.6 Public Houses

In Crich, as everywhere in Britain, the public house was a well-established meeting place for local people.

In the nineteenth century the following inns and alehouses were strung out along the main routes in and through the parish*:

> Lord Nelson at the bottom of Bullbridge Hill
> Canal Inn in Bullbridge
> Red Lion in Fritchley
> Shoulder of Mutton in Fritchley
> Kings Arms on Crich Common
> Royal Oak opposite the Parish Room
> Rising Sun at the top of the Dimple
> Black Swan at the foot of Bown's Hill
> Jovial Dutchman at the Cross
> Greyhound on Roe's Lane
> Wheatsheaf on Wheatsheaf Lane
> Bulls Head opposite the Church
> Cliff Inn at Town End on Cliffside
> Miners Hack at Wakebridge

Watkins also records that there was an inn called "Last Drink Out" near Causeway Lane[44] - on the Drover's road to the north - and there was, at one time, a "Bluebell Inn" at Fritchley thought to be at what is now called Church Farm on Church Street. At Whatstandwell there were the Wheatsheaf Inn and the Derwent Hotel and, at one time, an inn on Chadwick Nick Lane. (Section 4.5).

An earlier inn in Crich, near the Market Place and at the foot of Bown's Hill just south of the Black Swan, was a coaching inn called the "White Swan". The archway into the premises still exists and it may be this inn which was called the "Nether Black Swan" in advertisements in the Derby Mercury in 1799. The swan seems particularly associated with inns at the foot of Bown's Hill and since the existence of a black swan was not known until Captain Cook returned from his journey to Australia in the 1770s it is possible that the White Swan was renamed in recognition

---

* In the 1839 Rating Survey the Rising Sun, the Black Swan and the Greyhound (and several unnamed Beer Shops) were rated on the basis that they had 'Brewhouses', i.e. made their own beer.

of the novelty.[45] Legend has it that there was a subterranean passage linking the "Swan" inns with another old inn on the other side of the Back Lane which goes down behind the Bottom School and past the Comrades Club to Hilts cottages. Buildings on the "Swan" site can be seen on the 1728 painting of the Market Place and Bowns Hill that is held in Chiddingstone Castle.

Two other village inns, about which but little is known are spoken of. The first "The Victory" is said to have been in what is now Victory Cottage immediately to the south of the junction of New Road and the Common . The other, "Iron Gates", was at Crich Carr to the south of the upper part of Ludway Carr Road , on Glen Road towards the foot of Bryan's Steps.

Most of the public houses had clubrooms, many still in use for public meetings in the 20th century (Section 10.9) and evidence about the use of such rooms as public meeting places for the conduct of business and commerce is preserved in advertisements and notices in the Derby Mercury. Some examples are:

- an announcement on 28th February 1789 of a sale of timber to be held at the Canal Inn on Bullbridge. About 300 oak trees in each of three woods, Culland Wood, Caldwell Wood and Shore's Wood were to be sold.

- on 14th March 1799 notice was given of a meeting to be held in the Bulls Head at Crich by the Trustees of the Cromford to Langley Mill Turnpike to consider the propriety of erecting a chain or a side gate on a road leading to the turnpike between Bullbridge and the Tollbar House.

- on 18th January 1799 an Auction Sale was to be held at the Nether Black Swan in Crich of a freehold estate at Plaistow currently occupied by Ralph Wild and Samuel Orme.

- on 3rd October 1799 an auction was to be held at the Bulls Head, Crich for the letting of toll-gate rights on the Cromford to Langley Mill Turnpike.

- on lst August 1799 a sale of messuage, garden shop, cowhouse and four acres of land at Edge Moor, Plaistow was handled by J. Walker (the schoolmaster who opened the new school at the Bower on the Common in 1799 (Section 5.4))

Meetings other than sales and auctions were also held in the local inns. The Derby Mercury of 28th February 1799 gave notice of a meeting, at the "Peacock", Oakerthorpe (it being an annual meeting) of the South Wingfield Association of the Prosecution of Felons. The largest group of members of this association from a single village, eleven in number, came from Crich Parish. They included Jos Bowmer and Thomas Travis, local farmers and millers and Sam Turton of the family that owned the cotton mill on the Dimple Brook. Other members of the Association included Francis Hurt of Alderwasley; Outram, Wright, Beresford and Jessop of Butterley; Peter Nightingale and Joseph Wass of Lea - all of whom had business interests in the quarries and lead mines of Crich. The Mercury reported that at a meeting on 28th November 1798 there had been agreement on the rewards to be granted to an informer, for evidence leading to a conviction, for the following crimes:-

£5   5s   0d for burglary or highway robbery

£3 3s 0d for stealing a horse, or a cow, or a pig or any other capital offence
10s 0d for stealing poultry, cutting trees, hedges, etc., or destroying or stealing utensils or peas, beans, cabbage, etc. or any other petty larceny

In 1799 the average weekly wage of a labourer would be about 8s 0d (Figure 5).

   The Derby Mercury of 27th February 1800 carried a notice from the South Wingfield Association giving details of break-ins at Bullbridge and Chase Cliffe and an offer of rewards for information leading to conviction.

The public houses were also the places where the Friendly Societies met. In 1793 when these began to be formed four were organised in Derbyshire, the first registered at Sessions being at Alfreton, Crich and Ashford.[46] By the following year there were 98, by the end of the century 143 and by 1830 399 had been filed by the Clerk of the Peace - in those days the senior bureaucrat of local government.

In 1803 there were three "Mens Friendly Societies" in Crich. Together they had 106 members - about 44 % of possible contributors. There was also a "Female Friendly Society" with 60 members - which covered about 9% of those possible. Typical objectives of a 'female' society (this example is for the Glossop Female Friendly Society) were:-

"For the purpose of support of such members of this society as shall at any time be rendered incapable of work by means of Sickness, Lameness, Old Age or Casualties and for the decent interment of deceased Members, their Husbands and Widowers".[47]

The first society in Crich (a copy of its rule book is still extant) was the Independent Friendly Society and was instituted "For the Benefit of Sick and Infirm Members" and it met formally for the first time on 4th October 1794.[48] For some years its meetings were held at the Black Swan in Crich. Later it held meetings in its own Clubroom, built in 1835 - in what became the Parish Room. The Society was operated under a constitution comprising some 43 Articles and the formalities almost matched those of a London Livery Guild (on which, indeed, they may have been based). Eligibility for entry, the monthly subscription, the dates of monthly meetings (on the "First Saturday in every month between the hours of six and eight o'clock in the evening, from Michaelmas to Lady-Day and between the hours of seven and nine o'clock in the evening from Lady-Day to Michaelmas") and the functions and control of the Society were defined in some detail. The Society was governed by a Master, two Wardens and twelve Assistants, who included one to act as Constable, another as his Deputy and two others to officiate as Butlers. The posts of Constable and Butler were to be "chosen by rotation as they stand on the Roll", any member refusing such office had to pay fines to the Master and other officers. The duties of the Master required him to call over the Roll at specific times, the Wardens and Assistants to help him as necessary and to execute other business. The Constable's job was to preserve peace and good order, and that of the Butler was "to deliver Liquor out in due Proportion". If the Butlers brought in more ale than authorised by the Master and Wardens (the cost was covered by levy of twopence - included in the monthly subscription of a shilling) then "they must pay for the Overplus". On Whitsun Tuesday the Master and Wardens were required to organise a dinner for all members of the Society residing within six miles of the Clubroom - and a member was required to attend in decent apparel "with a pair of good white gloves, and a ribbon, provided at his own expense". (Business for framework knitters ?)

After the dinner the Society was required to parade the town. Before the dinner they went to church to hear Divine Service - each member carrying a wand provided by the Wardens. Officers and members failing to attend meetings or failing in their assigned duties were subject to forfeits:

for example, for a shilling if neglecting to attend a meeting at the specific request of the Master or Wardens - three days notice having been given. When a member had been in the Society for twelve months, and if he became sick, lame or blind and unable to follow his occupation, he was entitled to receive seven shillings for each week that his inability continued, for a period not exceeding ten weeks, provided that the cause did not proceed from a "vicious course of life" or from some infirmity concealed from the Society at the time of his entrance. After then, if the disability continued, the sufferer got six shillings for ten weeks more, then five for another ten weeks and if he needed help beyond thirty weeks he could receive four shillings a week for so long as his inability continued. If members lived outside the Constabulary of Crich they were required to provide certificates about the continuance of their state and the Master and Wardens were empowered to visit the sick members at stipulated times to keep an eye on those drawing benefit. (Infectious diseases could prompt exemption from a visit). A member who attained the age of 70 could draw four shillings a week for life, provided that he made no other claims, e.g. for sickness, on the Society. Provision was also made not only for widows but for widowers, who could get help for funeral expenses. Officers and assistants were required to attend the interment of a deceased member, decently dressed and each carrying a "Black Wand and Scarf - and a Pair of White Gloves provided at his own Expense". Again there were forfeits for non-execution of these duties and there were fines on members who misbehaved by brawling or behaving 'indecently', by refusing to be silent during the transaction of business or by proposing to break-up the Society. Other Articles covered items concerning administration, elections and interpretation of the Constitution. As noted elsewhere, the Clubroom of the Independent Society became the Parish Room in 1894 following the Local Government Act of 1894.

Another public house which provided a clubroom for a Friendly Society was the Jovial Dutchman. Here met the Cleft in the Rock Lodge No.123 of the United Ancient Order of Druids, who in 1838 had their byelaws printed by T. Turner of Pentrich and who, in 1856, led the procession celebrating the end of the Crimean War.

On Whit Monday 10th June 1867 Denman Mason, who returned from a holiday in Matlock (Well Dressings were viewed at Matlock Bath), noted that he: "Saw three Clubs marching through the Township of Crich today with three first class brass bands". It would seem that these Whitsuntide marches by the Friendly Societies were the origin of the later Whitsuntide Walks by the religious organisations in Crich (Section 10.12). No mention was made by Mason of church or chapel organisations taking part in the Whitsuntide Walks - though he does note the Anniversary Services at various chapels.

5.7 Clubs

Public sports clubs were a product, in Crich, largely of the 20th century (Section 10.9). However, as perhaps befitted an Australian, even in the 1860s, Denman Mason was very keen on cricket. He noted, on 26th May 1868, that the London Telegraph reported that there never was so much money taken at any time before on the cricket ground at Lords as in the current match between the Australian black eleven and the All-England team. The All-England team went in first and made 222 runs; the 'blacks' made 84 first innings and 132 in the second - thus losing by an innings and 6 runs. On Thursday 3rd September 1868 Mason recorded that he'd been to Derby to see the Australian blacks play against a South Derbyshire eleven. Again the blacks lost, this time by 126 runs. Denman thought the Australians did not play a winning game in the second innings in consequence of their having to go through other sports in the same day, "namely throwing the 'bowmerang', sham fight and Dick a Dick dodging the cricket ball, etc - which he accomplished in first-rate style, four men throwing at him at a distance of about 8 yards, each trying to strike him for about 20 minutes, but all failed to strike him for he took care to guard each ball".

He was comforted a little when the blacks won a game with Burton-on-Trent but noted that several had been ill when they arrived in England and one had died soon after. He declared that: "There is no mistake but that they are good fielders and Cuzens is a good round-arm bowler".

At about this time during his visit Denman Mason started recording details of cricket matches in Crich in which he played. At the first general meeting at the Bulls Head of the Crich United Cricket Club on 21st April 1869 he was appointed Secretary of the Club for the year. The annual subscription was fixed at 2s 6d. The opening match of the 1869 season was played on Richard Bryan's green (probably on Benthill) and was between the married and the single members of the Club. The single won. Before the formation of the United Cricket Club the last match of the 1868 season had also been between the single and the married men of Crich: again the single men had won, by seven runs. It is notable that this match took place on 14th October 1868, which nowadays would be regarded as a very late end to the cricket season. That match was followed by the customary supper at the Bulls Head. On the previous Monday Crich had beaten the Ripley Club on B. Taylor's ground near the Cliff and on the Tuesday Crich had triumphed over Riddings by 103 runs. It was Crich Fair time ! Mason pointed-out that the landlord of the Bulls Head, Benjamin Taylor, (of the Cliff Cricket Ground!) had had a fair share of custom, having had three suppers in succession. A cricket festival at Crich Fair was good business and a good end to the season !

In the previous season there had been several intra-village cricket matches, nearly all ending with a supper at the Bulls Head, usually at a price of 1s 6d each. Apart from the single/married matches, there was a match on July 30th - again on Taylor's field between North Crich and South Crich, the South being victors by six runs. On 24th August 1868 Crich Carr played Crich Common, for 1s 0d a man, the Common being victors by nine runs.

There were also challenge matches with clubs from other villages and townships; for instance, Riddings challenged Crich to play for a new ball.

No doubt that the cricket matches, based on the Bulls Head, were of some importance in Denman Mason's life in 1868.

5.8 Crich Reading Room

The 'foundation stone-cum-plaque' on the Crich Reading Room in Sandy Lane [349541] says that the building was erected by public subscription in 1889. The names celebrating the erection of the building are:-

   H. Dyson of Crich (Headmaster of the British School)
   R. Wildgoose J.P. of Holloway
   J. A. Jacoby M.P. of London
   E. Kirk of Crich
   J. Dawes of Crich (friend of Denman Mason)

In Kelly's Directory of 1895 it says that the Reading Room was built at a cost of £300, raised in 1887.[49] It is likely, therefore, that the village effort involved in collecting the £300 was made to celebrate Queen Victoria's Golden Jubilee. The village certainly built a stone circle (marked

VR 1887) on the common ground at the top of Sandy Lane [349540], which was allocated for common use by the 1786 Enclosure Commissioners, and planted trees in it to celebrate the Queen's long reign. The village did the same again in 1897 at the Queen's Diamond Jubilee, marking the second circle VR 1897. The area of ground around these two memorial stone circles and their trees - at the beginning of the footpath over the Tors and the track down to Bennets Lane - is still known as The Jubilee.

5.9 Footnote

In the parish of some 3,000 inhabitants at the end of the 19th century there were, apart from meeting places in the schools and in the Parish Room and the Reading Room, eleven places of worship and about fifteen public houses at which assemblies were held. Many of the public houses no doubt had come into being originally to serve the needs of travellers using the traditional 'high ground' routes in the district and were not solely to satisfy the more convivial villagers. In any case, traffic 'through' the village was on the wane and the heyday of the public house was nearly over. Nevertheless, it must have been some comfort to the more pious villagers, so many of them non-conformist, that they could look to their Sundays regularly spent in places of worship which, in numbers certainly, could nearly match the weekday influence of alehouses in the parish !

[1] Watkins A. (1952) *The Manor of Crich*. Manuscript. p.57
[2] Butler R. (1977) *A Short History of St. Mary's Church, Crich*. Bakewell. Smith.
Cox J. C. (1879) *Notes on the Churches of Derbyshire*. Chesterfield. Edmunds.
Done A. B. (1912) *History of St. Mary's Church, Crich*. Belper. G. Gibson
Pevsner Sir. N. (1978) *Buildings of England:Derbyshire*. Harmondsworth. Penguin
[3] Cox. Ibid. p.52
[4] Done. Ibid. p.6
[5] Cox. (1879) Ibid. p.57
[6] Cox J. C. (1890) *Three Centuries of Derbyshire Annals*. Derby. Bemrose. I. p.79
[7] Cox. (1879). Ibid. p.61
[8] Cox (1890). Ibid. II p.67
[9] Cox (1890) I. p.325
[10] Cox. Ibid. I. p.335
[11] Cox (1879). Ibid. p.60
[12] Dawes J. G. (1983). *The Crich Tales*. Cromford. Scarthin. p.58
[13] Done. Ibid. p.12
[14] Cox J. C. (1911) *Woolley Manuscripts*. Derbyshire Archeological Journal. Vol.33. p.172
[15] Camp J. (1975) *Discovering Bells and Bellringing*. Aylesbury. Shire. p.9
[16] Done. Ibid. p.20
[17] Watkins. Ibid. pp.1-2
[18] Cox (1879). Ibid. pp.45-49
[19] Watkins. Ibid. p.2
[20] Cox (1890). Ibid. p.290
[21] Cox. Ibid. p.291
[22] Trevelyan G. M. (1942). *English Social History*. London. Longman. p.255
[23] Cox. (1890). Ibid. I. p.345
[24] Davidson T. *Margaret Lynam:Quaker*. Derby. Sainty. p.2

[25] Trevelyan. Ibid. p.260
[26] Watkins. Ibid. p.27
[27] Hodgson J., Hodgson S. & Cooper D. (1977). *Non-Conformist Chapels in Crich.* Crich Silver Jubilee p.5
[28] Cox. (1890). Ibid. I. p.369
[29] Bagshaw S. (1846) *History & Gazetteer of Derby and Derbyshire.* Derby Local Studies Library.
[30] Watkins. Ibid. p.65
[31] Wragg J. (1985) Lecture : Fritchley OAP Friendship Club
[32] Ripley and Heanor News. Ripley.
[33] Cox. (1890). Ibid. I. p.340
[34] Lowndes W. (1980). *The Quakers of Fritchley 1863-1980.* Fritchley. Friends Meeting House
[35] Cox (1879). Ibid. p.57
[36] Done. Ibid. p.10
[37] Watkins. Ibid. p.66
[38] Crich Rating Survey (1839). Derbys Record Office. D.1281/PI
[39] Johnson M. (1970). *Derbyshire Schools in the Nineteenth Century.* Newton Abbott. David & Charles. p.29; p.65 et seq
[40] Johnson. Ibid. p.161
[41] Johnson. Ibid. pp.131-135
[42] Dawes. Ibid. p.26
[43] Garlick S. L. (1966). *How Crich Celebrated Peace in 1856.* Derbys Miscellany Vol.3.6. p.602
[44] Watkins. Ibid. p.45
[45] Watkins. Ibid. p.44
[46] Cox (1890). Ibid. II p.297
[47] Farey J. (1811-16). *General View of the Agriculture & Minerals of Derbyshire.* III p.565
[48] Independent Friendly Society (1794) Rules and Articles. Derby. Drewry.
[49] Kelly's Directory of Derbyshire. 1895

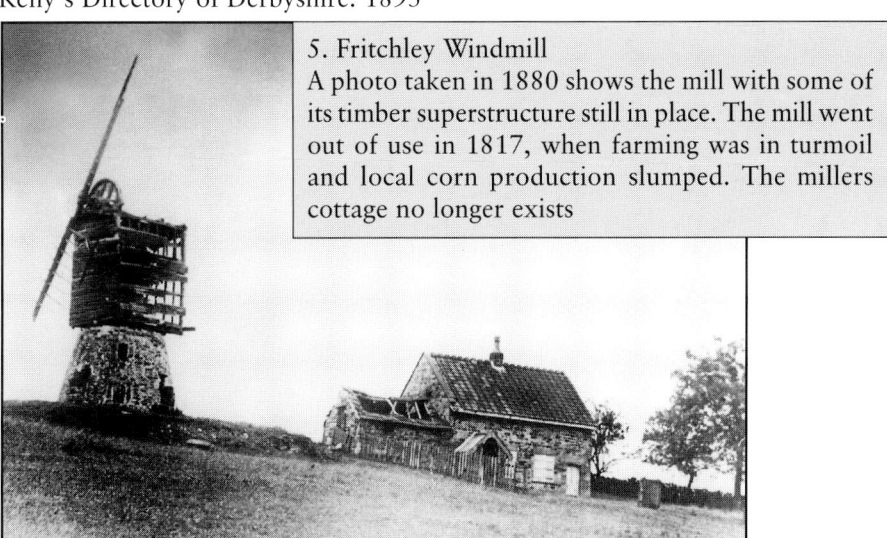

5. Fritchley Windmill
A photo taken in 1880 shows the mill with some of its timber superstructure still in place. The mill went out of use in 1817, when farming was in turmoil and local corn production slumped. The millers cottage no longer exists

PART II
THE STORY OF WORK

6. FARMING

6.1 Villein's and Freeholder's Lands

The earliest record of farming in the village[1] shows that Ralph Fitzhubert, the King's local tenant-in-chief, had on his home farm (or demesne) a plough and land for a plough. There were, under his control in Crich and Shuckstonefield, ten villagers and two smallholders who between them had three ploughs; there was a three-acre meadow and a woodland pasture three leagues long and one league wide. A league in Domesday Book[2] is usually about one and a half miles and since the extremities in the parish at present are about four miles apart north to south and about two miles east to west it is clear that in 1086 a very high proportion of the land in Crich could be classed as woodland pasture.

Unlike the sokemen in Crich (Section 3.4) who were comparatively independent the villeins, who were peasants with a toft and croft (a house plot and a smallholding) in the village and a share in the common land of the village, were required to work for two or three days a week on the Lord of the Manor's farm and more often when there were seasonal jobs to be done. They would be required to plough, to sow, reap, make hay, transport goods and carry-out repairs to the Lord's hall and mill. A group of villeins owning a plough, usually drawn by a team of eight oxen (but the number would depend on the type of soil), was obliged to work the Lord's farm with their own equipment. A plough team represented a considerable 'investment' and was recorded in Domesday[3], for it could be used as a basis for tax.

In addition to providing labour the villeins were 'bound to the soil' in the sense that they had no right to leave their land, they had to grind their corn at the Lord's mill and they could not give their children in marriage without his consent. (The future prosperity of the Manor and of its Lord might depend on how the rights of villeins were combined or divided by intermarriage between local families !)

Each farmer, or villein, had a certain number of arable strips in the common land of the village. These were usually scattered about over the 'open' fields so that each got a share of the good and of the less good land.[4]

In a wooded region like Crich in medieval times, and certainly in nearby Sherwood Forest, there was but little permanently enclosed land - either arable or pasture - much away from the very centre of the village: beyond this sheep and cattle pastured with the King's or the Lord's deer.[5] The villagers as a group, or occasionally individuals, would sometimes enclose portions of grazing land, tilling these 'breaks' for five or six years and then letting them revert to grazing. These 'outfields' would get but little manure and after cropping for a time would need a rest. The breaking-up of an outfield that had gone back to rough pasture for ten years or so was always a heavy job and when broken it would be doled-out to those tillers of the 'infields' whose oxen had done the work.[6]

Most of the manure available would be allocated to the infields in and near the Lord's demesne. As indicated in Section 2.7, the Canons of Darley Abbey had a grange (i.e. a pasturage for sheep) and a meadow near their 'court' by St. Thomas' Mount and the Lord of the Manor had an orchard in the same area.[7] There was also an area of common pasture and a common field in the Edge Moor-Plaistow Green area (see Figure 8).

Some of this land was still unenclosed as late as 1786. Apart from the centre of cultivation to the east of the line from Crich Cross to the peak of Crich Hill - where St. Thomas' Mount formed the centre of the village until well into the 17th century (apart from a few houses like Roger Beler's Manor on what is now the Market Place) - there is an area (identified on Figure 7 as Furlongs) where modern field shapes suggest that strip-field cultivation was carried out. This area had all been enclosed by 1786. It lies between the Canons Wood (see Appendix) and present day Coddington, to the north and north east of the Fridensti (Appendix). In the 1847 Tithe Apportionment Survey there are in this area: five fields called Furlongs; two Furlongs Pingles; and a Near Furlongs, a Little, a Far and a Nether Furlong (see Table K). In old English a furlong is furlang, from furh: furrow and lang: long and so the field names as well as the field shapes are consistent with strip cultivation in the area. It is quite likely that the Lord of the Manor would have, apart from his compact 'home farm', strips in the common open fields in the manor.

The strips in the open fields would be surrounded only by moveable hurdles. When the corn on the arable land and the hay on the meadow had been cut the land was thrown open for common pasture. The community as a whole came to the decision, usually in the manorial court and later in the Court Leet assembly of freeholders, which parts of the open fields were to be left fallow. This was, perhaps, the beginning of the jury and of 'democracy'.

From the earliest days some Lords of the Manor started accepting money rents from the local peasants instead of requiring them to provide labour.[8] Their bailiffs had discovered that the demesne was better cultivated by hired men working all the year round than by the grudging service of the farmers called off from working their share of the common land. When in the extensive woodlands some peasants cleared areas of timber, fenced them and started to work them the problem of labour for the demesne became even more acute. Even in Hubert FitzRalph's day, at the end of the 12th century, some of these clearings in the woodland (which were quite separate from the village common fields) - which were known as 'assarts' - were quite well established. A number of them were located in the area between the Church and a line extending from Edge Moor towards Culland. Here, in the shallow valley there is a water supply from the stream which rises near Fishpond House and flows down to meet the Dimple Brook near Millgreen, possibly descending a waterfall on its way. Such a waterfall is mentioned as near the assart of Hacon.[9] This was one of a number of land holdings in the village in the 12th and 13th centuries. Some are listed in Table F and where possible their situation is identified in Table G. Many of these holdings were granted - for ecclesiastical favour such as prayers for the souls of dead relatives - to the Canons of Darley Abbey and the annual rents for some of them were recorded in the Cartulary of Darley Abbey (Table F).[10]

The bovate identified in the table was a standard peasant holding. In the East Midlands it was usually between fifteen and twenty acres; however, there is one shown in the record of Crich as of twelve acres.

Apart from the assarts mentioned in Table F two others are identified in the Darley Abbey Cartulary, those of Robert de Wilde and of Petitpas. All that is known of Petitpas is that his forename was William and that he was a witness to a 12th century charter [11] relating to Crich. Robert de Wilde's assart extended from near the boundary of South Wingfield towards Edge Moor and Robert may have been an ancestor of the Ralph Wild who, together with Samuel Orme (who could have been a descendent of the family of Swain, son of Orm: Table F), occupied the freehold estate at Plaistow sold by auction at the 'Nether Black Swan' in Crich in July 1799.[12] Such a long tenancy in a particular family should not appear strange: John Kirkland's family (Section 10.8) was supposed to have farmed in Wheatcroft for over 500 years.[13] In the early 1980s the Lynam family who had been tenants at Tithe Farm [369532] for over 300 years had to surrender their rights, for there was no male successor to take over. Again, long associations on the land are illustrated in Table G, where names of places have persisted, almost unchanged, for at least 600 years.

6.2 Use of Woodlands

Large areas of the parish were, of course, unsuitable for farming, except marginally for grazing. Apart from the river valleys - Derwent and Amber - which were probably heavily wooded and with very wet ground, two such instances would be Crich Carr ('ker' is a Viking word for a marsh) and Crich Chase which, reserved for hunting deer with hounds, was the preserve of the Lord of the Manor. There was also a fairly large area of woodland (see Appendix) which Hubert FitzRalph had granted outright to the Canons of Darley Abbey.

In addition to rights on the common land of the village, the local peasants could also gather wood for building, hedging and fuel in the local woods. It was a dispute about these rights in the 'Canons Wood' that caused the friction between Hubert FitzRalph and the Canons and led to the lawsuit held before the Bishop of Worcester in 1175. (Section 2.1).[14]

The wastes and woodlands of early medieval times were full of game and the ground was not only encroached on for cultivation, with 'outfields' and assarts, but the lords and gentry increasingly enclosed warrens and woodlands as game reserves. One such could have been Le Hey (Section 2.7).[15] Crich Chase was a reserve for deer as early as 1212. Occasionally deer were seen there even as late as the 1920s - when they may have escaped from Alderwasley Park.

The deer and lesser game were protected by severe laws and hunting them was normally restricted to the upper classes. In 1389 a Statute decreed that no layman with less than forty shillings a year in land and no priest or clerk with less than ten pounds income a year should be so bold as to keep sporting nets or dogs.[16] But, of course, poaching went on - for it was a passion with all classes.

Rabbits were snared and dug out; small birds (thrushes and larks) were limed and netted and taken for food in great numbers by both the peasants and the sporting gentry. The gentry, additionally, made great sport of flying hawks at pheasant, partridge and heron - and of netting fox or badger.

In courts and manors dovecotes were widespread. It is likely that Hubert FitzRalph had such a dovecote for there is a Dovecote Close - later Dovehouse Croft - on the ground occupied by his demesne on the edge of St. Michael's Mount (see Figure 6). The peasants enjoyed secretly catching and eating the doves, for had the birds not fed and grown plump for the Lord's table on their corn ?

The Lord of the Manor would, of course, make his own arrangements for protecting his game against poachers. (Robin Hood committed the crime of poaching in Sherwood Forest and roused the wrath of the Sheriff of Nottingham !!) Eventually in 1682-83 Lords of the Manor were empowered to appoint, under their own authority, gamekeepers who were to have the power within that manor to seize dogs, guns, nets and 'engines' for destroying game, which were kept by unqualified persons and in 1693-4 Parliament gave gamekeepers protection against arresting offenders at night.

At about that time, in 1694, game rights were beginning to be exploited for profit: there is a record of that date in the archives at Chatsworth[17] noting negotiations between the Earl of Shrewsbury and Lord Halifax on the lease, for a year, of rights both in Culland Park and in Crich Chase. In 1707 - 1711 two further 'game' Acts were passed. The earlier permitted any Lord of a Manor to authorise gamekeepers to kill game within the Manor; the later to restrict the Lord so that he could only appoint one gamekeeper with power to kill in his Manor and requiring him to register his name with the Clerk of the Peace. The Derbyshire Clerk records: "Timothy Halton appointed on 14.7.1707 by the Dowager Duchess of Halifax - Gertrude - to be Gamekeeper for the Manor of Critch".[18]

Thus, in an area such as that of Crich Manor, the woodlands and waste were not only valuable as sources of building materials and fuel, of pasture for cattle, sheep and pigs, but also for the abundant game relished by the wealthier members of the Parish. Such game was, of course, also enjoyed by humbler members of the community - adding, no doubt, a spice not only to diet but also to life !

6.3 Effect of the Black Death

After the early part of the 13th century there was a slow growth of population in England and prices rose continually (Figure 5). Towards the end of the century there was a more rapid increase in the population and plenty of labour became available to service the Lord's land. As a result the bailiffs could select amongst those they could call on and they became more demanding, particularly on the large church estates. By about 1300 the Lords of the Manor, the Priors and the Abbots were in a strong position and it became even more usual to replace service on demesne lands with compulsory money rents or 'fines'. With rising prices and such demands there was widespread misery amongst the peasantry. The population increase slowed down in the reign of Edward I (1307-1326) and this, together with some improvements in farming technique lead to a fall in prices.[19] One of these came at the beginning of the 14th century with a realisation of the benefits of spreading marl on the fields. Marl is natural rock of mud and limestone which is usually soft and easily powdered and often available in a district like Crich with limestone near the surface of the ground or present as an outcrop. At this time too there was a growth in the control of sheep flocks by 'folding', so that the manure could be deposited where it might bring most benefit to the land.[20]

That landholders were beginning to realise the benefit of land-management is illustrated by a record in the Darley Abbey Cartulary about an agreement made between the Darley Canons and Sir Roger Beler, the younger, Lord of the Manor of Crich.[21] Sir Roger acknowledged the rights of the Canons to put twelve beasts in his park at Crich, between Edge Moor and Culland (Section 2.1), without payment. Nevertheless, Roger got the Canons to agree that, for four years, they would put no beasts in the Park, which had been cut and burnt, so that "the new wood would the better grow and not be destroyed by the beasts aforesaid". For this concession Roger agreed to pay the Canons 12s 0d at Pentecost during the said four years.

In 1348-49 the Black Death devastated the country. Perhaps a third of the inhabitants of the Kingdom died.[22] The survivors amongst the peasantry then had the whip-hand of the Lord and his bailiffs. Instead of there being too many labourers and a shortage of cultivated land, there was now a shortage of men to till what was available. The value of farms fell and the price of labour went up rapidly.

The situation in Crich is revealed in a deed of 1st October 1361 in which Sir Roger Beler rented a parcel of land in his Manor of Crich to the Knights Hospitallers: "Each messuage is hardly worth sixpence clear value as they are only cottages and untenanted because of the 'universal pestilence'. Each acre is hardly worth twopence clear value: they were newly assarted from the great Moor in the Peak".[23]

And again: "A messuage and two bovates in Fritchley, held by Felley Priory - at an annual rent of 8s 4d are held in alms from Roger Beler; 2 messuages and ten acres in Plaistow and Wheatcroft are held from Roger Beler (tenant-in-chief) for 3s 0d annually as a parcel of the Manor of Crich. The aforesaid three messuages are hardly worth 3s 0d per annum. The 2 bovates and ten acres are hardly worth 8s 0d - as they are uncultivated". (Compare these rents with those given in Table F).

Thus it was that Sir William de Wakebridge, who had accumulated money from his 'public services' (Section 2.3), was in a favourable position to pick up a number of bargains (land values being depressed at the time) to endow his chantries in Crich Church.[24] In October 1394 Sir William was able to buy a messuage and a croft in Crich and two bovates at Shuckstonefield with the intention that they become part of the endowment of his chantries in St. Mary's Church. The juries appointed by the Crown to consider his application permanently to transfer land held by him (under the Crown) to a trust to finance the chantries supported de Wakebridge's proposal on the grounds that the Black Death had had a crippling effect on property values and that the messuages and cottages in question were untenanted and the land was uncultivated.[25] There was an aura of desolation over the countryside.

The shortage of labour meant that many a Lord of the Manor could no longer cultivate his demesne land and that many strips in the open fields were back in his hands because the families who had farmed them had died of the plague. As time went by the number of strips in the open field held by a single villein increased as they took over derelict holdings. The peasant cultivators of these larger units started hiring labour (often itinerant - see below) and they began to rebel against their servile status and the demands of the bailiffs that they should perform their 'work-days' on the Lord's demesne themselves.[26] Not infrequently, when hard pressed by the bailiff to perform his field work, a villein would flee through the forest to better himself. Everywhere there was a shortage of labour and high wages were given to wandering labourers, with no questions asked about where they came from.

The free labourers on a manor could, of course, demand higher wages than before and all these pressures led to a rise in prices. Within thirty years of the Black Death the price of wheat increased by about 60 % (Figure 5).

As time went by more and more Lords gave up the attempt to cultivate their land by 'forced' labour and consented to accept money instead of service. Such money could pay for hired labour but the landlords could not always cultivate all their land because the price of labour was so high. It then became more usual for the landlords to lease land to those peasants who could afford to pay rent. This, because of lack of demand was, of course, at a depressed level.

In 1350 the wages of a farm labourer were 2d a day and 3d in harvest, a total of perhaps 50s 0d a year at a time when the annual rent asked for a peasant holding was of the order of 3s 0d to 4s 0d.[27]

6.4 Life on the Medieval Farm

After the Black Death, as the population steadily rose again, there was an increased demand for bread corn and although there was some clearance of woodland and more wastelands were brought into cultivation, in general the arable acreage was increased at the expense of pasture. In the absence of fodder crops for winter feed or of temporary leys to provide good summer feed for cattle and sheep there was an inadequate supply of manure to sustain continuous arable cropping broken only by periodical fallow. With a rotation of one or two straw crops and a fallow the arable lands became 'plough-sick' and the comparatively low yields of those days fell even further.*

For the ordinary peasant good cultivation was especially difficult for even though the Lord of the Manor made less demands for service from the local population (he took their rents instead) he usually retained the perquisite of folding the villeins sheep on his demesne. Even the small amount of manure available to the poorer villeins was frequently used as a fuel[28] (as today it is so used on the Indian sub-continent).

The peasants of the 14th and 15th centuries lived in farms and cottages built of logs or planks or with wooden uprights and beams supporting rubble and clay. The floors were earthen, the roofs of thatch. Their oaten bread and the ale made from barley they grew themselves depended on the uncertain harvests on the common field and in bad seasons there could be famine.

The farmers of the open field, either serf or free, each had his own oxen on the village pasture and, after harvest, on the stubble in the common field.[29] These beasts - half the size of modern cattle - were lean with scant fare and tough with years of tugging at the plough. Some were slaughtered at Martinmas to be salted for winter's food or killed fresh for Christmas feasting. Bacon was the most common meat dish and the number of pigs in a village herd depended on the extent and character of the local wastelands in which they roamed.

Often a peasant with a cottage (a toft) would have a small plot of land with it, on which he could grow such crops as peas and beans and perhaps keep his own cow or pig. Many certainly kept poultry, and eggs were part of their diet. Perhaps the most important item in the peasant's budget was the sheep's wool he could sell for cash. Sheep flocks could be pastured on the wastes, in the woodland and on the common field after harvest - when the landlord often got the benefit of the manure.

In the north Midlands, in the Crich area, the wool was of good quality and in great demand by the wool merchants.[31] The coin the peasants got for the wool they were able to sell to a rising cloth market was a valuable supplement to their income and since, after the plague, there was more coin available per head of the reduced population it became less difficult for a villein to save or borrow enough shillings to buy his freedom from the Lord's service and to pay the money rent for his farm. The better-off peasants, renting their land and free to work it as they chose, began to emerge as a new class - the independent, yeoman farmer.

It was the break in the servility of the peasant to the Manor after the Black Death that led to so many important developments in England in later years. It sowed the seed both for future mercantile success and the creation of democratic institutions.

6.5 Tudor Inflation

In the 15th century, as the population recovered from the catastrophe of the Black Death, there was a period of relative stability in farming. There was no great increase in the amount of wasteland or woodland taken into agricultural use, and no radical improvements in farming methods. For the workers on the land it was a period of prudent consolidation.

The next century was very different. Henry VIII's various adventures, the Elizabethan naval forays and the opening-up of colonies had, as a background, a fairly vigorous rise of population after about 1500. There was an increasing movement of people from the countryside to the

---

* In the Middle Ages a harvest yield of 4:1 was regarded as satisfactory. Even in the 18th century a satisfactory yield for corn was an average of 10:1. In the mid-20th century the figure was probably between 25:1 to 40:1.[30]

towns and the effects of Henry VIII's debasement of the coinage began to take hold.[32] As a result prices rose rapidly (Figure 5). Between 1500 and 1560 food nearly trebled in price and the things a landlord had to buy for himself and his household cost more than double.[33]

When possible the landlords took in more woodland and more waste for cultivation and there was considerable pressure on them to increase rents and to explore new methods of farming.

When the landlords started to raise rents they couldn't do it all around, with moderation. Some tenants were fortunate enough to have long leases of their holdings and legal forms of tenure which might involve only a nominal rent, perhaps in kind. As a consequence those peasants and farmers whose leases were renewable annually, or fell in on death or after a period of years, suffered extortion at the hands of the landlords trying to maintain their standard of living.

The yeoman freeholders and those tenants insulated from escalating rents could make a lot of money without paying an extra penny for their land. Such fortunate farmers were able, over sixty years, to sell their corn and cattle at three times the price their grandfathers had been able to ask.[34]

The more successful yeoman farmers amalgamated more and more holdings into larger farms and accelerated the process of enclosing wastes and of encroaching on common ground. These fortunates, using the opportunities which came their way, accumulated the wealth which enabled their descendents to buy shares in the manorial rights of villages like Crich (Section 2.5) and, like the Kirklands, to endow charities in the village.

6.6 New Farming Practices

Although new ideas in farming would be adopted in Crich later than in the softer arable lands of the east and the south where often they were developed, the village was one of those in the Highlands most nearly bordering those plains and, in the Cromwells and the Shrewsburys, it had Lords of the Manor who were in constant touch with the Royal Court and the sophisticates of London Society. It is not surprising then that the successful yeoman farmers living in the period following the Renaissance when, with improving communications able to spread experience widely and with the increased intellectual activity of the time - and as a result of their own acute observations - began to appreciate that the old division of land between permanent pasture and permanent arable was a bar to progress. In particular it resulted in a shortage of the fodder necessary to maintain cattle stocks over the winter.[35] It was found that old, plough-sick, arable land could be made profitable again if it was laid down to permanent grass or long leys. Again, commons and areas of rough hill grazing, often overgrown with weeds or bare through continued over-grazing, could be improved by ploughing-up and putting them under a suitable crop rotation.

It has been suggested that it was a combination of hard grazing and dressings of marl, chalk or lime which would encourage the voluntary entry of indigenous white clover into old pastures.[36] This led eventually to the discovery of the value of clover in fixing atmospheric nitrogen and of its benefit to later crops. Whether this is so or not the practice developed of sowing fodder crops, and particularly legumes. Parts of the arable land were laid down in temporary leys of grass and, on others, such crops as clover, lucerne and sainfoin were sown. Further, the practice of alternating arable and pasture on the same ground increased.

In these ways the fertility of a holding could be greatly increased while yielding heavy crops of hay. The arable crops had the double advantage of an increased supply of animal manure, for more cattle could now be fed on the open field, and an improvement of the fertility of the soil through the fixation of nitrogen.

Again, there was an extension of the practice of feeding sheep on the arable land after they had fed on the new succulent grass in the leys before these were closed for meadow and the production of hay for storage.

Such developments began to solve the problem of the winter feeding of stock and, at last, farmers could now save, with confidence, their best animals for selective breeding.

The use of fodder crops for cattle, instead of them depending only on permanent pasture, began expanding in the 17th century. By about 1620 clover seed was being regularly imported into England and turnips, which in Elizabeth's time were a garden crop, were being introduced to the farm. By about 1650 turnips were a regular field crop in counties like Suffolk, although it is likely that they would not by then have been a familiar crop in Derbyshire.

Another development of the late 17th and early 18th centuries, although it had originated in Tudor times, was that the farm horse was beginning to share the work of ploughing with the ox. To work well a horse was more expensive in feed than an ox, but it was stronger and faster and when replacing an ox team by a smaller team of horses there was a saving in feed and the horses could be used for a wider range of work more efficiently - particularly in speedier transport. Somewhat later, with the horses, came an increasing range of iron implements: ploughs, harrows, hoes and rollers.[37] The most widespread innovation was the development of the Norfolk plough drawn by two horses. It was not, however, until the early 19th century that such 'modern' systems were in common use in Derbyshire. For Farey comments:

"On very strong and stubborn land on Moorwood Moor in Crich I saw two horses employed in ploughing but unfortunately did not learn who was setting so good an example to his neighbours".[38]

However, there was still a remaining, removable barrier to a truly efficient agriculture. In many places, over the years, the gradual piecemeal redistribution of open fields had resulted in an unwieldy complex of tiny 'closes': any given peasant could be working land in parcels that were spread over many different parts of the parish. As experience grew it became clear that a more profitable agriculture could develop if a farmer could work with a compact and larger holding and break away from the ancient style of landholding based on open fields. In this, as has been said, the work was done on a plan laid down by the whole community of those with rights in the open field. Usually the arable open field was opened as pasture to the cattle of the village as soon as the corn had been reaped.

In such circumstances it did not pay a farmer to sow clover or turnips on his strip; they would only provide food for the collective herd.[39] It became clear that when a farmer could assemble a coherent holding in one place and could fence it he could achieve, under his own control only, a better balance between arable and pasture and could adopt a profitable crop rotation as well as take better care of his animals.

It was considerations such as these that prompted the early enclosures of land noted as taking place in the local area when Henry Azard and Francis Coke, the Justices for the Morleston and Litchurch Hundred reported to Sheriff Bradshaw in 1631 that:

"new enclosures are being made and further pastures broken-up into arable land".[40]

Enclosures of common fields probably grew apace after the Shrewsbury heiresses parted with many of their manorial rights in Crich in 1660 (Section 2.5) when, for instance, Ralph Smith and Anthony Bennet bought rights in, amongst other places, Culland Park. It was about this time that the new landlords began enclosing and cultivating areas that had been formerly woodland. That there was ample scope can be seen from Morderns Map of around 1695 which shows that the compact settlements of Crich and Fritchley were practically surrounded by woodland.[41]

Inspection of Figure 8 ('Land Enclosed by the 1786 Commission') suggests that in addition to the land formerly held by the Lord of the Manor and the Canons (Kings Meadow, Lane End, Hays, Cross and Fishpond - as well as Culland, Parkhead, Calvercroft, Lees and Warmwell) a number of substantial areas, where there were once open strip fields and commons, were enclosed quite early on. There is strong evidence for this (Section 2.7) in the Nether Cliff and Plaistow Green area and the area of common ground - part of which, even today, is referred to as "on the common" - to the west of the erstwhile Fritchley Mill Road where, for instance, in the Riddings region the Smith family (descendents of Ralph Smith and ancestors of Denman Mason) owned land clearly enclosed from the common. The other main area of ground which must have been enclosed quite early on (Section 6.1) is to the north of the Fridentsi and the Canons Wood (see Appendix) and encompasses Furlongs, Stones, Scott Ashes, Coddington, Benthill and Coddington Bank. These early enclosures probably took place piecemeal over a fairly lengthy period of time beginning before the Shrewsburys parted with most of their manorial rights. The process was brought to a climax in the latter half of the 18th century, as will now be described.

6.7 The Formal Enclosures

Before about 1750, when the population was increasing only slowly and there were longish runs of good seasons, the prices of both grain and animal products tended to remain stable. Eventually, as a result of an increase in cultivated acreage and the use of alternate crops on the same ground, prices actually fell. (Figure 5).

After about 1750, however, there began a rapid rise in population (Figure 9) and prices rose (Figure 5) as output lagged behind the consumption of a rapidly increasing non-agricultural population. In this period the Industrial Revolution was getting under way and the demand for farming's secondary products - wool, tallow, hides and so on - also expanded alongside the need to feed the growing urban population. With improving living standards this meant not only corn but also more meat and dairy products.

In the 40 years after 1750 the price of wheat almost doubled as did that for barley and oats.[42] Beef and mutton rose by about 25%. Such conditions favoured the arable farmers. There was also a decline in the frequency of good seasons. The opportunities presented for improving farming efficiency encouraged many leaders of local communities to press for the enclosure of the remaining open, 'common', fields in their parishes. They believed that this was the way to meet the needs of the new markets and, of course, they could benefit from the high prices for food that could be demanded.

A usual method of achieving Enclosure in the 18th century was for the owners of the major part of the private holdings in the village to petition Parliament to grant them an Act re-allocating the common land. The aim was to re-divide all the land communally owned, including that in the strips of the open fields, so that each farmer would own, or could rent, an enclosure with an extent, on average, of about ten acres, in which, within new fields, he could work as he pleased, timing his operations to suit himself and growing whatever crops he thought best, quite independently of the rest of the village.[43]

Usually, after the petition to the House of Commons, a committee would investigate the case and if there was no serious opposition an Act would be passed which would appoint Commissioners with power to re-allocate the village land in such a way that every landholder in the village was given the equivalent of what he had held before, but in the form of fields rather than strips.

It was usually, of course, the wealthiest men in the village who would own the bulk of the land and push the enclosure through. It was not easy for the often more numerous poor and uneducated peasants to oppose the enclosures and, in the end, many lost out. Even when they had received their new allocation of land many could not afford to fence it, and drain it, as required by the Commissioners. Often they sold out to the larger farmers who were engaged in creating the compact farms that brought increased efficiency to the industry and increased profits to themselves.[44]

In 1786 Parliament appointed John Beighton, George Barker, Joseph Outram and John Nuttall to make an award:

> "For dividing and enclosing the several commons and wastelands within the Manor of Crich".[45]

The preamble named various Lords of the Manor including the Earl of Thanet, Sir Edward Wilmot, Bart (one time surgeon to Queen Caroline), Peter Nightingale and a number of lesser notables such as David Woodhouse. A total of 450 acres or thereabouts was to be enclosed. Kelly's Directory gave the area of the parish as 3498 acres,[46] so the amount to be enclosed under the awards of the Commissioners was about 13% of the area of the parish. The areas of land covered by the award are shown in Figure 8 and Table D lists some of the principal beneficiaries. These new 'capitalist-farmers' could afford to take advantage of the benefits of fencing and draining their allotments and also of the new markets opened-up by turnpikes established through the village between 1750 and 1800.

After the 1786 Enclosures in Crich many of the poorer smallholders who sold out the land allocated to them were left only with their cottage and croft and became farm labourers or moved into manufacturing (Section 6.9). In the area around Prospect Terrace and Bennets Lane a number were at least able to breed pigs, for styes in those areas were still in use in the late 1920s.

6.8 The War with Republican France

Although wheat was grown over much of England in the 18th century it was not possible in the more northerly parts to ripen enough wheat* to feed the population.[47] Oats, wheat, rye and barley were all grown and, in the high grounds at the foot of the Pennines, oats prevailed - although barley was also grown quite widely; much of that went into beer.

In a report in 1794 by J. Brown it was noted that in the high ground of Derbyshire about a fifth of the enclosures were arable and that the chief crop was oats.[48] The rest were in pasture, the greatest part being employed in dairying and the breeding of stock. The normal bread corn was oats. Oatcake was the chief food from day to day, with black bread made from rye occasionally. Even gooseberry pie was made with an oatmeal crust.

After 1793, at the time when the war with France was gathering momentum, there was a series of unusually poor seasons. 1795 was an infamously bad year. It followed one of the three worst winters of the whole 18th century and then the summer was unusually cold. The harvest was 20-25% down on normal.[49] There were serious food shortages and prices continued to rise rapidly in spite of the advantages brought by the Enclosures throughout the country. The

---

* Of the varieties then available

high prices encouraged not only a more widespread adoption of better methods of husbandry but also a considerable increase in the acreage brought into cultivation.*.

In Crich Parish the timber sales advertised in the Derby Mercury around 1800, mostly of oak trees to provide material for Nelson's navy (Section 5.6), resulted in the opportunity to clear ground to provide food for the nation. The conditions were right for a considerable increase in corn growing in the parish. Farms were already enclosed, lime for improving the land was readily available, millstones for grinding corn had been made in the local quarries for centuries and in the Dimple Brook there was, towards its lower reaches, a local stream which could be controlled to provide power for grinding corn.

Furthermore the turnpikes established in the previous half-century (Section 4.7) meant that it was comparatively easy to transport produce to the growing urban markets. By judicious husbandry the land could be kept in good heart by manure readily available. Crich had, for a long time, been in a cattle and sheep rearing area. The cattle fairs held between the Cross and the Church attracted farmers and drovers from some distance around, travelling to Crich along the well-established ways originating centuries earlier (Section 4.2).[50] Crich Fairs, in the 18th century held on 16th April and 11th October, were well established in 1569 (according to one Wryley who was a friend and kinsman of John Claye (Section 2.4)[51]) and were listed as amongst the important Derbyshire Fairs in 1770 by William Owen.[52]

So it was that the Crich 'farming gentry' began to do rather well for themselves as they increased their arable land and took advantage of the rapidly rising prices for corn. Their prosperity is still evident in the chest tombs and copestones in the churchyard and the plaques, inside and outside, on the church walls that started appearing in about 1800. The Smiths, the Bowmers, the Coopers, the Allens, the Woodhouses, the Turtons and the Towndrows - and their prosperity - are all commemorated (Section 5.2).

The poor did not do so well. There is an indicative passage in the Derby Mercury of 19th June 1800:

"We are glad to record the following worthy example - which we hope may become general. Mr. Thomas Bowmer of Fritchley, near Crich, is now selling his wheat (which is of a very good quality) amongst the poor working inhabitants in the neighbouring villages at 8s 0d per strike".

At Stafford in the previous week wheat had been selling on the market at 19s 0d to 21s 0d per strike of 38 quarts.[53]

Not only was wheat now being grown locally, as well as oats, but barley was sufficiently widely grown to justify the establishment in the parish of two Malt Offices, one at Crich and one at Bullbridge. The one at Crich[54] was established by 1811.**

Oats were, of course, not only important as a food for the human population. The increasing amount of trade facilitated by the turnpikes meant that the number of horses, for whom oats is a staple if they are to work hard, increased considerably; they were also being used in greater numbers in agriculture itself.

Farey, who was surveying agricultural development in Derbyshire, devotes several pages of his report to examples of farms and estates in Derbyshire who used Crich Lime, in particular, to the benefit of their crops.[55] He cites farms from those of William Jessop of Butterley in Pentrich to that of the Earl of Chesterfield at Bretby and notes the quantities they used.

---

* In the country as a whole about a million acres of common pasture and wastelands were converted to arable use over the period 1793 to 1815. (See Chambers & Mingay p.206).
** After the slump in agriculture (see below) there was no mention of the Crich Malthouse in the 1849 Crich Tithe Apportionment, although the Malthouse Croft at the position of Prospect Terrace was noted.

One interesting observation is that the Crich Lime was laid in large heaps, between the hay and corn harvests, and was then slaked and spread in the middle of September at the rate of about 12 to 14 quarters (of about eight level baskets) per acre. It was "ploughed in immediately before wet falls - or it burns the horses feet".

Another use for quicklime from Crich was to dry wheat seed which had been treated in various experimental ways, such as washing in clear water or in salt brine or by using an arsenic solution to try and overcome the problems of rust and mildew in wheat. Crich lime was very popular for this drying operation because it was comparatively pure.

Some consumers of Crich lime had the limestone itself delivered to their farms by canal (distances of thirty or more miles were not unusual) and had their own private kilns. One such, Richard Harrison of Ash, used to get his Crich limestone from the canal wharf at Willington.[56]

The experimental approach to the use of lime at the time of the Napoleonic Wars (so well documented by Farey) indicates how the pressures of the market were stimulating the farming community to try new techniques to improve their profit. It was, of course, good business for Crich.

Two other observations of Farey are of local interest. He noted that flax was being cultivated in Crich.[57] This could have been an old local tradition for, as early as the 13th century, there was an area in Crich called Flaxlondes. There is a record of this being granted by Nicholas Bithewaite of Crich to William of Ballindon and Roger of Ashleyhay.[58] The growing of flax had long been encouraged by statute and in the late 18th century a bounty was paid to the growers of flax.[59]

The other fact recorded by Farey was that the flail was still extensively used for threshing corn. As the amount of corn grown locally increased there was the need to thresh and to grind it. Even quite small holdings in the parish had their own threshing floors, many identified by Watkins who also found, near them, numbers of the stone pillars of the corn-stack saddles made with an overhang to keep rats out of the stored corn.[60]

The most easily visible index of the amount of corn grown in the district at one time is the number of water-driven corn mills. There were Bullbridge, Pentrich Weir Mill, Wingfield Mill all on the Amber; there were three on the Dimple (or Fritchley) Brook and there were a number of windmills. The one at Heage, not far over the boundary of Crich parish, was restored in the 1980s but the one on the Mainpieces [365533], of which only the ruined stonework is now visible, was abandoned soon after Napoleon's final defeat. In the 1847 Crich Tithe Apportionment[61] there are three other places where at one time there could have been a windmill. These are listed in Table K and were in the regions of Nether Cliff / Plaistow Green, Wakebridge and Furlongs/Stone (Figure 7). (Also see Woolley Manuscripts).

Corn, meat and dairy produce were not the only produce of the land in the village. Much woodland was not suitable for agriculture, for instance on the steep slopes of Crich Chase and places like Bowmer's Rough, Smiths Rough and Bilberry Wood (see Figure 7). As we have seen the sale of large timber from the ancient woods, for instance around Culland, was well established. Large trees, principally oak (in demand for the Navy) but also ash, sycamore, elm, beech, poplar, alder and Spanish chestnut were of major commercial value but, of course, such growths take time to mature. It was often profitable for the local landlords, on ground unsuitable for agriculture once the large timber had been cleared, to allow the 'underwood' to be exploited as a crop. Saplings and small trees of oak, ash, nut-hazel, birch, sallow and so on could provide a profitable sale. Such timber found ready application in the developing coal fields of the East Midlands for roof support and other engineering purposes, as well as in the lead mines which were flourishing locally.

The perceptive landowners*, like Francis Hurt with land on both sides of the Derwent,[62] divided their woodlands into 24 or 25 nearly equal parts or 'falls', one of which was cut every year so that by the time the last fall was cut the first was ready for cropping and so on in succession. By these means the leadminers, colliers and other consumers could be supplied, reliably, with nearly equal quantities yearly.

Throughout the war with France the landlords and the farmers did well but when Napoleon was finally defeated and trade with the continent was restored to its previous levels, the situation changed radically.

6.9 The Times of George IV, William IV and Victoria

By 1818 large imports of corn flooded into England and the home price fell sharply (Figure 5). The tenant farmers, the freehold yeomen and the receivers of tithe and rent who had benefited so much as a result of high prices and the extension and improvement of land cultivation were now in trouble. Many were ruined and rents could not be paid. The poor who had suffered from the high price of bread were, however, to get but little relief. In 1815 the first of the protective Corn Laws had been passed by Parliament elected, of course, from and by those in the prosperous classes. The Corn Laws aimed to restore agricultural prosperity at the expense of the consumer. (The situation was not dissimilar to that created in the 1980s with the support, by the European Common Market, of agricultural prices). The Corn Law of 1815 prohibited the import of foreign grain until the price of English corn reached 80 shillings a quarter, and to quote Cobbett writing in 1833:

"In the north there were unnatural efforts to ape the farming of Norfolk and Suffolk - it was only playing at farming. It was a most lamentable thing that the paper-money price of corn tempted so many to break-up their fine pastures".

{Here was a situation, again rather like the 1980s, when farmers in the highlands of the White Peak were recently growing corn (which probably then went into the 'grain mountain') on land not really suitable, but which attracted subsidy}.

Cobbett was scathing about the poor crops grown on rather unsuitable land and being sold at an artificially high price to the disadvantage of the less well-off people. He did, however, greatly praise northern beef saying that "on the hills it was a country of graziers and not of 'farmers': a country of pasture, not of the plough".

In the end the distortions produced by the war with France receded and production of corn in the less favourable areas decreased. In Crich Parish there was a move away from corn production. An indicator of this was the closure of the windmill on the Mainpieces, which went out of action in 1817 and it was probably at this time too that the Mill at what became the Bobbin Mill changed over to woodturning instead of corn grinding. The only mill on the Dimple Brook working within living memory was the Bowmer Corn Mill. This, reputedly, was built in the second decade of the 19th century because Farmer Bowmer was dissatisfied with the service he got at mills higher up the brook. (Section 9.5).

The shift in agriculture from arable to grazing in the village is reflected in the census returns for the Overseer of the Poor for the Anglican Parish of Crich.[63] During the war with France, in 1811, out of 380 families in the village 51% were employed in agriculture. In 1821 not long after Napoleon had been sent to St. Helena only 30% were classed as 'agricultural' families out

---

* It is sad that, in the 1930s when the Hurts sold out at Alderwasley and went to live in Kenya, the mature woods in Crich Chase were felled and the land was left to be invaded by scrub. Had it then been replanted the mature timber that would now be standing in Crich Chase would be worth a fortune.

of a total of 394. Thus, whereas in 1811 194 families had been employed in farming, by 1821 there were only 118 such - a reduction of 40% of the number of families working on the land*. Until the Repeal of the Corn Laws in 1846 the arguments about agricultural protection divided England.[64] The town poor, in particular, were paying artificially high prices and were in some distress (Section 9.7). In the 1820s probably under 5% of home demand was supplied by imports. In the 1840s, when the population was about 17 million, it is estimated that about 12% were fed by foreign wheat.[67] A picture of the production of corn in Crich at this time can be built up from the 1847 Tithe Apportionment Award.[68] It is stated that:-

a) The area of land under cultivation in the village was 3667 acres of which 1347 acres were arable land (Section 3.14)

b) The output of corn registered for tithe was:
   Wheat   273.6 bushels
   Barley   485.3 bushels
   Oats   498.5 bushels

Data given by Farey for wheat and oats shows,[69] for Derbyshire, yields per acre for wheat and oats of from 35-40 bushels per acre and with weights of about 67 lb per bushel.

Thus the output of the wheat registered for tithe could be grown on about 7.4 acres, the barley on 13.1 acres and the oats on 13.5 acres - a total acreage of 34. If the tithe was 10% the implication is that in 1847 only about 340 acres of the 1347 down to arable were growing corn, i.e. 25%. The other 75% must have been growing fodder crops and other consumer products, perhaps peas, beans and brassicas.

Assume that the total output of wheat in the parish was of the order of 273.6 x 67 lb, i.e. about 183,000 lbs. The yield on milling to flour is about 70%[70] so that the local farmers could produce about 128,000 lbs of flour which could make, say, 128,000 one-pound loaves of bread. The local population was about 2400 at the time (Figure 9); hence the local wheat production could provide about 53 loaves a year for each man, woman and child in the village. A wheaten-bread consumption of a loaf each, each week, suggests that the parish must have been nearly self-sufficient in wheat: no doubt oatcakes were still being consumed and oatmeal used in cooking, for it had been so common as a basic part of country diet only fifty years previously. Thus Crich, at least, in the 'Hungry Forties' could have been self-sufficient in cereals.

As Britain recovered from the hard times of the 1830s and 1840s not only did industry prosper as the population grew rapidly (largely as a result of improved hygiene and medical care: it wasn't that the numbers of births increased but rather that the number of deaths was reduced) but more normal supply conditions returned to agriculture. It became possible, profitably, to use the acreage which had been greatly expanded by the wartime enclosures.

By the later 1830s agricultural incomes were improving, costs had been reduced as there had been an abandonment or putting down to grass of the high-cost marginal arable land - especially in such hilly, upland areas as Crich. Again the exchange of tithes for rents and the reduction in the local rating charges arising from the reform of the Poor Law (Section 3.13)[71] all led to an improvement in agricultural prosperity.

After about 1850 meat production and dairying became markedly more profitable than grain

---

* In the mid-1980s there were about 1100 households in the parish and a population of about 2800.[65] In 1984 only 61 people were engaged in farming, including farmer's families and casual and seasonal labour.[66] Thus less than 2% were working in farming in 1984 in contrast to the 50% or so in 1811.

as living standards rose and as more cheap grain was imported, especially from the Americas. The balance in Crich tipped markedly in favour of the natural propensity of the village to put its agricultural effort into grazing, stock rearing and dairying.

It was at this time too that the new 'machinery' of the Industrial Revolution was beginning to have an impact on agriculture. Even in comparatively remote areas like Crich railways were not far away and this meant that cattle could be shipped in good condition to the urban markets*. No longer was the drover employed to take his herd many weary miles to the main centres of population. Again, although mechanical farm machinery had been invented generations earlier, it had made little impact before materials like iron were readily available and ultimately before new power sources to replace the ox, the horse or the human could be applied to farming.

Even on the flat lands of the Midland Plains and of East Anglia developments like threshing machines[72] (originally invented in 1784 and coupled with steam engines as early as the 1820s and 1830s)[73], Jethro Tull's Drill or mole-drainage systems were not much used generally until after about 1870. The sickle had been replaced by the scythe but otherwise the enclosed fields in districts like Crich were, for most of the 19th century, worked by and large with the same tools as had been used on the medieval strips.[74]

In his diary (Section 2.9) Denman Mason gives some glimpses of the economics and of the hard life of farming in Crich in the later 1860s. Thus on 6th July 1867 he records that he and his two brothers mowed the greatest part of the field below the house called "The Drumble" [353536].

"Self tired out, with my hands well blistered with the scythe, having been in the field from 5 am till 10 pm".

Even so, two days later they had finished the hay by 10 o'clock in the morning ("It was a warm day with a powerful sun") and on the following day they "headed all the hay and have a very good stack of about 7 tons well got and in fine condition".

Mason was in Crich to supervise the sale of some of his grandfather's property and he notes the results of a number of public sales of agricultural property, usually held at the Jovial Dutchman". Thus on:

> 16.10.1866 The Pothouse Farm [352564] and 57 acres were sold with a reserve price on the land of £55 per acre.
>
> 22.2.1867 Land on Nether, Upper and Middle Cliff (consisting of 11/24 shares - grandfather's share in the Manorial Rights of Crich) - just over 7 acres was sold for £60 per acre.
>
> 14.1.1868 Cliff Land was sold to the Butterley Company at £62 per acre - fetching £450. The Malthouse was sold to R. W. Smith for £243. The Common Farm was sold to S. Radford of Bullbridge for £751.
>
> 2.4.1868 Some of the Mason's family possessions at the Common Farm were sold:
> A pony trap and harness   for   £10 11s 0d
> Two cows   for   £30   5s 0d
> A heavy dray   for   £5   10s 0d

* In the middle of the 19th century Friday was the principal market day, for all goods and provisions, in Derby, which was easily accessible from the railway stations and sidings at Whatstandwell and Ambergate. Markets were also held on Wednesdays for butter and vegetables and on Saturday for meat and vegetables. The market for cattle, sheep and pigs was held in the Derby Morledge on Tuesdays. [75]

One of these cows may have been the milch cow mentioned in the entry of 20th December 1867 where Denman records that he "sold a barren cow and calf to Mr. Burton for £17. Brothers Henry and John bought a fine cow in Derby Market - new calved and giving a good quantity of milk for £17 thereby providing a good supply of milk during the winter".

The Mason brothers had been obliged, because of frost and snow, to bring their cattle in on 4th December 1867 and then began to cut their stack of hay. Later in the month they went on a pigeon shoot with "Mr. Abbot...........Joseph Kyte was the victor killing all his birds".

In those days Crich Fair was a day of importance in the village calendar. Denman Mason noted on 11th October 1867 that there had been a "good show of sheep and fair sales: No cattle in the market". The next Fair Day, 12th October 1868, was recorded as having been a "day fine: a good show of sheep, cattle and pigs but not many buyers: sales generally were flat". Perhaps even by then the railways were beginning to affect Crich Fair, which was ultimately killed by the cattle lorry.

Two observations in Mason's diary give an idea when planting was being done in those days. Thus:

"22.8.1868   Plenty of rain in past week and grass growing nicely. Many farmers sowing turnips.

27.4.1869   Brother John and self set 5 rows of potatoes in Mr. Lee's field at the back of the hill - formerly grandfather's land.

14.5.1869   Self assisted Isaac Bowmer to set two rows of potatoes in Staffords field."

- rather late in the year, one would have thought !

The 'high-farming' of the later 19th century did not bypass farming areas like Crich. Improvements continued in animal and plant breeding; better crop rotations and pasture management were devised, seed drills, iron ploughs and drainage systems improved. Above all there was the impact on the farm - made possible by improved transport systems - of both feed for stock (some imported from the Americas) and of fertiliser. In the late 1850s, 100,000 tons of guano a year were imported into Britain and sources and application of superphosphates, nitrates and potassium fertilisers were expanded.

These 'imports' meant not only more fertility for arable production but also the ability to carry more stock per acre of ground.

Although threshing by steam engines and mechanical reapers and binders had been patented, some as early as the 1820s, by English and Scots engineers, they were not widely used until after the time of the 1851 Exhibition when McCormicks American machines received wide publicity. Thereafter there was a growth in mechanical harvesting and a lowering of costs to the farmer and a consequent general growth of prosperity in agriculture.

Just after 1870 agricultural wages reached a peak, and in the north of the country near to the coal mines and the better-paid industries, in places like Crich, the agricultural wages were better than in the south. For instance, in the West Riding they were about 14s 0d a week when they were 7s 0d in Wiltshire and Surrey.[76] (A century or so later the situation is quite reversed, with a prosperous South and a poor North !)

After 1875 agriculture began again to be a depressed industry. Its prosperity was destroyed by the effects of 'Free Trade', which was so beneficial to the industrial manufacturers of Lancashire.[77] As can be seen in Figure 5 the price of wheat - an indicator of agricultural prosperity - was quite low at the end of the 19th century and farming had to wait for the exigiencies of the 20th century World Wars to have the opportunity to regain prosperity.

[1] Phillimore (1978) *Domesday Book (27) Derbyshire*. Chichester. Phillimore
[2] Phillimore. Technical Terms.
[3] Roffe D. (1986) *The Derbyshire Domesday*. Derby. Derby Museum Service.
[4] Trevelyan G. M. (1942) *English Social History*. London. Longman.
[5] Clapham Sir J. (1949) *A Concise Economic History of Britain*. Cambridge. Camb.Univ.Press.p.86
[6] Clapham. Ibid. p.48
[7] Darlington R. A. (1945)*The Cartulary of Darley Abbey*.Kendal.pp.545-546; p.551
[8] Trevelyan. Ibid. p.7 and Clapham. Ibid. p.97
[9] Darlington. Ibid. p.544
[10] Darlington. Ibid. pp.470-570
[11] Darlington. Ibid. p.548
[12] Derby Mercury Newspaper. 18.7.1799
[13] Hackett R. R. *Wirksworth and Five Miles Round*. Wirksworth. Brooks. p.112
[14] Darlington. Ibid. p.xvii
[15] Woolley W. (1710-15).*History of Derbyshire*. Derbys Record Soc.Vol.VI [1981 Ed. Glover & Riden] p.75
[16] Trevelyan. Ibid. p.23
[17] Chatsworth Archive (1694). Lease L/17/59.
[18] Cox J. C. (1890) *Three Centuries of Derbyshire Annals*. Derby. Bemrose.
[19] Trevelyan. Ibid. p.8
[20] Chambers J. D. & Mingay G. E. (1960). *The Agriculture Revolution 1740-1880*. London. Batsford.
[21] Darlington. Ibid. p.564
[22] Trevelyan. Ibid. p.8
[23] Saltman A. (1976) *The Cartulary of the Wakebridge Chantries at Crich*. Derbyshire Arch. Soc. Record Series p.125
[24] Saltman. Ibid. p.7, 65.
[25] Saltman. Ibid. p.10
[26] Trevelyan. Ibid. p.9
[27] Felkin W. (1867) *History of the Machine-Wrought Hosiery and Lace Manufactures*. David & Charles reprint. 1967.
[28] Chambers & Mingay. Ibid. p.6
[29] Trevelyan. Ibid. p.22
[30] Min. of Ag. (1987) Private Communication
[31] Felkin. Ibid. p.62
[32] Trevelyan. Ibid. p.98
[33] Trevelyan. Ibid. p.119
[34] Trevelyan. Ibid. p.121
[35] Chambers & Mingay. Ibid. p.79
[36] Chambers & Mingay. Ibid. p.8
[37] Mathias P. (1969) *The First Industrial Nation*. London. Methuan.
[38] Farey J. (1811-16) *General View of the Agriculture and Minerals of Derbyshire*. II p.95
[39] Trevelyan. Ibid. p.299

[40] Cox. Ibid. II p.190-191
[41] Watkins. Ibid. p.15
[42] Chambers & Mingay. Ibid. p.111
[43] Parker M. St. J. & Reid D. J. (1972) *The British Revolution 1750-1970.* London. Blandford.
[44] Trevelyan. Ibid. p.379
[45] Crich Enclosure Award 1786. Derbyshire Record Office:Hugh/RI 2
[46] Kelly's Directory of Derbyshire (1908)
[47] Trevelyan. Ibid. p.144
[48] Hey D. (1980) *Packmen, Carriers and Packhorse Roads.* Leicester. Leicester University Press
[49] Chambers & Mingay. Ibid. p.39
[50] Glover S. (1829) *History of the County of Derby.* Derby. Mozley.
[51] Cox J.C. (1879) *Notes on the Churches of Derbyshire.* p.62
[52] Hey. Ibid. p.162
[53] Derby Mercury Newspaper. Derby Local Studies Library.
[54] Farey. Ibid. I p.127
[55] Farey. Ibid. I p.108-118
[56] Farey. Ibid. II p.433
[57] Farey. Ibid. II p.168
[58] Darlington. Ibid. p.569
[59] Fraser W. (1947) *Field Names in South Derbyshire.* Ipswich. Adland
[60] Watkins. Ibid. p.39
[61] Crich Tithe Apportionment (1847-9). Derbyshire Record Office. D 2365 A/PI
[62] Farey. Ibid. II p.223
[63] Overseer of the Poor Census 1811:1821. Parish of Crich. Derbyshire Record Office D.2365
[64] Trevelyan. Ibid. p.465
[65] Register of Electors (1984) Amber Valley. Crich Ward. Crich Parish.10th October 1984
[66] Ministry of Agriculture (1987) Agriculture Returns:Sheet 117:Form 601/SS
[67] Mathias. Ibid. p.71
[68] Crich Tithe Apportionment. Ibid.
[69] Farey. Ibid. II p.119
[70] Taylor's of South Wingfield (1987) Private Communication
[71] Chambers & Mingay. Ibid. p.110
[72] Parker & Reid. Ibid. p.259
[73] Mathias. Ibid. p.341
[74] Parker & Reid. Ibid. p.40
[75] Derby Market Hall (1966) Centenary Handbook. Cheltenham, Burrow.
[76] Trevelyan. Ibid. p.540
[77] Trevelyan. Ibid. p.541

7. QUARRYING

7.1 Early Quarries

Limestone has been worked on Crich Hill since the Romans went mining for lead. First burnt and then slaked, it was a prime part of the mortar used for building before cement was 'invented'. Thus one essential for erecting permanent buildings in the parish was immediately available. Furthermore when building in stone got under way - FitzHubert's Manor, St. Mary's Church, the Canons Court, Wakebridge Manor and then Roger Beler's Manor House on the present-day Market Place - there were also, ready to hand, good outcrops of gritstone at Robin Hood, at Crich Carr, along the Tors, along Edge Moor and into Culland. No-one knows where the first quarries proper were, though it has been suggested[1] that Beler's Manor was built with gritstone from Culland where dressed stone similar to that in old walls near to the Baptist Chapel has been found. Wingfield Manor was also probably built using stone from Culland.[2]

Certainly quarrying was done on a commercial basis in Crich in the 14th century for it is recorded, at that time, in the Rolls of Barlow Manor (between Chesterfield and Sheffield) that millstones from Crich had been obtained. Since Hathersage is so much nearer to Barlow than Crich and since in those days transport of heavy goods was not easy,[3] it is likely that the later, and famous, quarrying and manufacturing of millstones near Hathersage had not started by then.

7.2 Building Stone

The Parliamentary Commissioners entrusted with the division and enclosure of the several commons and wastegrounds within the Manor of Crich, in 1786, made provision for six acres of land to be reserved for use of local freeholders to obtain stone for building and the upkeep of roads and bridges in the parish.[4] Included was not only the land on which the Jubilee Monuments to Queen Victoria were eventually built (Section 5.8) and the gritstone quarry on the eastern edge of the Tors, but also the area including the outcrop of gritstone along Edge Moor. When responsibility for upkeep of the main roads was taken up by the Turnpike Trusts and, eventually, for all roads by the county highway authorities, more Crich parishioners started using stone from the Tors quarry for building individual houses and walls. They only had to supply labour to get the stone, but could take none beyond the parish boundary. This privilege exists to this day, but there is now little new stone to get and access to the quarry faces is very restricted by new building.

In the days when the cleaning and fortnightly decorating of stone floors, yards, window sills and doorsteps depended largely on 'elbow grease' and local materials, the location of the best fine-grained, softer 'rub-stone' in the Tors Quarries - and on the outcrop on Edge Moor - was a subject of local argument and picking rights were sometimes falsely claimed.

Another principal centre of quarrying, for the fine-grade Chatsworth Grit, was below Coddington and Bent Hill. Here the Dukes Quarries, in land owned by the Duke of Devonshire, for many years produced sawn sandstone for sale for high quality building work.

Again, there were quarries from which building components were made, at the other side of the parish at Fritchley and at Bullbridge. The artefacts made there are described in Chapter 9.

7.3 Limestone

Before substantial limestone-working companies moved into the village towards the end of the 18th century there must have been a number of small locally-run quarries and local limestone kilns, not only for local building but also for the 'export' of burnt lime by packhorse. That such trade was carried out in the 16th century is known for the Hardwick Hall accounts for 1596 list "one horse load of Crich lyme to whyte with".[5] A small quarry such as that adjoining the north side of the churchyard [348547], perhaps started to produce lime for use in building the church, may have been selling lime for some distance around. William Woolley, writing in 1710 to 1715, said that Crich was famous for its very good lime, which was sold in Derby at about 16d or 18d per horse load.[6]

The Enclosure Acts in Derbyshire from about 1730 onwards, and a consequent general improvement in agricultural practice (Section 6.8), led to a greater demand for burnt lime and this was coupled with a great expansion, somewhat later, of house building in the towns which blossomed at the time of the Industrial Revolution. With these demands a number of small quarries was opened up on the east-facing hill to the north of Roe's Lane and below the Church. Remnants of a kiln can still be seen, from Roe's Lane, at the side of the original Baptist Chapel of 1839 (Section 5.3) - recently used as a woodworking shop. Although it is now filled-in, as late as the 1930s there was a disused, early but important, small quarry at the side of the path from the Cross to Hogg Nick on Edge Moor. It was near to the south-east edge of the churchyard and to the east of the much larger, and later, Church Quarry - roughly at [350547]. At the side of the path from Hogg Nick there were then remains of a hearth and a cavernous 'oven'[7] which were probably parts of an early kiln.

In the Tithe Award of 1847-9 there are a number of crofts and fields with names associated with lime burning[8] (Table K). This list of established field names suggests that lime burning was an active local occupation, even before the major installations in the parish were created. They could have depended on the local coal supply (Section 9.1) rather than as the later ones did on fuel brought in by canal and then by railway.

7.4 The Butterley Company Quarries

The first major limestone quarrying activity in the parish was probably that on land between the Dimple Brook and Culland. This was originally owned by the Gray family*, after whom Gray's Lane was named. This road, eventually destroyed by the Hilts Quarry, led towards Park Head over "Le Lewes" (or The Lees) towards the position of the Mount Tabor Chapel.

It was in this region of the parish that, by about 1780, a quarry known as Warner's Quarry[11]

---

* The Grays were descended from John Gray of Codnor who married Margaret, sister of Sir John Swillington (Section 2.2)[9]. In 1405 Margaret was left rights in the Manors of Crich and Wingfield by Sir John and land in the area remained with the Grays for centuries. In 1775 James Turton (Section 9.6) bought land near the Dimple from Hannah Cooke who had inherited it from Anne Gray. This included Lees Close and Great Close which were, roughly, the site of the 'Old' Quarry.[10] Then in 1779 James Turton leased land from William Robinson (who was son and heir of a cousin of Anne Gray) which included the Hilt Pingle, the site eventually of the Hilts Quarry.

was supplying limestone down a tramway to Edward Banks' kilns and wharf near to Bullbridge. They took limestone to Derby where they had kilns and sold burnt lime at a cost of 3s 7d per quarter of eight bushels.

In 1789-90 when William Jessop was building the Cromford Canal he used Crich lime for mortar and it must have been carried on horseback to the working sites. Burnt lime was certainly being transported by packhorse as late as 1789.[12] In 1792 the 80 ft span arch carrying the canal over the Derwent below Wigwell Grange failed. Jessop accepted the blame but attributed the failure to the purity of the lime from Crich[13] - which did not contain enough of the clay-like materials which, when fired, and after slaking, helped to bind the mortar.

The big development in limestone quarrying in the parish took place when Jessop and Outram and their partners in what eventually became The Butterley Company took over the Warner quarry in 1793.[14] The entrance to this quarry was off the Dimple Lane (the Fritchley Mill road) near to where the Hat Factory was later built. The stone was mined from under the deep layer of the Dimple boulder clay. In 1802 the galleries were extended and an open pit - about 70 ft deep - was created. The tramway for taking the stone down to the kilns at Bullbridge entered the workings through a 100 yard tunnel.

At the start of the journey the trams were pulled in groups of five by horses along what is still called the Gang-road (a name once in use for routes travelled by 'gangs' of packhorses).[15] It was on this gang-road, in 1813, that trials were carried out of Brunton's "Patent Steam Horse"[16] - which achieved a speed of $2 \frac{1}{2}$ miles an hour and which was propelled by steam cylinders actuating ski-stick-like legs pushing in turn on the track behind the engine. Nearer the kilns a self-acting incline was developed and at Bullbridge itself the railway was continued to six 'tipples' for overturning and shooting the contents of the trams.[17] Four were adapted to send stone straight to the wharf below, and to the side of the canal, and two tippled the stone down an inclined plane straight into the barges. These were made entirely of wrought iron plates to sustain this 'violent' mode of loading, and stout planks of deal were laid on their bottoms to absorb the shock of the first layers of stone arriving in the boats. The trams used on the railway also had plate-iron bottoms and sides and each held about 34-35 cwt of stone in blocks of a half to three or four cwt each. The tram wheels were cast with round holes in them instead of more conventional open spokes. Through the holes short truncheons of wood could be put to lock the wheels when the trams were descending down the steep 'hurries' from the higher parts of the quarry. Levers could also be put in these holes to turn the wheels when a tram became stuck.

At the Easter Sessions in 1827 The Butterley Company obtained a licence for a powder magazine at the Amber Wharf at Bullbridge[18] and in 1857 this was in the charge of Curtis and Harvey.[19] At a later date, and used until the end of World War I, there was a strongly-built stone powder magazine with an iron door near the stream at the edge of the Old Quarry and just below Culland Wood [362544].

In 1844-5, after the purchase of land including Hilts Pingle in 1842-4, The Butterley Company opened a new quarry; the Hilts Quarry. The new branch tramway left the older gang-road at the Hat Factory [357537] and a self-acting incline operated from there up to the level entering the new quarry [354540], where horses again took over to get the wagons to and from the working faces.

The Butterley Company didn't only burn limestone from the Crich quarries at Bullbridge. Once the quarries were fully developed they used to take some unburnt stone, by canal barge, to their kilns in Codnor Park.

The total length of track from the Hilts Quarry to the Bullbridge kilns and wharves approached two miles and when more efficient steam traction became available a 0-4-0 tender engine, built at Butterley, was introduced in about 1860. At that time it was recorded that the Bullbridge kilns had produced 8000 tons of burnt lime and that 30,000 tons of unburnt stone had been shipped from the wharf.[20] The original quarry - known then, and latterly, as the Old Quarry - was closed at this period.

Watkins recorded that he remembered the locomotive "Fitz" in action as far back as 1896, when it was making three or four trips a day to the kilns, pulling a train of sixteen trucks loaded with limestone.[21] It continued to work until the quarry closed in 1933.

At the end of the 19th century the demand for lime was growing apace. Burnt lime had been used since the 15th century for agricultural purposes and its value was more and more appreciated. There was also a considerable increase at the time in the building of houses for rent. These factors together with the improved ease of transport by canal and rail (the Bullbridge kilns were quite near to the Sheffield-Derby line of the Midland Railway) resulted in a rapidly growing market. Burnt lime was even sent to the farmers of the Cheshire and Lancashire plains and to the mill towns there, using the Cromford and High Peak railway at one stage of the journey. One result was that in 1899 the Old Quarry was re-opened.[22] The tunnel from the excavated pit to the Dimple was opened out and a branch railway was laid on the track of the old gang-road. At this, the time of the Yukon gold rush, the quarry was nicknamed "The Klondyke" (presumably someone hoped for windfall profits) - by which name it is still known to older villagers. During World War I some labour in the Old Quarry was provided by German prisoners of war stationed in the village. After that war the lime trade, like its major customer farming, had its ups and downs and the Old Quarry was closed.[23]

Eventually the limits of economical working in the Hilts Quarry too were reached in the 1920s, when the working face approached houses and roads, and the whole of The Butterley Company operation, including the Bullbridge kilns, was closed in 1933.

7.5 The Cliff Quarry

The principal quarry for Crich lime, certainly after the mid-19th century, was the Cliff Quarry - made originally on the western side of the peak of Crich Hill. The area had been enclosed from waste ground in 1786 (see Figure 8) and was the site of much lead mining activity (see Figure 3). George Stephenson, the railway pioneer, appointed as engineer to the North Midland Railway,[24] had overseen the building of the Clay Cross tunnel in 1837 and had discovered several rich seams of coal. Under the trading name of Geo. Stephenson & Co. he started coal mining near Clay Cross. The prime product was shipped by the new rail system to the markets of London but Stephenson sought a profitable outlet for the small coal and slack produced as a by-product. He saw the market for burnt lime and realised that a source of limestone on Crich Hill could be linked by a downhill mineral line to a level site alongside his railway between Chesterfield and Derby, at Ambergate, to which he could bring coal for burning the stone.[25] In 1840 he started negotiations to establish a right-of-way through Crich on which he could build a tramway, and where appropriate, self-acting inclines, to get the stone from Crich Hill to the site at Ambergate where he was to build his kilns alongside both the NMR railway and, incidentally, the Cromford Canal. Stephenson also negotiated to extract limestone from strata under about 75 acres of the enclosed common land, the mineral rights of which were then owned by the inheritors and purchasers of the manorial rights in Crich.[26] These included the Earl of Thanet (descended from Mary, Countess of Pembroke, the 6th Earl of Shrewsbury's daughter), Richard Arkwright of Willersley Castle, Samuel Travis of Crich, gentleman, and three members of the Towndrow family (Section 6.8, Section 5.2). One of these was farmer Thomas Towndrow who owned a piece of land known as Wheeldon's Croft through which Stephenson wanted to lead his tramway. The delay in getting way-leaves north of the Weaver Brook at the bottom of Wheatsheaf Lane [348544] resulted in Stephenson - in order to get his kilns into operation - transporting limestone not at first from the Cliff Quarry but from the already existing Church Quarry [349546] to the east of the road between the Cross and the Church.[27] This stone was probably bought from the owners and brought out to the main tramway through a tunnel under the road - which was still open in the 1940s.

Carriage of limestone to Ambergate started in March 1841 and at about the same time extensive quarrying also started from about the position of the Jovial Dutchman to the Wheatsheaf Lane, to the west of the Cromford to Langley Mill Turnpike Road.

Eventually, in 1846, it was possible to extend the tramway up to the site of the Cliff Quarry and the originally planned operation was able to develop to the full.[28] By then Stephenson was not well and was feeling old. However, the Crich Mineral Railway was one of his loves and he was a regular visitor bringing cronies on tours of inspection: he spent his later years at Tapton House near Chesterfield. They usually ended with a visit to the Wheatsheaf Inn for refreshment.

In the late 1850s 120 men were employed in Crich limestone-working by Stephenson's Clay Cross Company, and before the quarry eventually closed in 1957 some six million tons of high-grade limestone had been carried down the line from Cliff Quarry to Ambergate, a distance of 2 miles. Construction of that line (interesting detail is given in Dowie's "The Crich Mineral Railways")[29] had involved raising embankments and making cuttings, the building of a handsome arched bridge over the lane from the Market Place to Bulling Lane [349542], the construction of a 65 yard tunnel (unlined) through the solid Ashover Grit under the Oakerthorpe to Wirksworth Turnpike Road leading from Crich Market Place to Whatstandwell [349540] and a number of self-acting inclines.

The most spectacular of these, the Steep [353524], was 550 yards long and went down a gradient of about 1 in 4 and over a small bridge spanning the Cromford Canal to the lime works alongside the canal. The original group of twelve kilns, built in 1841, was soon enlarged by a further eight and they could handle an output of about 50,000 tons of burnt lime a year. On the Cliff Face, as it was called, the quarrymen worked in small teams, often of two men, each allocated a particular section.

Their task was to bore holes for explosive (black powder in the early days) using a hand-held crowbar type of drill driven in by hand. One man held the bar, which had a shaped end, in the rock and rotated it between blows delivered by his companion using a heavy sledge hammer. It was hard, exposed and dangerous work and, with heavy exertion, precarious working positions and uncertain weather there were, of course, fatalities from time to time. Even the quarry floor had its dangers. Thus the "Ripley Advertiser" of 27th October 1866 reported an accident at Crich to one John Piggin who was moving limestone wagons when his foot slipped and one of the wagons crushed his foot. He was attended by Dr. Dunn and no bones were broken. (Dr. Dunn built The Tors - the large house between Bulling Lane and Sandy Lane which is now converted into a block of flats for senior citizens).

Eventually pneumatic drills were introduced to the quarry face and iron piping carrying the compressed air ran mostly along the Cliff Top with connections down to the working places. There was, even as late as the 1930s, a climbing chain up the southern end of the face to facilitate access to the Cliff Top for men to get more easily to the work place (to which they lowered themselves by rope) and to couple on their drills to the air supply. Each team, sometimes with the help of specialists using heavier equipment, having released a block of stone to fall to the quarry floor, were then required to reduce the block to pieces of a size - ideally about 8" in any direction - suitable for transport and for use in the kilns. They then loaded the wagons by hand for transport to Ambergate. The engine-drivers and the train attendants who looked after 'Dowie' and the other engines and operated the inclines were among the aristocrats of the workforce.

The more recent story of the Crich Cliff Quarry will be given below in Section 10.15.

[1] Wragg J. (1985) Lecture: Fritchley OAP Friendship Club
[2] Watkins A. (1952) *The Manor of Crich*. Manuscript. p.17
[3] Hey D. (1980) *Packmen, Carriers and Pack-horse Roads*. Leicester. Leicester University Press. p.140
[4] Crich Enclosure Award (1786). Derbyshire Record Office. Q/RI2
[5] Hey. Ibid. p.147
[6] Woolley W. (1710-15). *History of Derbyshire*. Derbyshire Record Society. Vol.VI (1981.Ed.Glover & Riden) p.76
[7] Cox J.C. (1890) *Three Centuries of Derbyshire Annals*. Derby. Bemrose.II 305.
[8] Crich Tithe Apportionment (1847-9). Derbyshire Record Office. D 2365 A/PI.
[9] Woolley W. (1710-15) *History of Derbyshire*. Derbyshire Record Society. Vol.VI. (1981 Ed.Glover & Riden)
[10] Butterley Records. Derbyshire Record Office 503/B.Boxes 1 & 2.
[11] Farey J. (1811-16) *General View of the Agriculture and Minerals of Derbyshire*. II. p.422
[12] Hey. Ibid. p.149
[13] Nixon F. (1969) *The Industrial Archaeology of Derbyshire*. Newton Abbot. David & Charles. p.147
[14] "Dowie" (1976) *The Crich Mineral Railways*. Crich Tramway Publications. p.5
[15] Garlick S. L. (1966) *Further Notes on Crich*. Vol.3.8 Derbyshire Miscellany. 8.11
[16] Nixon. Ibid. p.155
[17] Farey. Ibid. Vol.II. p.338
[18] Cox. Ibid. II.300
[19] White (1857). *History, Gazeteer and Directory of Derbyshire*. Sheffield. White. p.255
[20] "Dowie". Ibid. p.10
[21] Watkins. Ibid. p.33
[22] "Dowie". Ibid. p.11
[23] "Dowie". Ibid. p.12
[24] Smiles S. (1874). *The Lives of George and Robert Stephenson*. London. (Folio ED.1975) p.226-228
[25] "Dowie". Ibid. p.15
[26] Garlick. Ibid. p.13
[27] "Dowie". Ibid. p.16
[28] "Dowie". Ibid. p.21
[29] "Dowie". Ibid. p.24

6. Old End Lead Mine
A photo taken in 1964 shows the remains of the gritstone engine house where a steam engine formerly raised water to allow lead ore to be won from deposits at great depth. The shaft was 912 feet (300m) deep. The mine closed in 1864

8. LEAD MINING

8.1 The Liberty of Crich

The finds of Roman coins on Crich Hill, as well as on the routes from its northern side and Wakebridge to the Roman Camp at Pentrich (Chapter 1), are consistent with the view that the Romans, known to export Derbyshire lead, were involved in lead mining in Crich. The first documented record is, however, in the Domesday Survey[1] where Ralph FitzHubert is said to hold a lead mine in Crich. Since the time of Edward the Confessor (1004-1068) most of the Derbyshire lead field had belonged to the Crown, and indeed remained so as the "Kings Field of the Low Peak":[2] it contained most of the Wapentake of Wirksworth where the Barmote Court - purely ceremonial these days - still meets.[3] ('Wapentake' was a word from Viking days denoting a division of a county (Section 3.1)). The mineral rights in what became the Liberty of Crich were transferred from the Crown by King John to the 2nd Baron of Crich[4]. About 100 years later in 1325 the Kings Mine at Crich was granted by Edward II to Roger de Belers I. As an independent mining field Crich had its own mining laws and officials.[5] The articles of "The Custom of the Lead Mines" in Crich put the Steward of the Court Leet and the Court Baron (Section 3.2) in control of organisation and disputes in the Liberty. Any man, with the consent of the landowner (who would take an agreed portion of the output 1/4 or 1/3), could dig where he chose, except on roads, in gardens or orchards or in the churchyard. If he found lead it had to be reported to the Barmaster and the claim properly staked-out and a duty of a 'lot' had to be given to the owners of the mineral rights - these were by no means necessarily the owners of the land on which the claim was made.

In the 17th century the Lot was 1/9th of the ore, cleaned and made merchantable. There was also a 'Cope' of 6d a load which had to be paid by the buyer of the ore for access to the claim. The Barmaster supervised activities and if a claim was not worked for three weeks, without good excuse like illness or bad weather, after the Barmaster had noted that the claim had already not been worked for three weeks, he could consent to the claim being 'jumped' by a newcomer.

The Barmaster could requisition ore to cover debts for wages or materials like timber, smith work, candles, powder or bread and cheese and ale: "but ale without bread and cheese he cannot". When the ore was measured the Barmaster took the money and paid the debt, returning the remainder to the owner. No unlawful weapons were allowed in the mines and if there was a fight which "drew blood" there was a fixed fine of 3s 4d - to be paid before the sun set - or the Barmaster could impose a fine of 6s 8d and 'arrest' the culprit's ore to cover the amount. If a miner sold ore other than through the Barmaster's dish, or measurement, he could be fined £2. The Barmaster had the right to go into any man's mine or grooves to search for any stolen things belonging to the mines and he could take three or four "honest" miners with him to examine accusations of trespass and value the amount the miner should pay to redeem himself if he was judged to have driven into another man's claim. Another rule stated that "If any miner be damped* or killed in the mines within this liberty the Barmaster is instead of the coroner".

* i.e. suffocated; an indication of the dangers of lack of controlled ventilation.

In 1846 Joseph Mather was the Barmaster.[6]   At that time the Steward of the Court Leet in Crich was John Charge. (He still occupied the post in 1857;[7] he had been Derbyshire Clerk of the Peace from 1830 to 1849, then the industry was in decline and the post somewhat of a sinecure. The Barmaster in 1857 was Luke Alsop[8]). The records and responsibilities of the Crich Court were eventually transferred to the care of the Wirksworth Barmote Court[9].

Ownership of lead mining rights in the Liberty followed the Manorial rights from the Belers through the Cromwells and the Shrewsburys to the Earl of Thanet and to a wide group of local landowners including such as the Hurts, the Smiths, the Towndrows, the Nightingales and, at one time, Sir Richard Arkwright (Section 2.8).

8.2 Getting the Lead to Market

Although, as has already been noted (Section 4.6), Derbyshire lead had been transported to the South coast as early as 1443-4 by 'waynes', according to the Southampton Brokerage Book of that time[10], it is virtually certain that the Romans took their lead abroad from the East Coast.[11] This was the way to the market chosen in Elizabethan days by George, the 6th Earl of Shrewsbury[12]. He not only owned the mineral rights in Crich, and also in parts of the High and the Low Peak, but he took a lease of the Manor of Bawtry from the Crown and built a warehouse there to store the lead which he was exporting from Derbyshire to London and to Hamburg. This movement of lead to the east arose for two reasons. Firstly, there was plenty of timber available in the Sherwood Forest area on the Derby-Notts border to make the 'white-coal' used for smelting lead ore[13] ('White-coal' consisted of slivers of wood baked in a kiln. It was a cheaper fuel than the alternative, charcoal, which, although capable of being raised to a higher temperature in a blast of air, was not really essential for smelting lead ore*): secondly, from Nottingham on the River Trent and especially from Bawtry on the River Idle sailing barges using the Ouse and the Humber could trade with British sea ports and, through the Humber quays, with the continent.

With the establishment of this easterly route Wirksworth, above the western bank of the full and fast flowing River Derwent, which had but few crossing places nearby, and facing a steep climb by transport up the eastern edge of the Derwent Valley, was somewhat at a disadvantage. Much of its output incurred transport cost before it reached and passed through Crich, which was well placed geographically for getting its lead to market. The packhorse tracks from Crich, not only north and south but also towards the east and to the lead smelting and distribution points, were relatively easy going and well established (Section 4.4, 4.5). To this extent at least the Crich lead industry was well-favoured.

George Talbot, the 6th Earl and Lord of the Manor of Crich (Section 2.2, 2.4) was the largest lead smelter in England and by the late 1570s he was sending 40 to 50 tons per year through Bawtry; by 1585 his exports had risen to over 100 tons a year.

A hundred years later, in 1692, John Houghton in his "Collection for Improvement of Husbandry and Trade" - cited by Hey - noted that the lead trade route to the east was still active.[14] Not only was lead, particularly from the more northerly smelting mills near Chesterfield being exported through Bawtry as in Elizabethan times, but he also recorded that lead smelted at Derby went via the Trent to Hull and that lead from Crich and the mills about Wirksworth was being taken to Nottingham and then sent down the Trent.

Although much lead ore was still being carried from the mines to the smelt mills by packhorses

---

*   Charcoal was used to smelt the rich slag left over after the initial smelting of the ore with white-coal.

once the turnpikes were established in the mid 18th century (Section 4.7) Crich lead lost some of its commercial edge.

8.3 The Miners and their Work

Before gunpowder was introduced into stone-working in the last quarter of the 17th century the lead miners had often to depend on their own muscular strength in using a pick or a wedge hammered or inserted into natural cracks in the rock to lever away blocks which could then be broken up by hammer or, later on, be ground in a gin mill.[15] There were two other methods in use too in the early days. One consisted of lighting a fire against the face being worked, making it very hot, and then pouring water over it: this resulted in cracking and fragmentation and the face became workable by hand tools. Fires were lit only as the men left work in the evening, as a safeguard against suffocation. But there must have been many fatalities through carelessness and ignorance. The other method involved boring a hole in the rock using a heavy hammer beating an iron bar with a shaped leading-edge and rotated between blows by a fellow worker. Into the hole was rammed a quantity of burnt lime and the neck of the hole was stopped by a driven wooden bung through which a small hole was bored and into which water was poured. The slaking of the burnt lime resulted in the release of a lot of heat and expansion of the plug and as a result the rock was split.

Once the workings got beyond the opencast stage and the veins of lead were followed underground the working conditions became truly appalling. There is a classic description by Daniel Defoe published in the first years of the 18th century[16] of a visit he made to a 'North Midland' lead-ore field on his way to Buxton. Defoe described his conversation with the wife of a lead miner who told him that her husband, if he had good luck, could earn about 5d a day. This was well below the average wage for the time (see Figure 5) and reflected a very low standard of living. She, when able, could also earn money by washing the lead ore and, if she worked hard, could earn threepence in a day. This woman directed Defoe and his companion:

"........to a valley on the side of a rising hill where there were several grooves, so they call the mouth of the shaft or pit by which they go down into a lead mine: and as we were standing still to look at one of them, admiring how small they were, and scarce believing a poor man that showed it us, when he told us, that they went down those narrow pits or holes to so great a depth in the earth: I say, while we were wondering and scarce believing the fact, we were agreeably surprised with seeing a hand, and then an arm, and quickly after a head, thrust up out of the very groove we were looking at. It was the most surprising as not only we, but not the man we were talking to, knew anything of it, or expected it.

Immediately we rode closer up to the place, where we see the poor wretch working and heaving himself up gradually, as we thought, with difficulty: but when he showed us that it was by setting his feet upon pieces of wood fixed across the angles of the groove like a ladder, we found the difficulty was not much........When this subterranean creature was come quite out, with all his furniture about him, we had as much variety to take us up as before and our curiosity received full satisfaction without venturing down. (!!)

First, the man was a most uncouth spectacle: he was clothed all in leather, had a cap of the same without brims, some tools in a little basket which he drew up with him not one of the names we could understand but by the help of an interpreter. Nor indeed could we understand any of the man's discourse so as to make out a whole sentence: and yet the man was very free of his tongue too. For his person, he was lean as a skeleton, pale as a dead corpse, his hair and beard a deep black, his flesh lank, and, as we thought, something of the colour of the lead itself, and being very tall and very lean he looked - or we that saw him ascend ab inferis, fancied he looked - like an inhabitant of the dark regions below, and who was just ascended into the world of light.

   Besides his basket of tools, he brought up with him about three-quarters of a hundred weight of ore, which we wondered at, for the man had no small load to bring, considering the manner of his coming-up; and this indeed make him come heaving and struggling up, as I said at first, as if he had great difficulty to get out; whereas it was indeed the weight that he brought with him.....We asked him, how deep the mine lay which he came out of. He answered us in terms we did not understand; but our interpreter, as above, told us, it signified that he was at 60 fathoms deep - but that there were five men of his party who were, two of them eleven fathoms, and the other three, fifteen fathoms deeper. He seemed to regret that he was not at work with these three; for that they had a deeper vein of ore than that which he worked in, and had a way out at the side of the hill where they passed without coming up so high as he was obliged to do".

As mining technology developed the shafts leading to the veins of ore were enlarged and fitted with footholes, ladders or wooden stemples. These were billets of wood set in opposite sides of the usually square section shaft; men would step from one to the other with one leg on one side, the other at the other and steady themselves by grasping higher stemples.

   In due course the ore was raised in buckets suspended on a rope and wound up to the surface by hand, or by a horse-gin. Eventually headgear was erected and steam engines and wire ropes were used to get ore out of the mine. In some cases men were lowered into the mine and brought out by the same means.[17] Nevertheless, in the 1880s a mining inspector reported his computation that in getting to and from his work in a deep mine a miner would use as much as one third of the physical energy he expended during the whole of his working day.

   Lead mining was a hard and rough life and it is not surprising that, even in 1772, a horrified visitor from the south, Prebendary Gilpin, could write: "The inhabitants of these scenes were as savage as the scenes themselves" - thus echoing Defoe's judgement of 50 years previously that the 'Peakrills' were a rude, boorish kind of people. A similar judgement was made about 60 years later, in 1829, when a visitor's account of a visit to Crich described the dress and attitudes of the women who were then working in the lead mines. The extraordinary garb they wore involved: "the head being much enwrapped and the features nearly hidden in a muffling of handkerchiefs - over which is put a man's hat - in the manner of the Welsh peasant. Their gowns were usually red, tucked-up, around the waist, into a sort of bag and set-off by a bright green petticoat. A man's coat of grey or dark blue completed the costume and to protect their feet they had rough shoes with soles three inches thick, tied round with cords or thongs"[18]. The writer frankly described the women miners as 'complete harridans'.

   Kirkham also gives a description of clothing worn in 1828 by a visitor to Pearson's Venture Mine at Crich. "He changed into clothes of flannel and bed-ticking, their texture being only dimly visible through the clay with which they were covered, and he was lent a flannel cap. He climbed down the shaft mainly on stemples; these were pieces of wood which were fixed about a yard apart on the sides of the shaft so that his legs straddled the narrow shaft as he descended. There was a landing-place about 120 ft down where he crawled through a hole into a level, then through a further hole to another shaft with stemples. These were sticky with clay, and were of irregular sizes, set at varying distances and some were nearly worn through, while others felt loose and rotten. At the bottom they went into Ridgeway Sough until they could see along it for about 3000 ft in a straight line with daylight at the far end like a large star".[19] They had then descended about 500 ft.

The 'rough diamond' attitude of lead miners was maintained to the last. Joe Cockayne, or Cocky, one of the great characters of the parish in the 1920s and 1930s, lived in Melkridge House near Dimple Hollow[20] for many years and although 'rough' in every sense was still called as an expert witness to court proceedings in London.

8.4 Some Crich Lead Mines

The war with revolutionary France stimulated the market for lead and as the Industrial Revolution got under way (with an expansion of house building and eventually with the provision of piped water) the demand for lead grew rapidly, as did the means for transporting the material to its customers (Section 4.7). Even as early as 1782 about 200 tons of lead ore were being won from Crich Liberty[21] and thereafter, for nearly 100 years, there was much activity in the local ore field.

There was, at the time of the 1839 Crich Rating Survey, a Smelting Works (paying rates) at a position which would now be in the Cliff Quarry below the Stand. It had cupolas and two reverberating furnaces.

Kirkham has given a detailed description of lead mining in Crich[22] and some of the mines she identified are shown in Figure 3. Here will be considered a few of some special interest.

The Old-End Mine [346558]
The deepest Mine in Crich, one of the deepest in Derbyshire and the deepest shaft sunk entirely in limestone, was the Old-End Mine - between the peak of Crich Hill and the northerly end of Edge Moor. It was sunk, eventually, to a depth of 912 ft. (i.e. to below sea level from the side of Crich Hill). Before the miners got so deep it became necessary to 'dewater' the strata[23]. At first a sough was tried down towards Hollins Farm [354560] over the tip of Edge Moor, but it proved inadequate in the longer term. Then a sough called Crich Sough - or Fritchley Level - was made which entered the shaft at a depth of 420 ft from the surface. This sough drained the water down to the Dimple Brook at Fritchley, two miles away. The arch at its outflow [359534] is dated 1753. It is thought that the sough, excavated with pick and crowbar, runs its course (to save labour) through the shales and clays of the ground below Culland and along the edge of the limestone area using that edge as one of the sough walls. The lower end of the sough was explored in 1980 and a description of the expedition and its findings has been published.[24] A number of spoil dumps from the excavation can still be identified, a large one being south-east of Fishpond Farm. At the bottom of a garden at the foot of Ludlam's Lane the sough, with its never-failing supply of water was used as a well before one of the Ludlam boys was drowned in it, after which it was covered over.[25] In the Culland fields there was, within living memory, a break in the sough through which calves and sheep occasionally fell to their death.

In 1862-63 Old End was one of the mines being worked by Squire Wass' company, but at about the time Squire Wass was being entertained by Denman Mason (Section 2.9), in 1868, the ore working was abandoned as, with depth, the veins became poor in quality. Nevertheless, pumping was continued for some time to bring water up to the Fritchley Level. In 1879 the owners decided to withdraw the pumping gear (a Cornish engine house was, for long - until after World War II - a feature of the local landscape) and to abandon the mine because of rising costs and the refusal of the Wakebridge Mine owners to pay an agreed share of the expenses.

The Glory Mine [340560]
The Glory Mine was worked intermittently for 150 years, eventually to a depth of 810 ft, at first for lead and then for fluorspar. In the days of the lead mining boom, in 1837, it was said that its output was worth from £30,000 to £40,000 a year[26]. (The Wakebridge Mine at that time

came a good second). A geologist, Adams, is on record as saying that when Glory was first opened the owner was offered £10,000 for it on first sight of the ore vein. When it finally closed down it had worked some 1000 yards in extension.[27] In 1870 the Glory Mine was the centre of a riot when two dissatisfied factions of miners had a dispute over the working of the mine. The Barmaster of the time imposed fines of 3s 4d on each of the men involved, at a time when the daily wage for an eight-hour shift was 2s 6d. At this time boys were earning 1s 6d a day and a carpenter could earn 3s 6d. (Two engine-men at the Wakebridge Mine were paid 4s 0d a day and worked a six day week). Within a month of the ending of pumping at the Old End Mine in 1879, the miners at the Glory Mine (about ¼ mile away) found the lower levels of their workings flooded and some lower levels of the Wakebridge Mine were abandoned six months later.

The Wakebridge Mine [339559]
This was one of the principal operations in the Liberty of Crich. It was the site of lead mining from the beginning of the 19th century and in 1846 was leased by Squire Wass (Section 2.9). A plan of 1829 showing a circular race suggests that ore was then being raised by a horse-gin.

As at other mines the Wakebridge operation hit water and, in 1811, a sough called variously the Wakebridge or Whatstandwell or Ridgeway Sough[28] was driven from the Wakebridge shaft to a point between the Cromford Canal and the River Derwent at Whatstandwell [331551]. Originally it was 2/3 rd of a mile long but was later extended along Cliffside to bring aid to other shafts sunk in the area, when it had a total length of about a mile. The 'level' was about 4' 6" high and was unusual in that the depth of water was kept at a minimum of 15" by a series of locks, so that boats could travel its length with supplies including, at one time, coal for an underground pumping engine installed at a depth of 420 ft from the surface. Another engine was installed in 1857 - on the surface this time - and used to pull water from about 650 ft depth up to the level of the Ridgeway Sough. In the 1880s the miners were working as far as 800 yards from the shaft bottom.

It is recorded that[29] in 1857 about 42 men were employed in the mine*. If this report is correct many of the men must have lived outside Crich Parish for, although it was said that at the time of the 1851 Census the boom in lead mining was over[30], the rapid decline in numbers employed in lead mining was said not to happen until the 1860s yet Varty has reported that in 1851 there were only 23 lead miners in Crich, one lead smelter and one lead-ore dresser.[31]

The water flowing from the Ridgeway Sough into the Derwent is warm; Kirkham measured the temperature as 64° F. The Crich Cliff mines were reported to have been particularly warm to work in and were described in the mid-19th century as being of the "warmth of new milk". In cold weather one can still see the Derwent 'smoking' near the sough outfall.

8.5 The Twilight of the Industry

As Kirkham shows there were quite a number of other mines worked in the Wakebridge-Cliffside area but by the middle years of the 19th century the industry began to fade as the costs of drainage increased, the ore veins became poorer and as the result of the export of cheaper lead from the Australian fields.

Two mines on the Cliffside, Pearsons Venture and the Rodney Mine, were engulfed in July 1882 by land slips originating in the thin clay bands in the limestone of the Cliff Quarry.[32] There were several land slips along the Cliffside in the 1880s: one of them blocked the Cromford to Langley Mill Turnpike Road and destroyed a row of cottages. Fortunately for the inhabitants it was Sunday dinner-time and as one family left their meal in the oven and escaped out of the

---

* Arnold Bemrose travelled through the Wakebridge Mine in 1892 and made a geological survey of great interest.

front door the sliding clay and rubble came in at the back.[33]

After lead mining on any scale finished there was still a lot of activity recovering minerals associated with the veins of lead. Fluorspar, known locally as ganister, used as flux in steel making was of particular interest (sales to the USA steel industry were common) but calcite and barytes could also be profitable when the market was right. Quantities of these minerals were recovered from most of the old mines long after lead had ceased to be important.

As late as the 1920s as many as 18 men were employed at Wakebridge, at the Gingler Mine [339554], getting out fluorspar at depths of about 250 ft (by then the lower depths were flooded and inaccessible). Even in the 1950s an old lead working in the Hilts Quarry was intermittently producing saleable materials, and long after the end of World War II there was a dump of ganister alongside the road at the Dimple Hollow - a memorial to Joe Cockayne and the Crich lead mining industry, which had been active since at least the 11th century when Ralph FitzHubert was Lord of the Manor of Crich.

[1] Phillimore (1978) *Domesday Book (27) Derbyshire*. Chichester. Phillimore. p.10
[2] Ford T. D. & Rieuwerts J. H. (1981) *Lead Mining in the Peak District*. Bakewell. Peak Park Joint Planning Board. p.8
[3] Ford & Rieuwerts. Ibid. 10.12
[4] Stokes A. H. (1964) *Lead and Lead Mining in Derbyshire*. Peak District Mines Historical Society. Spec.Pub.No.2. p.43
[5] Glover S. (1829) *History of the County of Derby*. Derby. Mozley. II p.316
[6] Bagsshaw S. (1846) *History and Gazateer of Derby and Derbyshire*. (Derby Local Studies Library). p.167
[7] White (1857) *History, Gazateer and Directory of Derbyshire*. Sheffield, White. p.254
[8] Cox J. C. (1890) *Three Centuries of Derbyshire Annals*. Derby. Bemrose. Vol.I p.29
[9] Watkins A. (1952) *The Manor of Crich:Manuscript*. p.30
[10] Hey D. (1980) *Packmen, Carriers and Packhorse Roads*. Leicester. Leicester University Press. p.91
[11] Nixon F. (1969) *The Industrial Archaeology of Derbyshire*. Newton Abbot. David & Charles. p.24
[12] Hey. Ibid. p.109
[13] Hey. Ibid. p.119
[14] Hey. Ibid. p.122
[15] Ford & Rieuwerts. Ibid. p.14
[16] Defoe D. (1724-6) *A Tour Through the Whole Island of Great Britain*. Harmondsworth. Penguin. (1971) p.465; Letter 8.
[17] Stokes. Ibid. p.18
[18] Firth J. B. (1905) *Highways & Byways in Derbyshire*. London. Macmillan. p.419
[19] Kirkham N. (1968-69) *Lead Mining in Crich*. Manchester Association of Engineers Session 1969-69. No.5 p.11

[20] Dawes J. G. (1983) *The Crich Tales*. Cromford. Scarthin. p.15
[21] Pilkington J. (1789) *View of the Present State of Derbyshire*. Derby. James Pilkington. p.126
[22] Kirkham. Ibid. pp.1-17
[23] Kirkham. Ibid. p.4
[24] Warriner D. J. (1981) *Exploration of Fritchley Sough and Old End Mine:Crich*. Peak District Mines Historical Society. Vol.8. No.1 pp.49-53

[25] Watkins. Ibid. p.46
[26] Tudor T. L. (1926) *The High Peak to Sherwood*. London. Scott. p.245
[27] Ford & Rieuwerts. Ibid. p.109
[28] Kirkham. Ibid. p.9
[29] Ford & Rieuwerts. Ibid. p.107,108
[30] Ford & Rieuwerts. Ibid. p.28
[31] Varty E. J. (1977) *Stoneworkers and Lead Miners in Crich Parish*. CSJ. p.13
[32] Ford & Rieuwerts. Ibid. p.106
[33] Watkins. Ibid. p.37

7. Royal Oak Cottages, The Common
A rare and welcome survival of a purpose-built framework knitters shop as evidenced by the long row of small window panes in the righthand cottage. The Royal Oak pub occupied the lefthand side of the building. As early as 1789 there were records of 18 persons being employed in framework knitting in Crich parish, rising to 270 people in the 1840s

9. The Friends Meeting House, Fritchley
Fritchley had a thriving Non-Conformist tradition for centuries and the Quakers have a fascinating history. Meetings were usually held at members homes but in 1897 the present Friends Meeting House was opened on Chapel Street in Fritchley

8. The 'Hat Factory', Fritchley
Built in 1801 by partners Thomas Kidder and William Downall the factory was always intended for the manufacture of straw hats. But it changed hands several times in the next few years and probably never made hats. Its water wheel was advertised for sale in July 1805. The Butterly Company bought the buildings in 1810 and converted them into tenements for workers employed in the Old Quarry

9. MANUFACTURING

9.1 For Parish Use

In the centuries up to the middle of the 19th, before the coming of the railways and especially before the motor car became common, firstly packhorses and eventually traffic on the turnpikes brought goods of many kinds into the village. Nevertheless the community was, by and large, self-sufficient and itself made most of the things it needed.

Although there were no known records of its being granted a charter there was a market in Crich in early times. By the early 18th century it had been discontinued for a long period. Then, later in the century, an attempt was made to revive it. In 1810 it was again opened, being held on a Thursday: provisions and consumer-goods made locally were on sale but, by 1829, "it was not much resorted to"[1]. As late as the beginning of the 20th century there were stalls selling manufactures, such as pots, on the Market Place at the times of Crich Fair, i.e. on 6th April and at the main Fair on 11th October.

In 1835, serving a population of about 2200 (Figure 9) and apart from the following retailers:[2]

3 butchers	Hickton, R. Smith, R. Taylor
3 grocers*	Lee, Witham, Elliot
2 bakers	Burton, Wheatcroft
1 druggist	Beardah
1 seed dealer	Hey
1 lead merchant	Alsop

there were:

4 shoemakers	Holmes, Piggin, S. Storer, G. Taylor
4 tailors	Bestwick, A. Higgot, J. Higgot, Wetton
4 limeburners	Greatorex, Pearson, Silvester, G. Storer
2 blacksmiths	Poyser, Jm. Smith
2 milliners	Brown, Kent (also a dressmaker)
2 wheelwrights	Hunt, Jn. Smith
2 joiners	Haines, Wyvill
1 candlemaker	Bownes
1 miller	Hall
1 scythestick maker	Shipstone
1 tanner	Wall
1 saddler	T. Taylor
1 framesmith	Jo. Smith

* Elliot also sold 'drugs' and Lee and Witham sold drapery. Witham also dealt with the local post (Section 4.7).

The only present trace of the candlemaker is a building, now a bakery, at the southern end of the Market Place. It is known to an older generation as "The Candlehouse" and it supplied domestic needs locally at the end of the 19th century, but may well have originated in the need to provide light for the lead mines on and around Crich Hill. Other links, in the present century, with the tradesmen of 1835 were the smithy at the Cross (demolished in the 1930s) and certain family names associated with particular trades. In the 1930s there was a blacksmith called Poyser, a shoemaker Holmes, butchers Smith and Taylor and a joiner named Haynes - as there had been in 1835.

All the craftsmen made things for use in the local community which at that time (Figure 9) was growing quickly. In the early years of the 19th century the proportion of the population engaged on activities in 'Trade' as opposed to those employed in agriculture was growing. As we have seen (Section 6.9) between 1811 and 1821 the number of families working on the land reduced by 40% whereas, although in 1811 there were 150 families engaged in trade[3], in 1821 the number had increased to 165 - an increase of 10% (admittedly from a population of 394 families in the village in 1821 as opposed to a total of 380 in 1811). Much of the surplus labour had moved into framework knitting (Section 9.7). Thus even in bad times there had been an increase in those making and handling goods.

The Tithe Map of 1849[4] identifies the area where the tanyard was. The "Tanyard Close", then owned by John Haynes and occupied by Thomas Dawes (a grocer, coal merchant and general dealer with a shop on the Market Place) for pasturing his horses, was at the top of what is now the Dimple Lane which had earlier been called "Tanyard Lane which leads to Millgreen and Fritchley Mill Road"[5]. To illustrate again the continuity of service by particular families in certain occupations, in 1940 James Henry Dawes also had a grocer's shop on the Market Place and until the 1960s, and in succession, several members of the Haynes family ran building, woodworking and painting businesses in the tanyard. Before World War II the original tanning vats were being used to slake lime for making mortar.

Wood for use by local craftsmen was, of course, readily available in the locality (References to timber sales at the Canal Inn at Bullbridge have twice been made (Section 5.6; 6.8)). There was a Turning Mill at Whatstandwell making bobbins and spindles for cotton and flax mills in the first quarter of the 19th century[6] and there was, near to Whatstandwell, for a long time, a steam joinery works. (In the early years of the 20th century it was run by Dawbarns Ltd.) It was built on a rather restricted area of level ground between the canal and the river (and the railway) below Robin Hood [331549]. It is at this site that the Ridgeway Sough enters the river and, in cold weather, to use a local expression, 'vapours' (Section 8.4).

At one time the factory had supplies of timber from Chase Cliff and Leashaw Woodlands but, in its latter years, before economic forces and a series of fires killed it, it brought timber from abroad to the site, especially through Liverpool and Hull.

Iron was also available locally. Burdetts Map of 1791 shows a forge at the side of the Derwent. This was a charcoal furnace for making pig iron and was owned by the Francis Hurt of the time. By 1806 Hurt was making 700 tons of pig iron a year at Morley Park[7] using a tall furnace heated with coke from 'pit-coal' and blown by a cylinder bellows worked by steam engines. The forge and puddling works in Crich, by the side of the Derwent, was used to convert the pigs into rod-iron, principally for the nailers of Belper, and to bar-iron for local smithies[8]. Hurt also produced mouldings for plough-shares and, later on, castings in iron.

The production of cheap castings in iron under the stimulus of demand from the cotton spinners - like Strutt and Arkwright who were business partners with Hurt - for modern mill-machinery was an important factor in the development of the textile industry in the United Kingdom.

The village even had its own supply of coal. In 1592, Wryley, John Claye's friend described Crich: "It is seated on a hill, fertile and well stored both for wood and cole near the ryver Darwen"[9]. In 1811 coal pits at Plaistow Green [351558] and Wheatcroft [351569] were recorded[10] and within present memory Moorwood Moor Colliery [356569], though now disused, was working. (In 1954 there was a large opencast coal site between Barnclose Farm and the railway line [362527]).

At the beginning of the 19th century good local coal cost about ten shillings a ton, about half a week's earnings for a typical worker (Figure 5).

Not only was coal used domestically but, of course, it was of value in lime burning. In 1835 there were four lime-burners with separate businesses in the village.

Lime had been burnt in Crich for centuries. There is a mention of Adam, a lime burner in the 14th century[11] and at the end of the 16th century Crich was sending burnt lime to Hardwick Hall "to whyte with".[12] In the 18th and 19th centuries lime was widely used in the humbler homes of the time, sometimes being tinted either red or blue (as anyone who has restored old property will be aware). A lime-wash was not only decorative, it was hygienic and a regular lime-wash was prescribed in the poorhouse regulations (Section 3.12). The church was at one time lime washed (it was removed from the walls of the church during the Hurt restoration of the 1860s). Even well into the 20th century a lime-wash each year in spring was a way of maintaining a reasonable standard of hygiene in domestic pantries and in privvies, as well as in farms and public houses.

The use of burnt lime in agriculture, building and for decorative and hygienic purposes was, of course, spread far beyond the confines of the village and its manufacture and export - originally by pack animals and ultimately on the turnpikes, and railways grew enormously in the 19th century. (Section 7.4; 7.5).

9.2 Stone Products

The first known man-made export from Crich was a mineral product - the millstones sent from Crich to Barlow Manor in the 14th century (Section 7.1). When the transport of heavy bulk loads became easier as the canals developed, the manufacture of building components from local stone became established. Quarrying for building stone, and dressing it, was a long-established local craft. The specimens found in Culland Wood of dressed stone that might have been intended for Ralph Lord Cromwell's Manor at South Wingfield, or Roger Beler's Manor at Crich, establish that dressing stone had been going on in the parish since the mid-15th century at least (Section 7.1).

Apart from the millstone grit quarry on the east face of the Tors where villagers have had rights to get stone for at least two centuries (Section 7.2) there have been a number of commercial quarries. "Delphs" where building stone could be won, were to be found at Fritchley and on Edge Moor at the end of the 18th century.[13] Larger enterprises, at Dukes Quarries [333546] near Coddington and the Bullbridge Quarry [359525] were near the Cromford Canal. The cost of delivery to the Canal from the Bullbridge Quarry was about 3s 0d per ton in the first decade of the 19th century. This quarry was particularly noted for its production of 'Grey Slate', so widely used for roofing. The stone, which abounds in mica in minute plates and forms layers at joints in the strata, naturally splits into forms which can be used for paviors or flagstones as well as for roofing. Paving stones, 2" to 3" thick were sold, in about 1810[14], for 20d a superficial yard and a rood of grey slating (about 44 square yards) cost from 50s 0d to 60s 0d.

The Duke's Quarries, which produced better stone for structural building, was selling 'square' blocks of stone, in rough, for about 7d per foot cube: dressed stone was 1s 0d per foot cube and the best kinds of ashlar were sold at 2s 6d per superficial yard.[15]

The quarries served by the canal and eventually by the nearby railways up the Amber and Derwent valleys provided stone for many 19th century building projects - from railway bridges, cutting and embankment walls to housing and commercial premises. London and Liverpool were two typical developing cities using building components made in Crich from local stone.[16]

In earlier times the small delph at Fritchley (The Rue Cliff Quarry) provided stone, in 1740-1760, for Shipley Park. When, in 1911, the Suffragette Wall at Shipley Park and two lodges designed by Edwin Lutyens were built by Gee, Walker and Slater of Derby, the stone was again obtained from Fritchley.[17] In the meantime the Primitive Methodist Chapel had been built on the edge of the site and in the 1920s two semi-detached houses were erected at the foot of the quarry face. Before then the steep road down from Fritchley Lane to the junction of Church Street and what is now called Amber View had been made across the 'bed' of the quarry. The original highway left Fritchley Lane between the position of two old dams[18] (which served a carpenters shop) on the site where Pello House and Cherry House have been built and Henry Chell's Millwright's Shop (commemorated by a wall plaque dated 1864) and continued on the level above the delph to meet Amber View some 100 yards above its present junction with Church Street.

As late as 1851 the Official Census recorded that there were 31 masons in the parish,[19] presumably engaged in dressing stone for building purposes. Even in the 1930s there were men alive in the village who suffered from silicosis as a result of working the local quartzitic rock.

9.3 Barge Building

Although in a sense not a manufacture for export, the Cromford Canal was provided with barges built by J. Hepworth, who had an agency at Bullbridge Wharf and used the local dry dock. The barges must have included those made of sheet-iron into which stone was directly tippled from the wagons brought down from the Old, or Warner Quarry. In 1800 Hepworth advertised for "two steady good workmen, who may have constant employment as Boat Builders".[20]

By 1846 Samuel Wheatcroft (brother of Thomas Wheatcroft the cornmiller, and of the family to which German Wheatcroft belonged (Section 5.2)) was in business as a boat-builder at Bullbridge.[21]

9.4 Pots

In the late 17th century Thomas Morley, a Nottingham potter, bought land [353564] at Moorwood Moor from Dame Marie Dixie a granddaughter of John Claye (Section 2.5).[22] Both at Moorwood Moor and at nearby Wheatcroft there were deposits of whitish, yellow and red potter's clay - of various hues - useful for making earthenware and stoneware of the various kinds typical of those found around the East Midlands coalfield.[23] There was coal available nearby (Section 9.1) and, at Wheatcroft, there was also a deposit of fireclay suitable for making bricks to line furnaces and to make saggers for china factories, as well as crucibles for the metal trades.

In 1690 Morley extended the old manor house (Tudor's drawings clearly show the two phases of building[24]) in which, it has been supposed, preparations had been made to receive Mary Queen of Scots (Section 2.4). He also built a Pot-House on the site.[25] Specimens of this pottery's output have survived. The earliest known and dated item is a jug in Nottingham Castle

Museum inscribed "Crich 1701". An extremely rare monteith with a scalloped rim to hold wine glasses by the stem and modelled as if it were made of silver is inscribed "Gulielmus Flint : Crich 1704". In 1725 the pottery was acquired by the Dodd family who still held land in the parish at the time of the Enclosure Award of 1784.[26] However, with the Dodds the pottery business failed and in 1764 John Reynolds and Jacob Redfern of Crich were disposing of the estate of "Thomas Dodd, late of Crich, a bankrupt potter" to amongst others "Peter Nightingale of Lea, Gentleman". The pottery was run for some time by George Bacon of the Alfreton Pottery and the latest recorded specimen is a posset pot inscribed "I.H.1777".

At the time of the 1784 Enclosure, the Pot-House Farm and Manor House were in the hands of the Marshall family, one of whom married Denman Mason's grandmother. (The sale of the property was one of the first tasks undertaken by Denman Mason when he arrived in England in 1867).

After about 1780 the site was used as a brickworks until 1810.

9.5 Various Mills

Minerals - lead, limestone, sandstone, gritstone, coal and clay - were not the only bases of manufacture in Crich. Woodlands were important, but especially so was a good natural water supply which could provide power cheaply and drive simple machinery.

The brook coming down from the dome encompassing Benthill, the Furlongs, and Stones (Figure 7), within recent memory, fed a cattle trough at the junction of Bulling Lane and Vicarage Lane. (It is possible that this brook is the "Cruchebroc" - the Crich Brook - mentioned in the Darley Abbey Cartulary).[27] The water has now been conduited, as has the Weaver Brook, after it has crossed Wheatsheaf Lane. The flow from those two brooks, or from one of them, feeds the cattle troughs on Crich Market Place and the small open stream in front of Hilts Cottages [352541]. Recent residents told of grandparents who played around the troughs in the 1840s, and even then the troughs were old and had served pack ponies, cattle and horses for generations.[28]

The stream from the Hilts Cottages eventually flows under the Dimple and joins another stream in the Dimple Hollow which has contributory rivulets draining the area under the Tors. Some go down Snowdrop Valley and some are from the area around the top of Dimple Lane and the northerly end of the Tors. (The pumps on Sun Lane and on Dimple Green may have drawn their water from this source). All this water then flows, nowadays in an underground conduit, to near the Hat Factory [357537] where it meets the stream which drains Crich Hill, Edge Moor and Culland, and on which probably was the "waterfall" near to Hacon's Assart: its lower reaches nowadays skirt the Old Quarry (Section 6.1). It was on this site - covered when the overburden from opening up the Old Quarry was dumped[29] and when the stream was conduited there - that a mill is shown on the 1839 Rating Map. This is the place nearest to the centre of the village at which most water would flow - collecting water from practically all the high ground of the parish. It is possible that this was the site of the medieval mill which made flour for the local community and which is mentioned in the Darley Abbey Cartulary[30] as existing in the 14th century. It is possible then that at this site flour was ground for four or five centuries using the water flowing down the Dimple Valley towards the River Amber. However, in 1752 work was started to build the Fritchley Level (Section 8.4) to drain the Old End Mine. The outlet of the sough into "Phyllis' Brook" - as that part of the stream was known in the early 20th century - is immediately below the presently-named Poplar Cottage. This is about a quarter of a mile below the position of the old mill and is marked by a small archway, dated 1753, in the side of the stream. So much of the water from Crich Hill, Plaistow Green, Edge Moor and Culland was now brought into the valley below the position of the mill that it was 'starved' of water and was no longer viable. Soon afterwards two local 'entrepreneurs' built cornmills to replace the now highly inefficient mill (which at the time of the 1839 Rating Survey was owned by Jos. Bowmer Trustees and occupied by John Bowmer).

In 1755 a cornmill was built alongside the Amber at Bullbridge [358522] by one Isaac Bowmer.[31] In February 1869 a later Isaac Bowmer sold it to a Charles Else of Lea for £830[32]. (Somewhat later, Else took over Isaac Bowmer's house and property at Ridgeway). The Bullbridge Mill was still working preparing cattle feed as late as the 1930s and was known as Beevor's Mill. A car park for Stevenson's Dyers, adjacent to the railway embankment now occupies the site.

In the 1760s Isaac Bowmer built a cornmill below the present Dimple Dam [359532]. This was later converted to other industrial use (see below), and Enoch Harrison built a new mill just below Millgreen [359534] - the shell of which can still be seen, as can the remains of the wall which formed the dam which provided the power for Harrison's grinding machinery. The Harrison Mill is listed in the 1839 Rating Survey and seventy-five years after his ancestor had built the mill another Isaac Harrison is registered as owning both it and two cottages at Millgreen. One of these was noted as a house and stocking shop; the other a house and beer shop was called Nunfield Cottage. (The Nuns Field just below Thorpe Hill [362535] has been mentioned previously (Section 2.8)).

In later years a steam engine was used at Harrison's Mill to supplement the available water power and it was still in position until 1912.[33] The mill worked for the last time using water power in 1906.

Another mill, Bowmer's Corn Mill, was built between 1810 and 1820. Again, at a later date a steam engine was used to provide more power. The site is now the basis of a farm and stables and is occupied by a semi-retired member of the Bowmer family.

The largest dam in the Dimple Valley still holding water lies between Dimple Lane and Kirkham Lane [359533] and below it and to the south-western side of the dam wall is an industrial site of some importance but of somewhat obscure history. Watkins says that a cornmill was built on the site in 1790 and that one of the millstones could be seen there before 1954. There is also the possibility that a cotton mill was erected in the same area somewhat later.[34] Premises "at Fritchley" were put up for sale in 1805 and said to consist of a newly-erected stone building, four stories high, built as a Cotton Spinning Factory with an over-shot water wheel of 20 ft diameter with an 8 ft head from the reservoir. This would fit into the topography of the site below Dimple Dam better than it would at the site of the Turton Cotton Mill at the Hat Factory (Section 9.6). The Hat Factory buildings (at least in the early 20th century and there was no evidence of re-roofing) were only three stories high and in the deeds available are repeatedly referred to as a "factory intended for the manufacture of hats". The July 1806 notice of sale included two other lots on the same "Fritchley premises" as the cotton mill and its over-shot water wheel in Lot 1. Lot 2 was a 7 horse power steam engine. Lot 3 was a newly-built three-storey dwelling-house in an orchard at the bottom of which is a stream - presumably the Dimple Brook leaving the dam - and near which there was a "Boil, Size and Die House" and a weaving shop of five looms. There were also two roods of rich land "freehold and tythe free". 'Sunnyside' and its outhouses on Kirkham Lane would fit this description. (There is, today, an orchard at Sunnyside which could have been the site of the one mentioned in Lot 3 in the 1805 sale notice). There was also much equipment used in the manufacture of cotton goods on sale.

Since the steam engine was known, later, to be installed not far from the Dimple Dam (if there was a steam engine at the Hat Factory site no mention of it has been encountered), and since

Lot 3 is a considerable property of which no trace is known near the Hat Factory (and the lie of the land would not be conducive to an extensive industrial complex) it seems reasonable to assume that Lot 1, the factory 'newly erected as a cotton mill', was indeed also on the Dimple Dam site. There are several buildings below the dam which might originally have been the two dwelling houses and the weaving shop for eleven looms listed in Lot 1 - together with the cotton mill, the water wheel and some 444 spindles of water-frame spinning, two mules containing 336 spindles, nine carding engines and much ancillary equipment, as well as two fields of rich grassland comprising, in the whole, five acres.

The weaving shop for eleven looms was presumably older than the cotton mill "newly erected" in 1805, for weaving of wool and flax had been a local industry for years[35] - although by 1800 it had virtually disappeared from Derbyshire and had been replaced by the weaving of cotton, spun in the mills of Arkwright and Strutt (Section 9.6).

The weavers in the parish obviously had their troubles. In the Derby Mercury on:

<u>26th December 1799</u> a notice appears about a boy who had absconded from his master's service: "Samuel Chadwick, a boy of about 14 years of age, apprentice to Wm. Peat, Calico Weaver, of Fritchley near Crich in this County. He is supposed to be in the neighbourhood of Repton. Any person employing or harbouring the said apprentice will be prosecuted. Fritchley Dec 24th 1799"

<u>30th January 1800</u> "I, Thomas Cheetham of Crich in the county of Derby do hereby caution any person or persons from giving my wife, Martha Cheetham, credit on my account as I will pay no debts she may contract. Given under my hand the 12th day of January 1800. Thomas Cheetham, Witness Saml. Cheetham".

<u>1st October 1800</u> "On Friday last, Anne Bunting, wife of Joseph Bunting, of the Parish of Crich was convicted in the penalty of Twenty pounds for buying one pound of Cotton Weft of Thomas Cheetham, weaver, which he had been hired to work up, the said Anne Bunting not having first obtained the consent of his employers".

There is no mention of Cheetham being prosecuted and a fine of twenty pounds for buying seems severe. It would take a cotton weaver, in 1800, about 15 weeks to earn £20 (Figure 10).

The sale of the quite substantial industrial enterprise at Fritchley (discussed above) first advertised on the 4th and 7th of July 1805 was postponed by public notice on July 25th[36] but no further public notice about the sale has been discovered. Watkins notes[37] that in 1812 all the ground from Kirkham Lane including the Sunnyside orchard down to what became the Bobbin-Mill Woodyard field and to the stream - was all one property and that the mill on the Dimple Dam site started wood-turning in the period 1815-1820. In 1839 the Bobbin Mill was being run by the Wightman family[38] and they employed some forty men and boys. The Ordnance Survey Map of 1836 shows a sawmill near the Dimple Dam and remains of a saw pit can still be found. These would be used to prepare timber for the bobbin turners. In 1863 the Bobbin Mill was taken over by a Quaker, John Sargent,[39] who had been living at Cockermouth in Cumbria and was there engaged in a wood-turning and bobbin-making business. Sargent was followed from Cockermouth by a group of his Cockermouth work people. Watkins was told, in 1948, by two old men who had worked at the Bobbin Mill in Sargent's time, that the workmen had actually walked all the way from Cockermouth to Fritchley.[40] Sargent's daughter, Mrs. Ludlow of "The Briars" (Section 10.6) who lived into her nineties, recorded that in her father's time the bobbins were made of mahogany and the principal customer was the silk trade.

In the early 1880s the Bobbin Mill was taken over by Edward Watkins of Birmingham (he was Arthur Watkins' uncle) and in 1885 the mill was burned down and the stocks of wood destroyed in what was a disastrous fire. (At this time a steam engine was being used at the Bobbin Mill as a source of power). Edward Watkins who had, in the meantime, built "Chestnut Bank" - a large house on Bobbin Mill Hill - was not insured and although he tried to revive the business at a small mill at the bottom of Bullbridge Hill where Stevenson's Dye Works now stands, it was not a success.[41]

And so ended the industrial activity in the lower reaches of the Dimple Brook and dependence on its water power. At the present time the flow of water seems hardly great enough to sustain much industrial activity and although some of the run-off from many new houses and tarmacadamed roads will now go down to the Amber through sewers and the sewage works below Bowmer Lane [361525] either there has been a reduction in the rain falling locally (as a result of deforestation or some other cause), a loss of water into unknown channels or the present-day flow is roughly as it was in centuries gone by. If this is so and it was able to sustain some small-scale industry only with assistance from rudimentary steam engines, it is not surprising that eventually the Dimple Valley could no longer compete as a site for industry - which could find good level sites with easier access to supplies of coal.

Had there been electricity, gas and oil (and water) grids in the 19th century, especially in its early part, small-scale industry relatively near to the centre of the parish, with labour from the local population, might well have developed. But it was relatively expensive to bring coal up "The Hill" from the railways and coal-fired power generation has to be on a relatively large scale for it to be reasonably efficient. It is not surprising that industrial enterprises were founded in more favourable situations than in Crich parish, certainly after about 1850.

9.6 The Hat Factory

Except in wartime, or with political subsidy, arable farming is not economical in high-ground areas like those in Crich. Certainly this was so before the agricultural revolution of the 20th century - plant breeding, chemical controls and mechanical operations. For centuries most agricultural activity in the village was centred on grazing (see Chapter 6). Although this provided work for some women and children, and some were also employed in lead mining (Section 8.3), the majority could only make a contribution to the family income if they could work at home using materials that could be easily carried to them and produce goods that could be forwarded to the customer or the market without involving robust transport. Certainly until the end of the 18th century, although much weaving was done on domestic premises in country districts, the most important employment for women, and children, was the spinning of yarn - poor though the financial returns were.[42] Several spinners were needed to provide yarn for one weaver, usually a man. Defoe repeatedly noted that many poor country people were employed in spinning wool for the cloth industry, one of the mainstays of the British economy in his day (the first decade or so of the 18th century).[43] Even children as young as four years old were expected to "gain their bread" by carding and spinning.

In the latter part of the 18th century, in 1797, Eden recorded that lead miner's wives were supplementing their incomes by spinning at home,[44] some on the older woollens and some on the newer linens. (As already noted (Section 6.8) flax was grown in Crich around 1800). However, by the end of the 18th century such developments as Arkwright's water-frame and Crompton's Mule began to change things. The new inventions had been developed, following a period when overall population growth had been small and there was a shortage of labour, by entrepreneurs looking for ways of speeding-up and cheapening the spinning process and so cope economically with the continuing demand for British cloth.

When, eventually, factories powered by the River Derwent and then by steam were built, more and more spinning of yarn was withdrawn from the domestic scene. Arkwright finished building his first mill at Cromford in 1777 and, by 1783, was employing about 800 'hands'.[45] By 1789 he was employing 1150 people at Cromford of whom only 150 were men. Employment in factories such as at Cromford and at Strutts at Belper provided good employment to women and children in the near vicinity. But, for Crich women and children who, because of age or of other domestic duties and in the absence of any form of public transport available to them, could not walk the ten miles or so each day to and from work, the concentration of spinning in large factories deprived them of a valuable source of income. This was at a time too when the weaving of wool and linen on domestic premises was also in decline (Section 9.5).

Many of the skills of the nimble-fingered domestic workers could be transferred to the new, vigorous cotton industry and this was a boon to the entrepreneurs over much of Derbyshire. Cotton mills sprang up almost wherever there was a suitable water supply to drive a water wheel. They were largely financed by local gentry and by farmers who had done so well financially as a result of the First Agricultural Revolution, the Enclosures and the rising agricultural prices of the second half of the 18th century, as well as from the profits of the then prosperous Derbyshire lead industry. Thus, the mills at Lea, built by Peter Nightingale in 1784 were, almost certainly, financed from the profits of Nightingale's lead-smelting activities, but he was not successful in cotton.[46] In 1818 Nightingale had to sell-out to John Smedley of Wirksworth. (The mills remained with the Smedleys until well into the 20th century). During this period too Dr. Edmund Cartwright's patent designs of 1785 for power-driven weaving had been developed to the stage where, in Manchester in 1791, a steam-driven mill for weaving had been built. At the same time the lead mining industry was in recession. Pilkington in 1789 commented on the decline in prosperity of Derbyshire lead mining villages - a trend which continued into the next century. Farey listed twelve villages, including Crich, in which the population was either declining or nearly stationary as a result of the bad times being endured by the lead mining fraternity. As indicated in Figure 5 the price of wheat rose by a factor of nearly three in the period 1750 to 1800 at a time when wages were relatively stable. Thus, around 1800, the standard of living of miner's households in a village like Crich deteriorated and people were looking for work. This was reflected in newspaper advertisements drawing attention to the fact that a cheap supply of juvenile and female labour was a considerable economic asset of a lead mining area.[47]

It was, possibly, such a newspaper advertisement that attracted the attention of one Thomas Kidder, a 'factor' of the parish of St. Albans, Wood Street in the City of London. Kidder was interested in the straw hat trade. In the 17th century good quality straw hats were imported from Tuscany (Milan in adjacent Lombardy is the origin of the word Milaner or Milliner).

Before the end of the 18th century Dunstable had established a reputation for providing the nearby London market with an acceptable product for the cheaper end of the market. In our present context the important fact was that straw-plaiting had become established as a spare time domestic industry in rural districts in the South Midlands where the whole household was not already engaged in the prosperous arable farming in the area. Indeed, in such areas straw-plaiting gradually expanded at the expense of the rival domestic industry of wool spinning. In 1801 plaiting was better paid in Suffolk than was wool spinning.[48]

The population of the country was rising rapidly in the period from 1780[49] (Figure 9), mostly due to the efforts of the 'good doctors', and the market for straw hats - as with many other things - was rising with it in the period of the war with revolutionary and Napoleonic France.[50]

In 1800 Edward Simpson of Lilypot Lane in the City of London took out a patent to cover the straw-splitting process used to provide material for producing plaits for making up into hats. (The original idea is actually attributed to Thomas Simmonds of Chalfont St. Peter, supposedly around 1785).[51]

Simpson's splitters proved to be of great value for they gave a finer medium and made possible a narrow plait. As a result, hats comparable in quality with those exported through Leghorn could then be made in Britain from British straw.

Also around 1800 when the expansion of the straw hat industry was at its greatest in Britain, the Italian supplies were cut-off by the war, and this was before import duties on straw and plait were imposed.

That the straw bonnet was, at that time, exceedingly popular is shown by a favourite song of 1802 "The Straw Bonnet", which made it quite clear that the possession of one was desirable for a maid who wished "to have a man".[52]

To return to Mr. Kidder, who lived not far from Simpson,[53] - he wanted to sell hats at a profit. A good profit was in prospect if he could meet the rising market with a product made by a hitherto untapped source of cheap labour anxious to find work, like plaiting, which could be done at home. There was, clearly, such a reservoir of cheap labour in Crich for framework knitting had not then established itself in the village on the scale it did later (Section 9.7).

Other factors could have stimulated his interest in Crich. There were already in the district some centres of straw hat making - at Alfreton, Belper, Matlock and Wirksworth.[54] The products were 'rough and ready' sometimes being made with unsplit straw. In the Dimple Valley there were a number of corn mills (Section 9.5) and hence, at the time, a generous supply of straw, even with threshing done on the farms and even though the straw available locally was not so good for hat making as that of the South Midland Plain.[55] In the Dimple Valley too there were quantities of water available, not only for power but also for wetting the stitched-together-plait for shaping. In the hat and straw product industry men usually did the blocking, stiffening and pressing of hats using powered machinery and so a factory was necessary.

A factory could also house women not restricted by domestic duties who could be employed in the sewing-up of the plait and in lining hats. No doubt the most important factor was that there was then no alternative paid employment which could be carried out by women and children and straw-plaiting was essentially an 'outwork' or domestic activity. Further, even with the relatively poor communications of those days, there were two turnpikes through the village, which meant comparatively easy access to the urban markets for the finished product. The turnpikes also meant that Crich could form a reasonable centre for collecting plait from a fairly wide area in order to feed a factory based near a suitable stream in the village.

In the event, in 1801, Thomas Kidder came to Crich and formed a partnership with William Downall, nominated in various Deeds as a "Hat Manufacturer of Crich Parish"[56]. On February 11th they purchased properties on The Dimple from Joshua Debanke and William Smith. Kidder advanced £2000 for the project to buy the land and erect new buildings in which to manufacture hats. After a year, however, although building was well advanced, Downall had not kept his side of the bargain and on January 9th 1802 he made over to Kidder all his rights in the property, including as yet unused building materials still remaining on the site. Nine months later (10th September 1802) Kidder transferred the freehold of his Dimple properties (the Deeds described the property as including "a factory intended for the manufacture of hats, lately erected and built by Thomas Kidder") to James Turton of Crich (gentleman) and John Turton (cotton manufacturer). On 14th December 1802 John and James Turton transferred some Dimple properties including the "Factory intended for the manufacture of hats" to Thomas Turton and John Curzon for £250.

Thomas Turton, who in 1803 was Captain of the Crich Volunteers[57] (Section 3.11) had married on 31st August 1802 and the announcement of his wedding in the Derby Mercury of 2nd September 1802 said he was a 'Cotton Spinner'. John Turton remained in partnership with Thomas for in the Derby Mercury of 24th March 1803 there is a public apology which reads:-

"Whereas we, the undersigned Isaac Beardmore and Thomas Beardmore of Haylor Bridge, near Crich, in the County of Derby did, on the evening of 9th Inst, maliciously break the windows of Messrs John and Thomas Turton's Cotton Manufactury, and in consequence of their lenity in not commencing a prosecution against us for the same do hereby publicly ask their pardon for our very unjustifiable conduct and promise never to offend in future".

Later in 1803 (Section 2.9 and 9.9) there was an advertisement in the Derby Mercury that John Turton wanted to sell a 20 ft diameter water wheel at the Hat Factory near Crich. (This may have been the same wheel that was later advertised for sale in July 1805 (Section 9.5)).

The advertisement gave John Turton's address as Fritchley Cotton Mill. It should be noted that Turton differentiated between his "Hat Factory" and his "Cotton Mill" at Fritchley.*

It would appear that business was not too good for on 8th December 1803 public notice was given, again in the Derby Mercury, that the partnership subsisting under the firm of John and Thomas Turton of Crich, Cotton Spinners and Calico Manufacturers, was dissolved on 18th November 1803 by mutual consent. It concluded: "The business will, in future be carried on by Thomas Turton of Crich, aforesaid, by whom all accounts will be settled".

Less than a month after the partnership was ended on 3rd December 1803, Thomas Turton conveyed the premises including "the Factory intended for the manufacture of hats" to one William Lister.

In 1810 the Butterley Company bought the buildings and converted them into tenements for workers employed in the Old Quarry.[58]

Until the 1930s there were two buildings, comparable in size, one on each side of the road near where it crosses the dismantled 'tramway' leading to the Hilts Quarry. Then the building to the south of the road was demolished.

The other, parts of which have been renovated and modernised to form attractive dwellings still has, as its official address, "The Hat Factory". It has been so known to at least five generations of villagers even though, it is reasonable to suppose, hats were never made there.

The failures of the cotton mills in the Dimple Valley must have cost the local owners substantial sums of money; such is the risk taken by those seeking a fortune - especially when technology is changing rapidly.

9.7 Framework Knitting

Hand-knitted stockings have been made at least since the middle ages and were popular amongst the well-to-do in Tudor times when both woollen and silken hose were available.[59] In about 1589 the Rev. William Lee of Calverton in Nottinghamshire, completed the development of his mechanical knitting frame and framework knitting began as an industry. It was based in London and Nottingham. After about 1640 the trade spread to Derbyshire[60] and followed

---

* The Turtons were an old-established family of substance (Section 7.4). An earlier John Turton had been a Justice of the Peace in 1720 and a Deputy Lieutenant of Derbyshire in 1745 and 1762 and in 1776 a William Turton had been a J.P. James Turton had in 1775 bought property on The Dimple and leased other property there in 1779. The new century was not very kind to Gentleman James Turton. He not only got involved in the failures of the cotton industry but he also lost his son James, who died in New York. In the Derby Mercury of 30th January 1800 James, Senior, stated that he would deal with any of James, Junior's, debts if creditors would send attested claims to him.

continually-made improvements to Lee's frame and the use of worsted yarn spun from wool grown in the neighbourhood of Sherwood Forest. This had the longest and finest staple in England and was probably the equal of any to be found in Europe. From such worsted yarn it was possible to make, on the frame, articles strong enough to compete in wear with hand-knitted hose, which were made from more expensive extra-twisted materials.

In 1700-1715 workmen making plain stockings earned 2s 6d to 3s 6d a day and those on embroidered work up to 5s 0d a day. This was at a time when meat was $1^1/_2$d a pound and bread 14d a stone. On average the hands only worked at the frame for about four days a week and framework knitting was a well-paid 'luxury trade'.[61]

At the beginning of the 18th century the centre of the industry was near its biggest market and in and around London. However, a desire to escape the regulation of the London-based Framework Knitters Company resulted in other places, particularly Nottingham, becoming centres for expansion and development. In 1727 although there were 2500 of Lee's frames in London there were at least 5,000 in the rest of the Kingdom.[62]

Cotton was first adopted for use on the frame in about 1730 and until about 1770 the cotton thread for hosiery was all imported from India.[63] The expense of the material limited the growth of the industry.

In the late 1750s Jedediah Strutt sponsored an addition to Lee's frame which meant that ribbed fabrics could be made.[64] The "Derby Rib" hose became very popular. In those days, when elegant men wore knee-breeches, fashion was important to the upper classes and long, fancy hose were in vogue; the demand for different types of hose was high. Also, of course, long-skirted ladies wore stockings and there was great demand for good quality hosiery.

With the development of factory spinning for cotton, the production of better cotton thread and a growth of demand which followed the increase in population beginning about 1780, together with a domestic labour force released from hand-spinning, the conditions were ripe for the rapid expansion of the cotton-hosiery trade.[65]

Framework knitting was established in Crich as early as 1789.[66] It was reported that eighteen hands were then employed in the village in the manufacture of stockings. The availability locally, at Cromford, Lea and Belper, of machine-spun cotton yarn and the greater ease of travel on the newly-built turnpikes meant that it was possible to exploit the labour available in places like Crich (Section 9.6) which would be cheaper than that at Nottingham.

At the beginning of the 19th century all was not well in Nottingham. In the prosperous times of the late 18th century there had been a great increase in the number of knitting machines available and by 1812 there were 25,000 in the three Midland counties of Leicester, Nottingham and Derby and 29,000 in the country as a whole. The numbers had grown rapidly, not only because of demand and technical development but also partly as a result of the intrusion into the trade by people with spare capital who bought frames for renting to the framework knitters, the vast majority of whom did not own the machines they worked on. In the 'good' days the frame rentiers made at least 5 to 10% clear profit on the capital they invested over and above the basic 5% interest they could normally expect on a long-term investment carrying little risk.[67]

Established hosiery manufacturers and factors and the middlemen (the 'Bag Men') they used as intermediaries in dealing with the domestic framework knitters also rented frames to those whom they supplied with material and who made the products the rentiers sold. With income from frame-rents an important element in the profits of those renting them out, it was in the interests of the rentiers to spread the work around as many frames as possible. Not only was there a considerable number of surplus frames by 1810 but, in the late 1700s, vast numbers of apprentices had been trained by the masters facing an upsurge in trade.[68] The situation was full of danger for the framework knitters in a period of sluggish trade partly due to changing fashions. Being committed to paying rent for their frames they began to accept lower and lower piece-rates in order to obtain any work at all. The effect on their income and standard of living is shown in Figures 10 and 5. By 1835 the income of framework knitters making cotton hose had fallen to between a half and a third of its value in 1780 and during much of this time food prices were much higher than they had been in 1780. The approach of the wage levels towards the cost of wheat in the presentation in Figure 5 is an indication of the reduction in the standard of living. (Clearly the higher above the wheat curve the wage is, the better is the well-being of the worker). The situation was so bad that in January 1812 nearly half the population of Nottingham, some 4250 families, was receiving 'poor law' assistance from the rates.[69] In 1811 the frame breaking had started and there followed the so-called "Luddite Riots" (Ned Ludd - or Ludlam - was a simple-minded Leicestershire lad who, when told by his father to "square-up his needles", that is, place them in a good straight line, took a hammer to them and smashed his frame). The frame breakers were active not only in Nottingham but also in the neighbourhoods of Ilkeston, Holbrook and Pentrich. They, and Crich, are reported as "suffering seriously from the violence of the stocking frame breakers"[70]. The frame breaking carried on until a series of executions in 1816-17 brought it to a halt.

No Crich men were arrested after the treachery of the hunger-driven "Pentrich Revolution" in 1817,[71] following which three of the ringleaders were executed. These three were:

Jeremiah Brandreth of Nottingham, the leader of the marchers and a framework knitter*; Isaac Ludlam, a Methodist preacher of Wingfield Park and who owned a quarry at Coalburn Hill [374539]; and William Turner, a stone mason from South Wingfield.

However, Crich men were probably involved in the uprising for George Weightman, a sawyer of Pentrich (who was tried and found guilty but was spared the death sentence, being transported to Australia for life, along with fourteen other local men **) told a surgeon at Eastwood who attended one of the 'rebels' who had been accidentally shot in the leg that:

".... men came from Heage, Belper, Crich, South Wingfield, Swanwick, Pentrich, Ripley, Butterley and other places".[72]

The march of the rioters (about fifty in number) began at Hunt's Barn at South Wingfield and went off through Wingfield Park looking for arms and recruits. They acquired arms from S. Hardwick of Manor View [368546] and went on to Henry Tomlinson's home at Park Farm [365542]. Although Tomlinson had hidden his gun they made him produce it and accompany them on the march; but Weightman let Tomlinson return, as he wanted, to his family after they had gone but a few hundred yards. Some marchers then went on to the home of a widow, Mrs. Hepworth [375523]*** where her servant, Robert Walters, was shot - the only fatality of the insurrection. These men then went on to Pentrich Lane End where they rejoined others who had cut back to Park Lane and knocked-up a Mr. Marriott at the Weir Mill [380535]. From there the band set off for Nottingham. The 'revolution' ended pathetically near to Kimberley in a tanyard

---

* When visited by a magistrate when he was in prison and being warned that what he had done was very likely to prove fatal to him, Brandreth, with great indifference, said: "I need not care whether I live or die, for there are no 'Derbyshire Ribs' now".[74] Such was the desperation of many framework knitters !

** Of the fourteen transported, eleven of them for life, five were framework knitters and there were two colliers, two labourers, a shoemaker, a foundry man, a stone mason, a clerk and a farmer.

*** Mrs. Hepworth's stone farmhouse was later incorporated in Wingfield Park Hall when it was built and where it, at one time, was used for housekeeper's quarters.

near a stream called the Gilt Brook when the marchers became aware of the approach of a detachment of mounted men of the 15th Regiment of Light Dragoons.

After the arrests following the collapse of the 'Revolution' William Lockett, the prosecuting solicitor from Derby, reported to the Home Office the claim that Hugh Wolstenholme, the Curate of Pentrich, had secreted George Weightman in his house at Crich and helped him to get away to Yorkshire, but nothing came of the accusation.[73]

A minor consequence of the Pentrich Revolution was that when a new barn, on the road side of the farmhouse, was built at Barnclose Farm [362532] it was designed rather like a fortress; there were no windows on the ground floor but 'observation and firing slits' were provided at intervals around the perimeter.

The Luddite revolts prior to the Pentrich Revolution were partly against low wages, partly in opposition to high frame rents, but also to hostility to the new 'wide' frames on which cheap and spurious cut-up goods could be made. These, by the end of the Napoleonic Wars, were usually housed in large workshops and were concentrated in the bigger towns.

As suggested above, in Nottingham itself the hosiery trade was in a parlous state and by 1819 men's wages were down to about five to six shillings a week - for which they were labouring some sixteen to eighteen hours a day.[75] The wages of women and girls were, not surprisingly, less than this. They worked as winders and seamers for sums between 2s 6d and 4s 0d a week.[76] At around this time the better-class workers in Nottingham were being attracted into the lace trade. When good framework knitters in full work could average 11s 6d a week on their frames, the best bobbin-net hands could earn up to 28s 0d and the average lace-worker could get 15s 0d.[77] When the better workers moved into lace they left behind a demoralised workforce with no pride or interest in their work, apathetic about improving their lot, unable to pay to educate their children, or to attend church or "enlarge their minds"[78]. As a framework knitter said rather later:-

> "a man becomes more like an ass than a man from his excessive labour
> and want of time to study and learn and intermix with social society".[79]

Because there was a source of cheap labour in country districts and rather less fear of organised frame breaking, more and more frames, and the problems associated with them, were moved there. The vast majority of these frames were of the older 'narrow' frames used for 'wrought' or full-fashioned work which, per unit of production (though the quality was higher), was more labour-intensive than the 'cut-up' product of the wide frame. It is likely that most of the frames installed in Crich were of the narrow type.[80]

By 1844 there were 245 frames in Crich and Fritchley and in a National Census[81] somewhat later it was recorded that 127 families in the parish were engaged in framework knitting and producing cotton hose. Altogether some 270 people were involved, over 10% of the local population. The women and children would be mostly engaged in winding yarn on bobbins before knitting on the frame could begin and, when the fabric had been knitted, there were the tasks of mending, stitching, seaming and making-up. A woman or a competent child was needed full-time to do the seaming work for two or three stocking knitters.[82]

There is, in Crich, in the Royal Oak Terrace [350340] across from the former Parish Room, a fine example of a 'stockiners shop' with its long row of windows - good light was essential. Quite a number of such shops in Crich and Fritchley are listed in the 1839 Rating Survey. One was to be found at Thorpe Hill Farm [361537] where, Watkins records, Tom Ludlam, an old man who was then running the farm, told him that the girls working in the stockiners shop built there "were serenaded at work by youths discoursing sweet music on a triangle, thus anticipating

BBC ideas of 'Music While You Work' by a good many years".[83]

By the 1840s poverty among framework knitters was rife, and probably worse than it had been in Nottingham before the Luddite Riots. In the period 1810-1845 the hosiery workers, especially those in the country, were in a truly miserable condition. By 1842 the price paid for making a dozen pairs of most sorts of stockings was not much more than half that paid in 1814[84] and country framework knitters were very liable to accept work 'below the list price', there being no alternative employment such as was developing in the towns as the factory-based Industrial Revolution got into its full stride. The country framework knitters and their families fed on bread and potatoes, sometimes for weeks together:

> "It became a widespread practice to still the cravings of hunger in the adult
> by opium taken in the solid form and by children as Godfrey's Cordial".[85]

Their furniture gradually disappeared, their clothing could scarcely be held together, nothing new had been obtained by many families for so long that they could not remember the time. The dwellings were mostly filthy and abodes of discontent and misery. Children had no scholastic education at all.

As can be seen by inspection of Figure 5, although in about 1700 a framework knitter could earn an income typical of a skilled artisan, by the 1840s his earnings, if he worked in cotton, had dipped to a level much below that of a labourer (the dashed-line - also see Figure 10). Even so he would be working cruelly-long hours each day and every day at his frame; it was truly a pauper trade.

Poor Law records in Crich show that relief was paid out to local framework knitters and the Census Return contains such entries as "pauper-framework knitter".

The change in the industry from the prosperity of the 1780s is well illustrated by Felkin's sketch of his grandfather, William Felkin's, life.[86] Grandfather William was born in 1745 and bound, as an orphan, as an apprentice framework knitter at the age of ten. At that time the charge to a journeyman knitter for board, lodging and washing was 5s 0d. Meat was 1½d a pound, butter and cheese 3d a pound and wheat 3s to 4s a bushel. A journeyman's income could be as much as 30s 0d a week if he were diligent and working at the top end of the fancy-quality scale.[87] In 1783 William bought a new frame for £25 and, over the next thirty-five years he made hose on it before selling it for £10. During that time he only spent £3 on maintaining his frame. When William Felkin began work the usual hours of work were ten on five days a week. One Saturday was allowed for taking-in work and marketing, the alternative was for gardening and domestic matters. In middle life it was necessary for him to work twelve hours and at the time of his death in 1838, aged 93, it was necessary for a framework knitter to work fourteen to sixteen hours a day in order to sustain bare maintenance.

The situation became a public scandal and a Parliamentary Commission of Enquiry was established under Richard Muggeridge. It reported in 1845. The biggest single grievance Muggeridge uncovered was the iniquitous 'frame-rent' system. The rent had to be paid (or the knitter could be deprived of his livelihood completely) irrespective of whether the knitter had work in or not.[88] The normal rent in the mid-19th century was 1s 0d a week and, in some villages, a man was paying more for frame-rent than for house rent. Muggeridge reported that by the time the knitters had paid for their materials and had covered the dues of the 'bag man', "they have to work, on an average, two full days a week for the charges before they begin to earn one penny for themselves or the support of their families".

The role of the bag man in framework knitting was crucial. In the 1850s they handled over half of the narrow-frame work and more of that from wide frames. The warehousemen, or 'hosiers', were content to accept their services for it enabled them to avoid dealing with large numbers of small-output employees and in practice they got the services of men who were, in effect, managers and foremen at no direct expense to themselves. The country framework knitters endured them for it saved them time in going to the warehouses to collect materials and to deliver their product. Many of the bag men also made an income as receiver or collector of rents, in addition to making a straight deduction from the knitter's earnings for delivering materials and work. Often they would conceal from the knitter the true piece-rate and pocket the difference. If they arranged for seaming and mending again they would deduct from the earnings of the women who did the work. It was alleged, even in 1783 when the trade was relatively prosperous and there was neither a surplus of frames nor of craftsmen, that bag men were deducting as much as 20% commission on the price being paid by the hosiers for the product of the framework knitters.[89] It was probably even higher when the bag men were in a more powerful position to allocate work to competing knitters desperate to get work.

The knitters were very aware of the bag man's indulgences in the various deductions he tried to make. There was continuous ill-feeling, but when trade was bad and too many knitters and too many frames were wanting work, the bag man was in a situation which many used unscrupulously.

In the early part of the 19th century many middle men doubled as both bag men and shopkeepers and the knitters were often paid in 'truck', i.e. in goods of nominal value bought from a particular shop nominated by the bag man and often owned by him. Again the system was prone to abuse, either by overpricing goods or providing ones of lower than standard quality. Nevertheless the wives of knitters often favoured the system of payment in kind for:-

> "it effectively keeps workmen from the public-house or beer shop
> because he is without money and therefore without welcome there and
> it ensures that his earnings are expended at home on articles almost
> exclusively consumed by his wife and children".[90]

The old, old conflict between husband and wife is well illustrated in some of "The Crich Tales" to which 'Ted the Post' contributed so handsomely.[91] Ted's grandfather, who appears in one of the Tales was a bag man serving Crich on behalf of Smedleys Mills at Lea. He also kept a 'truck shop' at the end of Prospect Terrace [351539] and was a prominent figure in the Primitive Methodist Chapel once on Sun Lane. Even after the passing of various Truck Acts in the middle of the 19th century the custom of payment in truck still persisted, even though by then it was illegal.

By 1850 or so there were about 40,000 knitting frames being operated on domestic premises and the frame-rent system attracted more and more hostility.[92] A Parliamentary Select Committee on Frame Rents was established in 1854 and eventually they were abolished.

Even by 1854 some hosiers, like Biggs of Leicester, had abandoned frame rents, which they compensated for by lowering their piece rates. For their 'out-workers' this at least removed a threat associated with lack of work. In the 1850s too there was a move towards factory production in the hosiery trade. Hine and Mundella opened their Nottingham factory in 1851[93] and even when, later, steam-power was applied to the so-called 'circular frames' (by A. J. Mundella and Samuel Morley of Nottingham) it was the wide frames producing the lower quality goods which the new machines superseded. In the best class of goods, in which fashioning in those days meant frequent stopping of the machines, there was no great advantage in the use of steam power, and the country framework knitters using narrow-frames still had a market. Nevertheless, whereas in 1844 there had been 245 frames in Crich, by 1857 the number had reduced to a hundred.[94]

The highest quality work had, of course, always been done on the narrow frame, and it depended greatly on the skill of the knitter. Henry Sulley, a Fritchley man born in 1820, became an expert stockiner and had his work exhibited at the Great Exhibition of 1851. Queen Victoria was so impressed with his product that she ordered a pair of fine cashmere stockings from him. There was a wall plaque commemorating Sulley (who died in December 1886) in the Fritchley Primitive Methodist Chapel at Fritchley until the chapel was converted into a dwelling. The plaque, then in the possession of Joan Wragg, was presented by her to Derby Museum.

Although there was still a place for the hand-operated frame in the production of the highest quality goods even late in the 19th century[95], the change in production in the period 1850 to 1860 towards the use of power machinery was matched by, and partly stimulated by, a change of fashion. Men were, increasingly, wearing trousers rather than knee breeches. Stockings were becoming 'under' rather than 'outer' garments[96] and when trousers are worn it is not possible to tell whether it is a full-fashioned stocking or a straight-down, or 'cut', lower quality and cheaper stocking that a man has on. Again, as Victoria's reign developed the fashion preference was for ladies to wear long dresses and long boots out of doors and this again reduced the demand for high quality wrought stockings.

The increased demand for lower quality stockings also came from a new market of working-class customers. Once the price was low enough they started buying stockings in the shops instead of hand-knitting them at home. The new urban wage-earners became a bigger proportion of the growing national population and they were less inclined and less able to have their clothes made at home.[97] They were not content with other people's 'cast-offs' if they could buy new, cheap goods and, of course, they could not afford high quality or 'bespoke' garments.

Hence, just as the problems of the hand-operated framework knitter were being tackled by Parliament - far too late to prevent suffering - at last offering regulation about frame rents and, in 1860, establishing a Board for Arbitration and Conciliation of the Hosiery and Glove Trades[98] (which was based in Nottingham and whose first president was A. M. Mundella) the market and the technology in the hosiery industry were changing rapidly. Times for hosiery workers in the newly established factories were a great improvement on those endured by the hand-frame knitters in the early years of the century. In his report for 1866-67 Mundella was able to report that the past year had been a prosperous one, the demand for hosiery for the last two years having been exceptionally large.[99] By 1880, thanks to the abolition of frame rents, compulsory schooling for children, easier migration, more alternative employment and more stable markets, even the remaining hand knitters had an improved situation, at least as far as regularity of work was concerned.[100]

In the late 1880s adult men on the highest classes of skilled 'wrought', or fully-fashioned work, could make 18s 0d and upwards per week.[101] The wage-curve on Figure 5 moved above the wheat-curve again and the standard of living had returned at least to something like its level in the days when framework knitting was a luxury trade. Indeed that was what it had once more become. Eventually, however, technological development of hosiery machinery rendered the frame operator redundant, even for the highest quality work. Nevertheless, a few frames were still in use at the beginning of the 20th century in Crich. James Henry's widow (Section 10.1) Elsie, born in 1896, who came to Crich in 1908, clearly recalled in 1987 that around 1910, stockiners could still be heard at work in the 'long room' at the top of the north-end of Royal Oak Terrace. It was early in the 20th century, in Crich, as in other villages, that the production of framework products slowly vanished.

Until the 1930s there were a few frames collecting dust in stocking shops in the Mount Pleasant area of Crich, but none working. Such textile workers as remained in Crich were then travelling daily to mills at Belper, Cromford and Lea - except for a few outworkers in the village who, as late as the middle 1950s, were employed using small specialist machines installed in their own homes by Smedley's of Lea Mills. Their task mostly was to link knitted components together and assemble them into garments for wholesaling by Smedleys.

[1] Glover S. (1829) *History of the County of Derby.* Derby. Mozley. Vol.2 p.315
[2] Pigot & Co. (1835) *Commercial Directory for Derbyshire.* Matlock. DCC County Library 1976. p.37
[3] Overseer of the Poor Census 1811:1821 Parish of Crich. Derbyshire Record Office. D.2365
[4] Crich Tythe Apportionment (1847-9). Derbyshire Record Office. D.2365 A/PI.
[5] Crich Enclosure Award (1786). Derbyshire Record Office. Q/RI 2
[6] Farey J. (1811-16) *General View of the Agriculture and Minerals of Derbyshire.* Vol.2, p.234
[7] Farey. Ibid. Vol.1. pp.396-404
[8] Chapman S. D. (1976) *The Early Factory Masters.* Newton Abbott. David & Charles.p.148
[9] Cox J. C. (1879) *Notes on the Churches of Derbyshire.* Chesterfield. Edmunds. p.62
[10] Farey. Ibid. Vol.1. p.207;214
[11] Wragg J. (1985) Lecture:Fritchley OAP Friendship Club.
[12] Hey D. (1980) *Packmen, Carriers and Pack-Horse Roads.* Leicester. Leicester University Press p.147
[13] Farey. Ibid. Vol.1 p.416
[14] Farey. Ibid. Vol.1. p.431
[15] Farey. Ibid. Vol.1. p.418
[16] Kelly's Directory of Derbyshire (1895) p.113
[17] Derby Evening Telegraph. Derby.
[18] Watkins A. (1952) *The Manor of Crich.* Manuscript. p.31
[19] Varty E. J. (1977) *Stoneworkers and Lead Miners in Crich Parish.* Crich Silver Jubilee Brochure p.13
[20] Derby Mercury Newspaper. 9.10.1800. Derby Local Studies Library.
[21] Bagshaw S. (1846) *History and Gazetteer of Derby and Derbyshire.* Derby Local Studies Library. p.167
[22] Watkins. Ibid. p.46
[23] Farey. Ibid. Vol.1. p.448
[24] Tudor T. L. (1926) *The High Peak to Sherwood.* London. Scott. p.244;259
[25] Bower J. (1977) *Pottery.* Crich Silver Jubilee Brochure. WEA/CSJ Committee. p.10
[26] Cox J. C. (1911) *Woolley Manuscripts.* Derbyshire Archaeological Journal. Vol.33. p.136
[27] Darlington R. A. (1945) *The Cartulary of Darley Abbey.* Kendal. p.139
[28] Varty. Ibid. p.9
[29] Crich Rating Survey (1839). Derbyshire Record Office. D1281/PI
[30] Darlington. Ibid. p.565
[31] Woolley Manuscripts - Local Studies Library. Matlock. Reynolds. 6707;17-18
[32] Mason D.(1866-69). Diary. February 1869.
[33] Watkins. Ibid. p.30

[34] Mason. Ibid. 4th & 11th July 1805.
[35] Chapman. Ibid. p.17
[36] Mason. Ibid. 25th July 1805.
[37] Watkins. Ibid. p.35
[38] White (1857). *History, Gazeteer and Directory of Derbyshire.* p.256
[39] Lowndes W. (1980) *The Quakers of Fritchley 1863-1980.* Fritchley, Friends Meeting House. p.3
[40] Watkins. Ibid. p.69
[41] Watkins. Ibid. p.71
[42] Bythell D. (1978) *The Sweated Trades.* London. Batsford.p.28
[43] Defoe D. (1724-6) *A Tour Through the Whole Island of Great Britain.* Harmandsworth. Penguin. 1971
[44] Blythell. Ibid. p.29
[45] Chapman. Ibid. p.62
[46] Nixon. F. (1969) *The Industrial Archaeology of Derbyshire.* Newton Abbott. David & Charles. p.193
[47] Chapman. Ibid. p.167
[48] Dony J. G. (1942) *A History of the Straw Hat Industry.* Luton. Leagrave. p.32
[49] Bythell. Ibid. p.44
[50] Trevellyan G. M. (1942) *English Social History.* London. Longman. p.470
[51] Dony. Ibid. p.36
[52] Dony. Ibid. p.51
[53] Guildhall Library (1986): Private Communication
[54] Farey. Ibid. Vol.3. p.481
[55] Dony. Ibid. p.19
[56] Butterley Records. Derbyshire Record Office. 503/B. Boxes 1 & 2
[57] Cox J. C. (1890). *Three Centuries of Derbyshire Annals.* Derby. Bemrose. Vol.I, p.404
[58] "Dowie" (1976) *The Crich Mineral Railways.* Crich Tramway Publications. p.5
[59] Felkin W. (1867) *History of the Machine-Wrought Hosiery and Lace Manufactures.* David & Charles reprint 1967 p.30.
[60] Felkin. Ibid. p.62
[61] Felkin. Ibid. p.72
[62] Bythell D. (1978) *The Sweated Trades.* London. Batsford. p.80
[63] Chapman. Ibid. p.147
[64] Felkin. Ibid. p.93
[65] Blythell. Ibid. p.44
[66] Pilkington J. (1789) *View of the Present State of Derbyshire.* Derby. James Pilkington. Vol.II. p.239
[67] Blythell. Ibid. p.87
[68] Felkin. Ibid. p.435
[69] Felkin. Ibid. p.239
[70] Cox. Ibid. Vol.I. p.213
[71] Stevens J. (1977) *England's Last Revolution - Pentrich 1817.* Moorland. Buxton.
[72] Stevens. Ibid. p.70
[73] Stevens. Ibid. p.80
[74] Stevens. Ibid. p.82
[75] Felkin. Ibid. p.441

[76]   Felkin. Ibid. p.460; p.511
[77]   Felkin. Ibid. (Ch) xxix.
[78]   Felkin. Ibid. (Ch) xxi
[79]   Blythell. Ibid. p.95
[80]   Felkin. Ibid. p.466
[81]   Howarth D. M. (1977) *Royal Oak Cottages*. Crich Silver Jubilee. pp.10/11
[82]   Blythell. Ibid. p.82
[83]   Watkins. Ibid. p.31
[84]   Blythell. Ibid. p.92
[85]   Felkin. Ibid. p.458
[86]   Felkin. Ibid. p.451
[87]   Felkin. Ibid. p.102
[88]   Blythell. Ibid. p.86
[89]   Chapman. Ibid. p.26
[90]   Blythell. Ibid. p.94
[91]   Dawes J. G. (1983) *The Crich Tales*. Cromford. Scarthin. pp.82-89
[92]   Blythell. Ibid. p.82
         Felkin. Ibid. p.516
[93]   Felkin. Ibid. (Ch) xxiii
[94]   White (1857) *History, Gazetteer and Directory of Derbyshire*. Sheffield. White. p.255
[95]   Blythell. Ibid. p.89, p.97
[96]   Blythell. Ibid. p.92
[97]   Blythell. Ibid. p.66, p.91
[98]   Felkin. Ibid. (Ch) xxxi
[99]   Felkin. Ibid. p.487
         Trevellyan. G. M. (1942) *English Social History*. London. Longman. p.558-561
[100] Blythell. Ibid. p.94
[101] Blythell. Ibid. p.93

10. Crich Stand 1851-1922
The predecessor to this tower was demolished in 1849 and Francis Hurt, Lord of the Manor of Alderwasley had it replaced in 1851 at a cost of £210. The simple round tower was struck by lightning in 1908 and badly damaged. In 1922 the tower was demolished when Crich Hill had been chosen as the site for a new war memorial to the Sherwood Foresters

PART III
THE TWENTIETH CENTURY

10. REMEMBERING

10.1 Introduction

Records and writings since the Norman Conquest have told of the many changes in village life over the eight hundred years to Victoria. In the four or five generations since the Queen became a widow there have, perhaps, been even greater changes. These can be recalled by grandfathers who remember their own grandfathers and can well recount what their fathers told them. Here we tell of some of the events in Crich since the time of 'Victorian' John, father of James Henry Dawes the grocer and grandfather of Peter the Parish Clerk of post World War II days - who all appear in the pages of "The Crich Tales", the collection of stories about Crich characters alive in the last hundred years.[1]

John Dawes, who once lived at Dimple House was, amongst other things, the local overseer* who, before the formation of the County Council under the Local Government Act of 1886 had the job, under a series of statutes dating from the Overseers Act of 1555 and under the supervision of the Justices of the Peace at Quarter Sessions, of looking after such local activities as highway maintenance and fire protection. John was also a stationer, a bookseller, a tobacconist, a hardware dealer and he kept an ale and porter store on Crich Market Place.[2] He had been apprenticed to his Grandfather Thomas who had kept the shop in the 1860s, and his horses in Tanyard Close. (Section 9.1).

John's five daughters and three sons were born in the house above and behind the shop. He attended church every Sunday dressed in top hat and frock-coat and he always occupied a seat at the back of the church on the two-seater pew to the south of the organ console. He was proud of a red waistcoat embroidered with railway engines which he liked to wear on social occasions. His father had left Crich around 1840 to work on building George Stephenson's Midland Railway and had settled for a time at Baldock when the construction was held up at nearby Hitchin while negotiations for the building of St. Pancras were being slowly completed. John was born at Baldock.

John's son, James Henry - often known as 'Jas H' - had three sons. At different times he had two different shops on the Market Place and was, several times, Chairman of the Parish Council in the 1930s. He inherited his father's seat in the church and for many years sang in the choir wearing a black coat, pin-striped trousers and spats. He walked to church with a silver-topped malacca cane - as much a part of his uniform as his black bowler hat.

True to family tradition, John's grandson Peter Dawes worked in the Rating Department of the Rural District Council and also attended church on Sunday mornings. As Captain of the Bellringers, he rarely stayed to morning service and led his team out just before the service started in what a caustic churchwarden called "The March of the Bellringers". He was clerk to the Crich Parish

---

* According to Bulmer's 1895 "History and Directory of Derbyshire" (page 647) John had also held the posts of assessor and collector of taxes and of collector of tithes.

Council for 25 years and collected council house rents in Fritchley, Crich, and Whatstandwell. Here is an example, from grandfather to grandson, of continuity in a village community in the 19th and 20th centuries.

10.2 Fairs and Farming

The later turnpikes in the local area - like the one financed by Arkwright, Strutt and Hurt along the Derwent Valley (now A6) and that from Ambergate up the Amber Valley (now A610) avoided the long climb through Crich. With the advent of the railways and, after World War I, of the cattle lorry, much of Crich's importance to local farming communities was lost. Even though Farmer Wilmot still brought his cattle up the holloway[3] on Smiths Rough [352523] and up the Top Hagg to the fair held near Crich Cross and other farmers drove their beasts to the fair along the old high-ground routes until the 1920s, it was during that decade that the Fair died*.

Over the last hundred years the farmers in Crich Parish - working on high ground which was often exposed and not very fertile - have tended to raise sheep and calves for fattening in lusher pastures and in providing the needs of the locality for dairy products. Before World War II it was common for local farmers to go to Derby Market by their own pony and trap or later by "Ludlow's Bus" (Section 10.6) to sell eggs and butter each week. Local men told of their journeys, in the 1920s, driving a herd of cattle or a flock of sheep to the good grass of Chatsworth Park - some 12 to 15 miles over Dethick Common and Middle and Beeley Moors. There, with cattle, and the walk back in a day was an arduous task!

During World War I, because of the Atlantic U-Boat Blockade, prices of food were high and the efforts of the farmers were well appreciated but prices went down again after 1925 only to recover at the start of World War II; for the same reasons yet again (see Figure 5).

After World War II, with beneficent Government support, farming prospered. The mid-20th century agricultural revolution encompassed many of the features of earlier progress. The use of the tractor and a host of associated mechanical devices; animal breeding (with artificial insemination playing a valuable part); the use of food additives; new methods of controlling stock and its feed; improved veterinary treatments; plant breeding both for increased disease resistance and increased yield in a wide range of growing conditions; improved control of fertiliser application and the use of sophisticated chemicals for disease and pest control have all played their part to an extent where yields have increased enormously and the United Kingdom has come near to self-sufficiency in temperate-zone agricultural products.

For many farms in the Crich area, raising and milking cattle on relatively small holdings, the main form of income since about 1950 has been the monthly 'milk cheque'. The local farmers and their families became relatively prosperous, but they provided but little employment for others in the village. Only one worker was hired full-time in 1984.[4] The rest of the work was done by the farmers, their families and by casual and seasonal labour (Section 6.9). There is, now, no real sense of Crich being the centre of a farming community as it once was.

Since the 1970s, when Britain entered the European Economic Community, there has again been a distortion - by support prices and food mountains - of the established national agricultural market.

But, as Cobbet observed over 150 years ago, such 'artificialities' entrain the seeds of their own destruction and with the onset of Milk and Grain quotas and talk of marginal land reverting to woodland it would seem that another farming cycle is about to start.

* Even in the 1860s Denman Mason was hinting that Crich Fair was not handling its earlier level of business (Section 6.9).

10.3 Manufacturing

In the 1970s the Crich Pottery was established in buildings below the Candlehouse [350541]. It did not, like its predecessors in the 18th century, use local clay - but it established a world-wide reputation. Its first outlets were Maceys in New York and Harrods in London. In 1983, in competition with some of the great firms of the Five Towns, the Crich Pottery was awarded the "Supreme Gift Award" by the Jewellery and Giftware Federation, having previously been given formal recognition by the London Design Centre.

Apart from the potteries and the local butcher and baker (the candlemaker has long gone!) the only 'manufacturing' near the centre of population in the village employing local people and actually producing things for sale was one near Dial Farm [352535] - the "Tors Spring Company" - which in 1987 employed about 50 people, mostly women. It was established in 1961 and made springs and wire shapes for a range of manufacturers - of domestic appliances, of motor vehicles and for British Telecom amongst others. *(Ed: In the 21st century Tors Spring moved out of the village and on to a nearby industrial estate. The site is being redeveloped for housing)*.

There is a joiner's shop on Cliffside and a number of local craftsmen (fibre-glass and plastic artefacts, upholstery, reproduction furniture, carpenters) who create custom-made items for sale.

The nearest places at which some numbers of local people find employment are either just inside or just over the present-day parish boundaries, on a few well-established sites in the river valleys, near main roads and the railways. Until recently Richard Johnson and Nephew operated a wire-drawing works on a site [342522] near the original Hurts Forge (Section 9.1). This works was always referred to as the "Forge". At the old Dawbarn's site below Robin Hood there is a small foundry making specialist castings (even for such firms as Rolls Royce). Perhaps one of the largest employers of local labour is the Stevenson's Dye Works at the foot of Bullbridge which occupies a site on which, at one time, Edward Watkins tried to re-establish his wood-turning works.

So far as the majority of the Crich population is concerned it is not things made in the village which are sent out to earn its living but the people who make things and provide services outside the village who go out to earn their keep.

10.4 Public Services

With a good catchment area from Edge Moor to Benthill and along the Nether Common (Figure 7) and a good bed of boulder clay extending down the Dimple, Crich was always blessed with a good supply of water. (Perhaps a reason for its early importance, for it meant that a community could be maintained on high ground).

Cattle troughs were to be found in many parts of the parish and village pumps abounded, many of them functioning into the 20th century. In Crich township itself the Holywell Pump [346545] supplied the mound on which the church is built: there were pumps on Dimple Green, on Sun Lane and at the top of Snowdrop Valley, as well as others in the smaller communities; as at Fritchley, where one was sited on Church Street.

Many private houses built at the end of the 19th century had their own pump too. In the yard at Peter Dawes' house at Dimple Villas a well some 16 ft deep was uncovered in the 1970s when building work was being carried out. This well also fed a pump in the attached house next door. Pumps were still in use in kitchens of the houses in this row in the 1920s.

The main pump in the centre of the village, on Dimple Green, was unlocked and brought into use as late as the mid-1930s when there was a drought. Piped water was first laid in the village in 1906. The header-reservoir, now abandoned, was near the road junction at Town End [346549] (Section 10.5).

Installation of piped water and the gas mains laid by the Ambergate, Crich, Bullbridge and Fritchley Gas Light and Coke Company Limited were the first steps taken to bring amenities in the village up to recognisably modern standards. The Gas Company, with its works at Bullbridge, was formed in 1865 but the laying of the principal mains was not completed until after September 1910.[5] It was then that an agreement was made between the Company and the Derbyshire County Council as to the opening and breaking-up of certain main roads and county bridges in the parishes of Crich and Heage for the purpose of laying pipes and other apparatus. At one time Grandfather John Dawes, whose duties as local Overseer had been taken over by the County Council, was Secretary of the Gas Company.

Street lighting was at first done by oil lamps fitted on brackets attached to buildings (as at the "Jovial Dutchman" at the Cross) or in a few special places like a wrought-iron arch over the steps immediately across from the "Rising Sun" which led down to the Dimple Green. These were lighted and turned-off each day; a job which, in his youth, was done by Skimps - one of the more memorable characters in "Crich Tales". The installation of gas street lighting in 1921 was a considerable improvement.

Main sewers were first installed in 1924 and earth closets (including the friendly two-seaters) and the night soil men slowly went.

In 1924 too a supply of electricity was brought up the Common as far as the Market Place. The cables were hauled along and up over the poles by teams of shire horses. At first there were nine subscribers in the village.

The first council houses were built in 1928 and at about the same time the surfaces of the main roads in the village were first tarred. This was a great benefit to the one or two cars running in the village. The doctor, who lived at "Rosskeen" off Dimple Green and Surgery Lane, was the pioneer motorist; for many years he employed his own chauffeur.

In the early years of the century, two policemen were permanently stationed in the village. The old police station (with its cell) on the Market Place was replaced in 1901 by a new police station, with its own lock-up, on The Common [351534]. A sergeant lived at the station and was in charge. The parish was regularly patrolled and the police knew what was going on, who was likely to get into trouble and if there were any strangers nosing about. Their principal occupation was with crime prevention and this meant using their eyes and talking to local people, not to each other on the radio. They certainly spent but little time in totting-up prosecutions for a bureaucracy to display in a Chief Constable's Annual Report. The last policeman to be stationed at the Police House with any direct responsibility for what went on in the parish was transferred elsewhere in 1960. For a time thereafter villagers had often to direct the occupants of panda cars to wherever they had been told by radio to go or to help them find whoever it was they were seeking.

In the early 1930s the last permanent 'civil' building in the village was put up. It was the urinal on Bown's Hill, known to many of James Henry Dawes' cronies as "Jimmy's Corner" (he was doing one of his stints as Chairman of the Parish Council when it was opened). It was declared that he had chosen the site so that he would not be caught 'short' in walking from the "Kings Arms" to the "Jovial Dutchman"!!

10.5 Reservoirs

At the beginning of the 20th century, Crich's position, on one of the first heights of the Pennine chain at the side of the Derwent Valley and overlooking the East Midlands plain, was exploited by a number of municipalities in order to provide their water supplies with suitable 'header tanks' or 'service' reservoirs. These not only held a reserve of water coming from the original source but meant that the 'head' on the mains systems was adequate to drive the supplied water through the many miles of mains water pipes required to bring the water to the population using it.

a) The Chadwick Nick Reservoir   [348532]

This was built by the Ilkeston and Heanor Water Board[6] to hold water treated at its works at Homesford Cottage by the side of the Derwent where the Meerbrook Sough discharges drainage water from the Wirksworth area.[7] This sough was started in 1841 to drain the lead mines around Wirksworth and on average discharges some 17 million gallons of good quality water a day into the Derwent.

At the time of building, in 1903, the Ilkeston and Heanor Water Board designed its system to supply some one million gallons during a working day of ten hours - keeping a reserve capacity of an additional ten hours to meet the requirements of the growing population. The water was pumped using steam power (it is now powered electrically) through an 18 inch diameter main up to Chadwick Nick - a height of some 500 ft.

The Chadwick Nick Reservoir is 700 ft above the ordnance datum and is 150 ft long by l00 ft wide with a working depth of 16 ft. It was excavated out of the millstone-grit rock in the southerly extension of the Tors beyond Chadwick Nick and the excavated rock was ground up to form an excellent concrete material, of which the walls and floors were constructed. The four walls are about 19 ft high, 3.6 ft thick at the base, tapering up to 2.5 ft at the top. It is divided by a concrete cross wall, l0 ft high, into two compartments, to enable one part to be cleansed whilst the other is kept in work. The reservoir is covered by a concrete roof covered with turf and supported by one-ring blue-brick arches; the arches being supported by about fifty free-standing blue-brick piers. It has a capacity of 1.4 million gallons. The water, on being pumped up from the treatment plant, descends to the bottom of the reservoir and is decanted from the top by two floating arms into the gravitation main. The main is 15 in. in diameter and passes across the Amber at Bullbridge on its way to the Ilkeston Reservoir. There is a junction near Codnor Gate from where a 10 in. main feeds the Codnor Reservoir (near Jessop's Monument) which is the highest point in the Heanor district.

By the early 1930s the gravitation main was found to be of inadequate capacity to keep the customer's reservoirs full during periods of prolonged dry weather or frost. With the increase of population and increasing demand it was found that a fall of several feet in the height of water was frequently occuring. When the balance was not restored during the night time the Codnor Reservoir, which was the one most affected, became empty. In 1932 the Water Board, under pressure from the Ministry of Health, and from the Ministry of Labour which was anxious to find work for the growing number of unemployed, and then enabled to borrow capital on favourable terms, initiated a duplication of items of plant and also the installation of a new 15 in. main from Chadwick Nick reservoir to Codnor so that, in effect, each of the towns of Heanor and Ilkeston had a separate trunk main.

b) The Bowmer Rough Reservoir [349527]

The Derwent Valley Water Board was incorporated in 1899 with the aim of supplying water from the Upper Derwent Valley to the corporations of Derby, Nottingham, Leicester and Sheffield and construction of the Howden and Derwent Dams in North Derbyshire started in 1901/1902. At the same time the Derwent Valley Aqueduct* was started, to bring water from the treatment beds at Bamford to the covered service reservoir above Ambergate - near to Bowmer Rough and Bilberry Wood. The water was brought by a series of syphons, cut-and-cover conduits and tunnels. The construction of the Bowmer Rough Reservoir started in June 1907.

To transport materials two railways were built; one, worked by a Hudswell Clark tank engine called "Crich", brought stone from a quarry created on the western side of the ridge which, further north, becomes the "Tors"; the other took spoil down the hill and delivered materials to build the Crich Conduit which brought water to the Bowmer Rough tunnel and then into the inlet well of the reservoir.

The reservoir in shape is a rectangle with an added semi-circle overlooking the confluence of the Derwent and Amber rivers. The rectangle is about 480 ft. by 360 ft. and the semi-circle is of radius 180 ft. The buttressed retaining wall is some 16 ft. thick at the bottom and 2 ft. 6 in. at the top and there is a dividing wall 10 ft. high about 280 ft. from the northerly wall facing Chadwick Nick. The floor is 12 in. thick concrete in a 6 to 1 Portland Cement mixture, and the roof is of reinforced concrete 4 in. thick covered with 12 in. of soil, which is grassed. The roof is supported by some 600 blue-brick pillars 2 ft. 8 in. square, spaced on a 20 ft. by 16 ft. grid and supporting 20 in. by 7 $^1/_2$ in. RSJs and 6 in. by 3 in. steel channels. The depth of water from the floor to the lip of the gauge well is 23 ft. and that is 640 ft. above ordnance datum.

The capacity is 28 million gallons. The main pipeline to Nottingham, of 29 in. diameter, crosses the canal, the river, the railway and the road near the railway bridge over the A 610 near Bullbridge. The Leicester and Derby pipeline, of 40 in. diameter, crosses the A 610 near Ambergate sidings and goes on over Thackers Chase. There is an overflow pipe which runs as far as the River Amber, where it discharges, alongside the Leicester and Derby pipeline.

At the peak of activity 56 men were employed on the site of the reservoir and steam cranes and rock breakers were used. Water commenced filling in June 1911 and the final construction work was completed in July 1911.

There are a number of other service reservoirs in the parish, of similar form to those at Chadwick Nick and Bowmer Rough. Some details of them are shown in the table below:-

TABLE A : SERVICE RESERVOIRS IN CRICH PARISH : 1987

Location	Date Built	Capacity Gallons	Source of Water	Customers Served
Stones Lane	1969	3,000,000	Meerbrook Sough	Stretton, Higham, Clay Cross, Chesterfield, N.E. Derbyshire
Lea Moor	1972	250,000	Meerbrook Sough - blended with Derwent Valley Reservoirs	Crich, Dethick, Lea & Holloway, Wessington
Parkhead	1910	60,000	From Lea Moor Reservoir	South Wingfield

The Severn-Trent Water reservoir at Lindway Springs was abandoned in 1980; it is now stocked with fish and is used for angling.

* The track of the aqueduct is often identifiable by robust iron gates let into stone walls.

10.6 Travelling

Although Macadam's methods of road construction had been used widely, at the beginning of the century the use of tar to bind the materials of the surface was not then common (Section 10.4). Watkins, who had been a keen cyclist, wrote feelingly about how bad the local roads were - even the main ones.[8] They were all made of limestone, thick with dust in dry weather or deep in sticky mud in wet. Usually there was not enough traffic to justify the frequent use of a heavy steam-roller for repairs, certainly not on the village roads.

Before 1910 or thereabouts cyclists could ride six-abreast on the Matlock Road (now the A 6) without any interference and, on the same road south of Derby (heading for London), Watkins had seen loose stones laid on long stretches of road that waited weeks for the arrival of the roller.

One of the reasons for this neglect was that for many decades before about 1910 it was quite unusual for a long-distance journey to be undertaken by road: the comprehensive network and frequent schedules of the railways met the need for travellers between most towns and many villages.*

Denman Mason described, in his diary, how much use Crich people made in the 1860s of the Midland Railway; walking, or going by pony and trap to Ambergate or Whatstandwell and then off on jaunts to Matlock, Derby, Sheffield or, a favourite with him, to Sawley. When James Henry Dawes, in about 1890, won a scholarship to Wirksworth Grammar School, he at first walked the six miles or so each way, though later on he caught a train at Ambergate and got to Wirksworth after a change of trains at Duffield. When later, at the turn of the century, he worked in a grocer's shop at Ripley he used to travel there each day by pony and trap: it was said that the pony could find its own way home, but that it stopped at every pub on the way !

Even in the 1920s there was only one way for the boys and girls from the parish to get to Strutt's School. If you lived in the centre of the village you walked the two miles down The Common, Bullbridge and The Hagg to Ambergate Station (and back again in the later afternoon) to catch a train from there to Belper. If you lived at Parkhead or Plaistow Green then another mile each way was added to the daily trudge to school, even if you used the Fritchley gangroad and then went on the canal-side to Ambergate. Indeed, the walk up and down the two miles to Ambergate Station was the price you paid before about 1930 for the privilege of using everyday public transport: you could walk the rather shorter distance to Whatstandwell if you wanted to go north or pay rather more to travel south. For a woman who wanted to go shopping in Derby and if she had a child in a pram it wasn't possible to use the whole of The Hagg, which was restricted by a number of stiles. Such travellers, when returning with their shopping had to start up The Hagg, push the pram through the canal tunnel and follow the canal path to meet Bullbridge Hill near the Canal Inn and face the push up the steepest part of the hill to reach Crich Common.

In the 1920s there was one bus each week - on a Friday - to Derby Market. It was run by Quaker Ludlow, who kept "The Briars" Guest House [352530] where Bernard Shaw and Mahatma Gandhi used to stay. This 'market bus' was a converted World War I lorry, and passengers sat facing one another on two bench seats one along each side of the passenger compartment. Farmer's wives with eggs and dairy produce were important and regular passengers.

In about 1930 Guy Else started a regular service, with a proper bus, from Crich Market Place to Ambergate Station. It ran about every $^3/_4$ hour at busy periods of the day and was scheduled to meet specific trains. These were, in fact, quite frequent - being several trains an hour to Derby at

---

* With the development of the internal combustion engine and the motor vehicle the situation is completely reversed; it is, nowadays, the railway system that has been allowed to deteriorate.

peak travelling times and there were regular services to Manchester and Sheffield and beyond as well as to Derby and London. This bus service was a boon, not only to Strutt's pupils but also to people who worked in Belper and Derby: quite a number, however, continued to walk to the railway station even as late as the early 1960s - from habit, for exercise and for economy.

Then the Pippin Bus Company at Alfreton bought out Guy Else and ran through to Belper. They were eventually taken over by the Trent Bus Company (a main shareholder in which was the London Midland and Scottish Railway). From then on there was no co-ordination between times of departure or arrival of trains at Ambergate and the travel of buses between Ambergate and Crich. It was the first, 'narrow-minded, immediate-profit', step downhill which lead to reductions in local train services and eventually to the Beeching Axe. Nowadays there is an infrequent commuter service from Matlock to Derby which stops at Ambergate, but the lines to Sheffield and Manchester through Ambergate Station are no more.

The Midland General Bus Company started a service in the 1930s between Alfreton and Matlock which used the Oakerthorpe-Wirksworth turnpike route to Crich Cross and the Langley Mill turnpike from there to Cromford where it joined the A6. This was valuable not only for the workers at Lea Mills but also for those who sought the pleasures of Matlock, particularly at the swimming baths.

It wasn't until well after World War II that there were more than a handful of private cars in the village. By then Ludlow's bus service to Derby Market had gone, but it had been replaced by the "My Lady Coach" service based in the village which also, on Saturdays, ran a service between Crich and Ripley. This eased the burden of a shopping trip to Ripley tremendously, but it didn't do the Crich shopkeepers a lot of good having to compete with the larger shops and with the weekly market on Ripley Market Place.

When the Hilts Quarry closed in 1933 and the Cliff in 1957 the village lost two of its frequently used, but illegal, highways. They were the Fritchley gangway to the Hilts Quarry, which was the standard route from Bullbridge and Fritchley Green to Crich Market Place (this, going up the Dimple Valley, avoided the steep inclines taken by the public road system) and Stephenson's Railway itself. This went from Chadwick Nick under the edge of The Tors, through the tunnel cut through the gritstone under Sandy Lane, over the archway spanning the end of Bulling Lane and on up to the Town End. It was not only an easy, comparatively level way from one end of the village to the other, being crossed by paths giving access at fairly short intervals, but also a favourite 'private' walk of courting couples. To accuse anyone of going 'tunnelling' may have had Freudian overtones, but it was not an uncommon pastime.

10.7 Schools

The pattern of schooling in Crich at the beginning of the 20th century had been established when the British School was opened in 1885. Its early records show that one of James Henry Dawes' brothers was a 'monitor', and that three of his sisters were pupil teachers there at one time and another. The only secondary schooling available before Strutts was opened in Belper in 1909 was well away from the village.

In about 1890 when James Henry won a scholarship to Wirksworth Grammar School (the only Crich boy to do so), he went on to take the "public examination" of those days and became a Licentiate of the College of Preceptors.*

---

* He hoped to go on to study medicine but John the Overseer got into money trouble and James Henry had to abandon his ambitions and was apprenticed as a grocer to his brother-in-law at Ripley. Then, and even until after World War II, it was not possible to study medicine unless you had private means. University scholarships lasted for three years: a medical course took a minimum of five.

After about 1910 pupils at the Crich Primary Schools competed for scholarships and free places at the Herbert Strutt School, Belper. In the twenties and thirties one or two pupils from the parish were successful each year. Peter Dawes was one boy who won a free place.

In the period 1920 to 1945, from a total village population of about 3,000, Crich pupils at Strutts won fifteen university scholarships. Two became Cambridge wranglers, another a Knight and a university vice-chancellor and two others university professors; all these, interestingly, in mathematical or science subjects.

With the advent of 'comprehensive' education in the 1950s Crich secondary pupils have been 'bussed' to Alfreton. *(Ed: For approximately five years Crich schoolchildren were transported to Frederick Gent School in South Normanton, before being sent once again to Alfreton).*

10.8 Welfare

In Grandfather John Dawes day the parish workhouse was remembered only by the name "Workhouse Row" - a group of cottages up Chapel Lane past the Wesleyan Methodist Chapel. Then, and until World War II, the destitute, the senile and the helpless were given indoor relief in Babington House (Section 3.13) at Belper, a place regarded with some dread by old people without means. But, before the Beveridge reforms in the 1950s there were still plenty of applicants for help from one of the many private charities in Crich, some of several centuries standing.

They were administered by village notables, acknowledged leaders such as the vicar, the doctor, the schoolmasters, the churchwardens and the chairman of the parish council. They knew which families needed help by personal observation. There are boards dating from 1774 in the church belfry which name some of the benefactors of the village and which record the origin of charities still alive today. They list:

John Kirkland of Wheatcroft who in 1562 left forty shillings yearly to be paid to 16 deserving widows - forever !

John Bradshaw, 1639, who from his estate required seven shillings and sixpence to be paid yearly by John Wetton's successors "forever" to benefit the church and the poor of the Parish.

Edward Lowe of Plaistow in 1694 gave 5 shillings to the Minister and 5 shillings to the poor forever - and the yearly rent of the Sheldon Pingle (off Coast Hill) was to supply five shillings yearly for the use of the Church and the Poor, 2s 6d to the Vicar and 2s 6d to one poor widow for a Christmas dinner.

In more recent times:

Gisbourne's Charity of 1817 supplied coarse Yorkshire cloth and flannel to the value of £7 5s 0d and is known locally as the "Flannel" charity even though, nowadays, the proceeds take the form of cash.

The Rev. Thos. Cornthwaite in 1838 left £200 in 3% Consolidated Stock - the dividends from which were to be spent for the benefit of the poor.

John Cooper in 1853 left the interest on £40 to be divided equally between 10 poor widows of Crich by the Vicar and Churchwardens on Christmas Eve yearly.

Until 1894 some of these charities were distributed by one of the churchwardens and the local 'overseer' . Thereafter the parish council took over responsibility. The other charities and the foundations established by the Hurt sisters were, and are, distributed under the authority of the vicar, churchwardens and parochial church council.

In the 1920s after the General Strike and early in the 1930s there was much poverty in the village. The 'dole' or the ten shillings a week 'Lloyd-George Pension' was not over-generous and not everyone was entitled to it. It was not unusual for old people, and some young in money trouble, and perhaps hungry and barefoot, to go to the vicarage and seek help. Often the vicar was able to countersign a note authorising them to collect 2s 6d worth of groceries. James Henry Dawes handled many of these each year at his shop on the Market Place. Since the inception of the Welfare State after World War II acute hardship arising from poverty has not been so visible. *(Ed: It is uncertain how many of these village charities are still active: there have undoubtedly been some amalgamations).*

10.9 Clubs

In the first half of the 20th century, and not surprisingly for there were a lot of healthy and vigorous youngsters about and little else to distract them (even if 'consumerism' had existed then they had no money!) there was much sporting activity in the village.

Four different football teams are remembered. Crich Rangers played on a field at the bottom of Stand Lane and stripped at the "Bulls Head". Crich United played on the Tors and changed at the "Rising Sun". Crich Athletic played on Chase Fields and patronised the "Black Swan" and Townend played on a field towards Coddington and used the "Cliff Inn". Not all existed at the same time but even just after World War II there were two teams competing for local talent. The Rangers side of 1932-33 was a classic team of local men which won numerous local and county competitions.

The Crich Cricket Club, founded as recorded in Denman Mason's diary in the 1860s and still playing until 1963, first had an excellent pitch not far from the Market Place where the Recreation Ground now is. The boundaries were a little short but, when its pavilion was moved in the early 1930s to a field on the edge of 'Stones', out of the centre of the village and its activities, it was not so easy to 'drop-in' on a match in progress; its 'characters' were less in public attention and from then on attendances and support declined.

The present Recreation Ground was taken-over from the Cricket Club by the 'Miners Welfare' and two tennis courts were built where the old wicket had been. An abortive attempt was made to make a bowling green and establish a bowling club but World War II intervened and afterwards the field was taken over by the Parish Council for the use of the village as a whole. In the middle 1930s the Miners Welfare Tennis Club ran a vigorous, if not particularly successful, team which represented the village in competitions and leagues formed amongst other Miner's Institutes in the Derbyshire Coalfield.

Tennis had been popular in the village for some time. Before the Miners Welfare courts were constructed there had been, in the late 1920s, at the same time, at least five different tennis courts within half a mile of the Market Place. At present there is not a single one in the whole parish.

In 1887, by public subscription, a Reading Room had been erected on Sandy Lane just above the Baptist Chapel. (Overseer John Dawes' name appears on one of the foundation stones!). It followed in the tradition of the Lending Library which was attached to the Church Sunday School in 1833 and the one in the small building opposite Victoria House. The Quakers also established the Fritchley Lending Library in the middle of the 19th century. Eventually the Sandy Lane Reading room was taken over by the Miners Welfare organisation: a billiard table was installed and it became a club for the local mining community and their friends. In the 1950s the building was taken over by the County Education Authority for the preparation of school meals (and for the "Meals-on-Wheels" service run by the W.V.S.) and is now used as a canteen by pupils at both the 'Top' and 'Bottom' schools. *(Ed: This is no longer the case: the canteen has been closed and the property purchased for private use).*

After World War I the men who had fought and survived and their friends and relatives formed a 'Comrades Association'. With money collected by public subscription and with funds raised by whist-drives, dances and other functions it built the "Comrades Club" down the lane at the back of the Bottom School. This too became a centre for billiards and other bar games (including Housey-Housey) and it is still vigorous.

A village institution which, alas, no longer survives, was the Crich United Silver Prize Band. Formed about 1900 it played in public for the last time at Christmas 1964 when it toured the village regaling listeners with a selection of carols. It used to practice on Sunday mornings in the Parish Room and to those living nearby the sound of the band and the aromas of Sunday dinner being prepared are an abiding and evocative memory. The Band played at Carnivals, Whit Monday walks and at Armistice Day parades when, at about 11 o'clock, the Last Post and Reveille on a solo cornet would echo down the nave of the church. For a long time its conductor was Sam Hollingsworth a man who, through his work at Lea Mills was given an introduction to the "Besses of the Barn" Band and was so accomplished a soloist that he was asked to accompany them on a tour of Australia and America. There, he and the Band had the privilege of being conducted by John Phillip Sousa.

A Baden-Powell Scout Troop was formed in 1924 by Captain Barker, who was then the manager of the Cliff Quarry. At first six boys were brought together in the Captain's sitting room in his house at the entrance to the Quarry (now occupied by the British Tramway Society). As the Troop grew, a floor in the joiner's shop in the Engine Shed at the Cliff Quarry was cleared and adapted as a Scout Hut. Eventually a Cub Pack was formed and in the 1930s the Scout Group met in the Clubroom at the "Black Swan". Joining the Scouts was an opportunity for the boys in the village to explore and visit places well away, at first to the English Coast and then, in the 1960s, the Scouts camped in Skye and in Norway - an enduring part of their experience and development. In 1965 a new, purpose-built, wooden Scout Hut was built on Jeffrey's Lane and shared with the Guide Troop (established in the 1920s by the local doctor's daughter). The money for the building was raised by waste-paper collection, barbeques, whist drives, jumble sales and with financial and other assistance from the Derbyshire County Council. The Scouts and Guides still thrive. *(Ed: There is now no Guide Pack).*

There are now a number of clubs, societies and associations active in the parish that have a history of some decades. One can list the Womens Institute at Fritchley (formed in 1923), the local branch of the British Legion (1924), the Workers Educational Association (1953) and a number of meetings organised by the church and the chapels where members of the Mother's Union, the Church of England Men's Society, the Womens Bright Hour and such groups foregather. There are too, nowadays, vigorous organisations running pre-school Play Groups and, for older citizens, the "Evergreens" who meet in The Glebe and the OAP's who meet as a 'Friendship Club' in the Congregational Chapel schoolroom at Fritchley.

10.10 Shopping

Before the local buses and then the private motor car made transport so much easier the village met many of its own needs. Before World War I there was a bootmaker and a tailor on the Market Place and another tailor at Victoria House (where the bakery now is). The 'emporium' there was run by Jimmy Tommy Lee who, as well as clothes, sold groceries and 'pharmaceuticals' - such as they were. Even in the 1920s there were three drapers shops in the village: one at the top of Bown's Hill, one on the Market Place and one where Surgery Lane meets the Common. Then too there were four butchers shops on the Market Place (and another on Fritchley Green) as well as a thriving Co-op opposite the "Kings Arms"- with a butcher's shop and counters for bread, confectionery, groceries and greengroceries. Even in the 1930s the butchers (excepting the Co-op) killed their own animals on their own premises in the village.

Milk was fetched each day by the children of each family from a chosen local farm, usually in a special enamelled can with a wire handle and a lid. Queues at popular farms were often tiresome to the children when they had to wait for the completion of milking. There was often more than a little 'horse-play', spilt milk and retribution.

In the 1930s too there were two cobblers and two full-time barbers. *(Ed: Now there is one hairdresser on the Market Place and no cobbler in the village).*

Apart from the several smaller 'kitchen table' shops (one next to the Royal Oak, a 'Truck' shop at the end of Prospect Terrace and one across from the church) there were four or five 'professional' grocers in the village in the 1920s and 30s. Each had served an apprenticeship and qualified as a journeyman in the trade. They received, at first by horse-drawn dray and later by motor van and lorry, flour, butter, sugar, lard, dried fruit, rice, treacle and many other groceries in bulk and they did their own 'weighing up'. Factory packaged foods, excepting some jams and some tinned goods, were almost unknown. A 'proper' grocer could weigh-up a pound of rice on a flat sheet of paper which was then folded and tucked-in in such a way that, with no fastening, it could be dropped from counter height on to a stone floor without spilling. The grocers delivered orders; most had permanent errand boys.

James Henry Dawes sons delivered groceries when not at school. It was a weekly task for one of them, when he was about 12, to make two trips down to Crich Carr on a Saturday morning each time carrying two baskets of bread and groceries to one large family. The eventual purchase by Jas. H. of a basket-carrying bicycle for delivery was a great boon and thrill to his sons.

After the General Strike in 1926 some of the families whose bread-winners were coal miners at pits at Oakerthorpe and nearby had a hard time. Then with the Depression in the late twenties and early thirties there was a lot of unemployment and much poverty (Section 10.8). Some of the grocers bills run-up in James Henry's shop by certain families reached £80 to £100. This was at a time when some were glad to get a 2s 6d voucher from one of the local charities to buy something to eat. Even when, with rearmament before World War II more prosperous times returned, these large bills were never paid off. James Henry comforted himself with the thought that his credit, which had saved many families from going very hungry, at least meant that they had to keep trading with him, or face court debt collection. Otherwise when the children grew up and started earning in the better times before 1940 they could have taken their trade to the Co-op with its 'dividend'.

James Henry was not only a grocer but made-up his own tea mixtures to suit the taste of particular customers on outlying farms with their own water supply. He also provided the local farmers and people who kept livestock with several kinds of corn and meal. His 'advertising' in the Parish Magazine and on a slide at the local cinema named him as "Grocer, tea, provision and corn merchant". After World War II most goods in a grocer's shop were delivered pre-packaged and simply handed over the counter by the shopkeeper, a job almost anyone could do. Nowadays the customer serves himself or herself in a supermarket.

Another indication of the village's self-sufficiency before World War II was that there were at least four building contractors in Crich who employed ten or more craftsmen each, including plumbers, masons and joiners. They each had their quicklime pit for making mortar and they sawed-up their own timber, using gas engines to power circular and band saws. They made up their own house fittings like doors and window frames, cupboards and so on.

When Jimmy Tommy Lee's emporium closed before World War I a shop on the Market Place at the side of the Baptist Chapel became the local chemists, its owner being a qualified pharmacist. He not only provided medicines and made-up prescriptions for the local doctors but he also supplied some basic medical treatment for those who couldn't afford to pay the doctor, even if they were members of the National Deposit Friendly Society. Even those who could have paid the doctor went to the chemist to have their ears syringed or boils lanced, or for simple remedies for illness: it was cheaper. Apart from his medical sales the chemist sold petrol from the first pump in the village. He also sold groceries and, after the advent of the wireless, the recharging of accumulators for his customers and other possessors of wireless sets was a profitable sideline.

10.11 Entertainment and Holidays

In the early years of the century not only did the local shops meet most of the villagers' needs for goods, but their leisure activities were also usually based in the parish.

It is true, nevertheless, that there were the annual "Butcher's Trips" - a day out in London, or a day at York Races was typical: there were also Choir and Bellringers Outings - by horsedray and open charabanc - or more adventurously by railway train to more distant places. Cathedral cities, Lincoln and the new Anglican Cathedral at Liverpool were favourites and were visited as a link with church activities. In the 1930s Blackpool, and its Illuminations, became a regular venue. In the early 1920s, perhaps as a relief from war, there had been an organised visit from the village, funded by local activities, actually to stay for several days at Blackpool. It took a whole winter to raise the money but it meant that many of the older generation saw the sea for the first time.

Some enterprising young men grouped together, even before World War I, to go on holidays together to Blackpool and eventually even to Paris. In both places they seemed to have spent most of their time playing billiards (at least that was the story they stoutly maintained!).

Overall, however, the villagers spent their active leisure in the village, even if they weren't members of the numerous clubs in the parish (Section 10.9). There were annual concerts in the schools and carnivals in the streets raising money for good works: the Derbyshire Royal Infirmary, church, chapels and the many sports and other clubs in the village benefited. There were the fairs in April and October, even after farmers had ceased to bring animals and produce for sale to the area above the Cross - when "Timmy Ray" brought his roundabouts, swings, booths and stalls to the Market Place and then, after the mid-1930s, to the "Dutchman Croft".

Whist drives and dances were regularly held. Before World War I potted palms, white gloves and cards for booking dances with ladies were the thing at the Bottom school where the parquet flooring was better than the older, knotty, planking at the Top School. In the 1930s there was hardly a Saturday night without there being, in at least one of the schools, a Whist Drive and Dance raising funds for some organisation and providing a chaperoned social meeting place for the local teenagers. Waltzes, foxtrots, quicksteps and veletas - sometimes even a polka or the Lancers were danced to a band of three to five local musicians. The Cricket Club Dance on New Year's Eve (which probably descended from Denman Mason's parties in the 1860s) was a well-established institution, with the singing at midnight, usually led by Peter Percy Taylor's tenor of "Oh who will o'er the Downs so free".

Sometimes a travelling circus - like that of "Young Sandow" - or a group of wandering actors would bring more exotic entertainment and their own marquees to the "Dutchman Croft" - or to the croft at the side of the "Kings Arms" where the "Calico Theatre" would put up its tent and thrill the locals with "Maria Martin" or "Sweeney Todd".

The cinema was opened in 1923 (a gas engine-driven generator in a room under the projector provided the power). Saturday afternoon matinees and cowboy serials opened new horizons for the young. Talkies arrived in the early 1930s.

Perhaps the signs of a more permanent change in entertainment were the ten and twenty-yard lengths of wire suspended from tall poles in gardens around the village which led to the house, like giant washing lines; these were the aerials feeding a signal from Daventry 5XX or London 2LO to the catswhisker wireless sets with tilting tuning coils that were powered by 120 volt high-tension batteries and 2, 4 or 6 volt lead-acid rechargeable accumulators.

10.12 Singing Hymns

When John Dawes and James Henry Dawes sang in the Church Choir it was seated around the organ at the west-end of the nave under where the old minstrel's gallery used to be before the church restoration of 1861. The organ and the choir were, unconventionally, placed at the west-end of the church so that the chancel could be reserved for the exclusive use of the local 'squire' and his family. They had their private entrance in the south wall of the chancel near to the sanctuary. For many years before World War II the Deacon family of Chase Cliffe (he was in charge of the Sheepbridge Iron Company), having acquired the local squirearchical rights by purchase, occupied, in sole splendour, the chancel. They sat under the window dedicated to the Hurt sisters who had been so active in parish affairs in the 19th century - and for whom Chase Cliffe had been built.

In the late 1950s the choir acquired surplices and moved to their rightful place in the chancel to lead the singing in church.

In the early 20th century and until the 1950s Whit Monday was a great day in village life. All the chapel and the church congregations, then numbering several hundreds, gathered together and, with banners at the head of each Sunday School, paraded around the village led by the Crich Band. At certain places - Town End near the church, on the Market Place, at the top of Snowdrop Valley (traditionally a village gathering place between the village and the Nether Common) and on Fritchley Green, they massed together to sing hymns in unison - for many years being conducted by the headmaster of the Top school, "Daddy Haywood". Having toured the centre of the parish the groups in the procession would disperse to their Sunday School for a 'bunfight' provided by the ladies of the congregation, and afterwards to a local field for sports. This was the day, traditionally, when those children whose parents could afford to buy them new clothes first wore them. A feature of the Church School Sports in the Vicarage Croft was the arrival of grocer James Henry Dawes with a tin of Nuttalls Mintoes which he threw by the handful over the heads of the scrambling pupils. A few sweets were held in reserve for the more timid ones; experience showed it avoided tears and misery.

Another long-established custom was for the principal chapels to hold a special series of services on a particular Sunday in spring or early summer. These were the "Anniversary" or Chapel Sermons; the "Sarmins" in local talk. The day was usually marked by an assembly on the Market Place (at Fritchley it was on the Green) in the afternoon or evening when the chapel choir and congregation would sing a series of hymns to the public before retiring to their own chapel for a special commemorative service celebrating the founding of the congregation. Certain accomplished tenors and sopranos - to be trusted with a solo - would help out at a whole series of "Sarmins" and their performances, as well as the ladies' hats and dresses, were the subject of regular critical comment.

10.13 Bellringing

In the Church Tower there is a ring of eight bells. Until 1910 there were only five: they were dated 1616, 1626, 1671, 1721 and 1771 {this latter being a recast of a bell made in 1583 (Section 5.2)}. A new bell was added in 1910 and in 1928 the five old bells were recast and tuned to the new bell, and two new bells were added by parishioners and the relatives of men killed in World War I. The recast bell of 1671 bears the inscription "Fear God and Honour the King". The largest bell, the Tenor which weights 12 $^1/_2$ cwt is inscribed:

> " All men who hear my monstrous sound
> Repent before you are in the ground" .

It is this bell that is used for tolling a death or a funeral. Early in the century the verger, as soon as he was notified of a death in the parish would perform a toll. A series of separated single strokes indicated the death of a child: strokes in groups of two a woman and three before an interval of repetition told of the death of a man. Parishioners often knew who was ill and were able to speculate on who had passed away.

The bells are still half-muffled each Armistice Sunday. On the death of a truly national figure like King George VI or Winston Churchill they were completely muffled except for one side of the tenor. The 'rumble' of the muffled bells followed by the clear, clean, deep strike of the tenor's uncovered metal clapper stroke is very impressive.

The custom of muffling has endured since World War I, and the Armistice Service is one of the few, together with Easter Communion and the Christmas Carol Service which, since the abandonment of the King James Bible and the Book of Common Prayer is nowadays attended by the ringers. There has always been - and still is - a traditional wariness between bellringers and the church authorities. After the Reformation, before which the clergy used to ring the bells, the bands of ringers - who were paid for their services - too often used to spend their fee on drink at the inn which in so many villages is found near the church. Too often there was open warfare between the vicar, churchwardens and the ringers. Around the early 1700s many bands of ringers were barred from the church on the Sabbath. The so-called "Quality" used to exercise and and enjoy their art on Saturdays only. Even as late as 1875 the "Ecclesiologist" could still print an article by a country curate on the best methods of dealing with "an ungodly set of ringers". A Cambridge church still carries a board in the ringing chamber which declares:

> "Do not ring and run away
> Leaving other folk to pray"

Until the mid 1970s - when services were held late on New Year's Eve, the Crich Ringers used to "Ring In" the New Year by firing all the bells simultaneously twelve times at the stroke of midnight. In the 1980s the Bell Captain was Peter Dawes - then in his sixties - who first started bellringing at the age of twelve.

10.14 Quakers

Quakers have been associated with Crich Parish for about three hundred years (Section 5.3) and even from the early days were subject to local harassment. As recently as 1914 Crich youths damaged Quaker Davidson's shop (The Fritchley Stores) on Fritchley Green as an expression of disapproval of the pacifist views of the "Friends". During World War I, several members of the Society were arrested and jailed though some, farmers, were excused on conscientious grounds. Even in World War II Edward Tomes was sent to prison and Donald Smith was arrested: others were exempt from military service provided they undertook specific employment and some served in field ambulance units in various theatres of war. Apart from their pacifism - greatly respected today on the basis of their unselfish service in world trouble spots - the Quakers attracted attention because of their objection to the payment of tithes. They regarded these as forced maintenance of the Establishment religion and contrary to the precepts and example of Christ and of his Apostles - and indeed of the Christian Church itself during its first 300 years of existence.

Even as late as 1930, Thomas Pye of Dimple House was served with a demand for a tithe of two-pence which he refused to pay. The officer serving the demand was so embarassed by this refusal that he paid the demand himself - against the wishes of Pye. A more celebrated case took place in autumn 1930.[9] Edward Watkins, who administered the affairs of the "Fritchley Meeting", was charged with a claim for tithe alleged to be due on some property owned, corporately, by the Friends. No tithes had been collected for fifty years but Watkins was sued for 1 shilling - fourpence more than the two years arrears for which the law allowed claim. The case was tried at the County Court at Alfreton and judgement was given for the recovery of the amount. The bailiffs moved in on Watkins and took a silver lever watch which had cost six or seven pounds many years earlier. This was put up for sale on November 11th 1930 - but no buyers came forward and the sale was adjourned. In 1931 the Governors of Queen Anne's Bounty withdrew the case and since then there has been no further antagonism.

10.15 Quarrying

Although the Warner Quarry had been re-opened at the time of the Alaska gold rush (Section 7.4) it was not worked after World War I during which German prisoners of war - billeted in Victoria House and in the Candle House - were put to labour there under the guard of a British Army Sergeant and his Section. The Hilts Quarry continued in full operation until 1933 by which time the spoil heap in Flower Meadow at the side of the gangway [355540] across from Dimple Hollow had grown to its present size. Quarrying finished there because the working faces were approaching existing houses and a main road (Bowns Hill) and the amount of clay overburden above remaining workable faces made the operation uneconomic. The Cliff Quarry, however, continued to thrive and in 1937-38 produced enough stone to enable over 70,000 tons to be burnt in twelve months at the kilns originally built in the 1840s by George Stephenson down at Ambergate. In the 1950s, however, using the technology of those days and with the need for stone for these kilns to be produced in a comparatively narrow - but largish-size range (8 in. average diameter), the combined operation of quarry and kilns became uneconomic and the quarry closed in 1957. The familiar sound of everyone's favourite engine, "Dowie", and the boom of blasting at the Cliff face were not heard again in the village.

Since then, and to win stone chiefly for roadbuilding, the quarry has been re-opened. Sophisticated low-intensity explosives and mechanical loaders and other new methods of working have been introduced, many fewer men are employed and the village is plagued by the traffic of heavy stone-carrying lorries. By the late 1980s new contracts had been won (it is thought to make concrete for building bunkers for American forces) which involved, in 1986, winning about 3000 tons of stone a day, 150 20-ton lorry journeys and the rapid erosion of Crich Hill to the north of the Stand. This short-sighted, quick, financial-return is not really sensible, though in tune with the spirit of the time. Crich Limestone (Section 7.4) is very pure: in the 21st century there is likely to be a shortage of alkalis and such a local resource would become more valuable: plenty of other stones (at the present day perhaps somewhat more difficult to get) could have been used for roadmaking or concrete.

The Duke's Quarries near Robin Hood continued to get building stone until the middle of the century and there has been talk of re-opening them to remove massive blocks to near Chesterfield to fabricate building components of high cost: so far the difficulties of transport and the unpleasant and obstructive traffic that would be generated have inhibited the project with the Planning Authority.

Two of the larger disused quarries, Church and Hilts are now used as rubbish dumps for industry. The former for heavy-metal residues, the latter for radio-active waste. *(Ed: Church Quarry has now been completely filled, restored to its former ground level and grassed over)*. The Old Quarry which was for two generations a quiet sanctuary and nature reserve - a happy hunting ground for the young; either camping, playing 'cowboys and indians', bird nesting or exploring the cave and the newt pond - or when a little older 'courting' and blackberrying, was being used, and its amenities destroyed, by the Derbyshire County Council which used it as a dump for rubbish from West Derbyshire; creating again an obstructive flow of rubbish-collecting vehicles pounding along the local narrow roads. It has now closed as a household waste tip.

The bed of the Cliff Quarry is now occupied by the National Tramway Museum. *(Ed: The name of the attraction has now become Crich Tramway Village)*. Here, balding, bewhiskered and greying 'adolescents' in overalls and peaked caps indulge their childhood fantasies of engine-driving with the benefit of charitable status and golden entrance fees from tourists - at the cost to village folk of pollution by traffic, parking, noise and incongruous piles of masonry.

10.16 Wars

From William de Wakebridge who fought in a Crusade in the early fourteenth century, to Sergeant Wetton of the 95th Derbyshire Regiment who lost a leg storming the Heights of Alma (Section 5.5): from German Wheatcroft who was killed at Lucknow in India in 1857 to Tommy Wood who fought the Boers in South Africa, there have always been Crich men who served their country on the battlefield.

But it was World Wars I and II that made as big an impact on the village as the introduction of modern amenities in the first half of the 20th century.

In World War I - from a population of about 1500 males of all ages (perhaps 600 between 18 and 40) some 390 men went on active service. Their names are recorded on a Roll of Honour in the Church; 63 of them were killed and very many were wounded. James Henry Dawes, called up to the Royal Garrison Artillery and serving in howitzers on the Western Front, was gassed and wounded in the legs by shrapnel: he was invalided out of the army at the age of 38.

In World War II the carnage was lighter but, even so, from about the same population some 22 men and one woman were killed on active service. Peter Dawes, eventually the Parish Clerk, was called up at age 18, was trained in Canada and served as a Warrant Officer Navigator in the Coastal Command of the Royal Air Force.

One day in the year, the first Sunday of July, is of particular significance in Crich. It is then that a service is still held each year in memory of the men of the Sherwood Foresters who fell in two world wars. The service is held at the Memorial on the peak of Crich Hill, known as the Stand - the site of two previous observation towers. The ceremony is attended not only by units of the present-day British Army but also by many British Legion Branches and by private citizens from quite a distance around. At the top of the memorial there is a rotating lamp which, at night, sweeps a beam over the countryside. It was intended to throw light on the homes - both in Derbyshire and Nottinghamshire - of the fallen of World War I. Before World War II, it was said, the beam could be seen clearly as far away as Hucknall in Nottinghamshire. The present installation, in a different world, is a feeble substitute and the light is soon lost in a background haze of local improved street lighting.

10.17 Epilogue

The two World Wars affected everybody alive at the time and for some the scars never healed. But the changes the wars hurried along were perhaps more fundamental. Crich may have been slow in following the provision of amenity and what are thought of as more civilised conditions but by the 1930s the real necessities - clean water, adequate sewerage systems, reliable means of lighting and heating homes - were available in the village. As with other places, labour-saving devices like vacuum cleaners, washing machines, telephones and refrigerators came in quantity after World War II - as did the affordable private car. With the advent of television in the 1950s and 1960s the possibility of readily available, home-centred, national-quality entertainment came within most people's reach.

It may have taken over 200 years for wheeled transport to be as common on the routes in Crich as it had been elsewhere, 100 years for gas lighting and heating to arrive, 40 years for electric light, 20 years for radio to be common after its first demonstration and 10 for the original television, but the arrival of colour television was as rapid in the village as elsewhere, as was the instantaneous appearance of video recorders all over the country.

The world is, indeed, now a village and the history of our village in many ways is, in miniature, the story of how the world has changed.

[1] Dawes J. G. (1983) *The Crich Tales*. Cromford. Scarthin.
[2] Kelly's Directory of Derbyshire (1895)
[3] Watkins A. (1952) *The Manor of Crich*. Manuscript. p.47
[4] Ministry of Agriculture, Fisheries and Food (1987). *Agricultural Returns:Sheet 117: Form 601/SS*
[5] East Midlands Gas Board (1983). *Private Communication. 28.4.83*
[6] Ilkeston and Heanor Water Board (1905 [?]). *The Works of the Ilkeston and Heanor Board*.
[7] Severn-Trent Water Authority (1987). *Private Communication*.
[8] Watkins. Ibid. pps.42, 53.
[9] Lowndes W. (1980). *The Quakers of Fritchley 1863-1980*. Fritchley. Friends Meeting House. p.250

11. IN CONCLUSION

Crich was once quite important. On high ground where ancient routes crossed, with a good water supply, plenty of wood, reasonable soil and wealth to be won from the local lead deposits, it is not surprising that it was attractive to the Norman conquerors. Even after the Barony was no more, local men like Roger Beler and William de Wakebridge played a large part in the county and in national affairs.

John Talbot, Earl of Shrewsbury, was Lord of the Manor of Crich at an important period of British history and his relative and aide, Sir George Vernon, one of the Conunissioners for the Muster in Derbyshire, used the village as a base in 1558 when he was in communication with the Lord Lieutenant of the North, the Earl of Westmorland.

In the 18th century Crich farmers and lead miners adopted new techniques and as transport improved, new markets brought prosperity to the village. For the less prosperous its virtue was that it was one of the first places in the country to afford a Workhouse and amongst the first in the county to establish a Friendly Society. Its lime was in great demand for agriculture, building and improving hygiene. Once framework knitting was no longer in its heyday the village became a centre of the trade: but it was the beginning of the end.

Arkwright, a few miles away, accelerated the Industrial Revolution but water power on an adequate scale was not available in Crich village: it was expensive to move coal 'up the hill' and industry went to low-lying, level sites, especially after the river valleys were turnpiked. Then when railways were built and factory production with easily accessible power and transport became the norm Crich began to lose its position as a place of substance.

True: the population grew in line with the national expansion until the end of the 19th century but then, with increased educational opportunities, the disturbance of World War I which revealed other worlds to local men, with the onset of mass production in large centres of population and the lack of local employment, young men went and raised families elsewhere. The number of people living in the parish declined.

Even many sporting and other social activities withered as the older children bussed out to school to form associations no longer based on their 'home' village.

Crich has become a dormitory - with a national tourist attraction. But it is a pleasant dormitory set in a fine position in a lovely countryside.

It is increasingly acknowledged that small is beautiful and with the internal combustion engine, electrical power, the micro-chip and the fibre-optic cable it is becoming realised that it is really no longer necessary to behave like ants in concrete canyons in order to earn a living.

It could be that within the 21st century more and more Crich people will be able to earn their keep once again without the burden of daily commuting with its expensive and unhealthy hassle.

It is a pleasant prospect that with luck and forethought increasing numbers of Crich villagers could revert to a more traditional way of life associated with a community in which it is possible to know most of the members and to put the more unpleasant features of the last 150 years behind them.

APPENDIX

The Canons Wood in Crich

The Latin text describing the wood in Crich granted to the Canons of Darley Abbey by Hubert FitzRalph on 22nd September 1175 is:

> "Pretera concessit Hubertus eisdem canonicis in manerio de Cruch
> partem memoris per metas subscriptas, scilicet per semitam illam
> Fridene sti ex transuero usque ad Fridesseford per aquam Derewent
> usque ad Cruchebroc, et per Cruchebroc usque ad cilitium montis per
> metas illas que facte sunt inter Sideweie et cilitium montis usque
> ad Fridenesti que uadit ad Turlokebode a parte boreali".

A translation of this is to the effect that Hubert granted to the canons the worth of the wood limited in the direction of the Manor of Crich (at that time near the Church -see Section 2.7) by the path crossing over the Fridensti all the way to Fridessford - by the waters of the Derwent - all the way to the Cruchebroc (Crich Brook -see Section 9.5) and from Cruchebroc on the skyline to the limit from there to the Sideweie (sunken way) and then by line of sight to a place on the Friden path where Thurlowbooth lies to the north.

It seems, then, that the Canon's Wood was bounded on one side by the route of the old "Fridensti". Friden could be from Friday, the day of Odin's wife Frigga. "Sti" is a Scandinavian word-ending indicating a path. This could have been the path followed by the canons on their way to Wigwell Grange (Section 4.5). On the 1849 Tithe map Field Nos.1313 and 1315 are denoted as "Hasland Fridings" and "The Fridings" respectively and help establish that the Fridensti, in its upper reaches, crossed what are now called "Chase Fields" [345537] between Bulling Lane and Chase Cliffe [342537].

Although it is likely that at a later date the monks on their way to Wigwell crossed the river at Whatstandwell where the bridge is now built, the fact that just below Thurlowbooth there is a field called Abbotswell Close [Field No.1484 on the 1849 Tithe Map] supports the notion that the original crossing of the river, i.e. the Fridessford, was there at a position roughly S.W. of Thurlowbooth. Also, Immanuel Halton's map of 1683 shows a ford there (Section 4.5).

The "Sideweie" - the sunken way on the skyline - is probably "Chadwick Nick" [348532] which was enlarged to take the improved "Fritchley Road" and was named after William Chadwick in about 1734 (Section 4.5).

TABLE B
MEDIEVAL CLUES TO THE LOCATION OF HUBERT FITZRALPH'S MANOR AND THE CANON'S COURT
(from The Cartulary of Darley Abbey)

Page in Cartulary	Grant to Canons by:	Details of Grant of Land	Items Thought to be identifiable (see Table C)
543	Hubert Fitzralph	"One acre under the hill of Crich and 6 acres by the road which leads to Wessington between Farmanescroft and the ditch towards Moorwood - to be enclosed for use."	The road to Wessington 6 acres by the road
545	Hubert Fitzralph	"One perch and a half of his demesne in Crich, extending from the Mount of St. Thomas to the Canons land, in front of their grange - in exchange for one and a half perches in the Canons Furlong extending from St. Thomas Mount to Merewelsiche."	Mount of St. Thomas Canons land in front of their grange Canons Furlong Merewelsiche
546	Hubert Fitzralph	"The place above which the Canon's oven is situated next to his orchard in Crich and an extension of 7 ft. in length and breadth stretching from the cemetery to the house which Tyrri held of the Canons."	Canons Oven Fitralph's Orchard Cemetery
551	Hugh Gurney	"5 acres of meadow in Crich below Le Hey, ie 4 acres between the Canons Meadow and the village pasture called Sauvegefelth and one acre between the Canons Meadow and the common pasture of Crich".	LeHey Canons Meadow Village Pasture Common pasture of Crich
554	Ralph de Frechecheville	"A plot of land pertaining to his demesne lying below the Canons Court for an enlargement thereof - in exchange for a headland in Wigesbutte above Ralph's furlong, which abuts his garden".	Headland in Wigesbuttes Ralph's furlong

TABLE C
PLACES NEAR FITZRALPH'S MANOR AND THE CANON'S COURT

Items Mentioned in the Items Abbey Cartulary	Identified on the 1839 Crich Rating Survey and shown on Figure 6
The road to Wessington	Path from the Churchyard to Hogg Nick and on to Wessington
6 acres by the road	Top, Far and Near Parson's Closes
Mount of St. Thomas	St. Mary's Church (on the peak) and the adjacent area
Canon's land in front of their grange	Possibly Fishpond Close and the eastern ends of Far and Near Parson's Closes
Canon's Furlong	Bottom Piece and the adjacent Hall croft
Merewelsiche	Area embracing Wig Meadow Pingle, Hays Land and Undertown Field
Canon's Oven	Kilncroft next to the smaller Hallcroft (i.e. Fitzralph's Orchard)
Fitzralph's Orchard	Hallcroft (the small unit near the Churchyard)
Cemetry	Churchyard of St. Mary's
Le Hey	Hay's Lane
Canon's Meadow	Possibly Fishpond Close and eastern ends of Far and Near Parson's Closes
Village Pasture	Undertown Field [Ref: grant (Cart 551) to canons of 4 acres (of "Hays Land")]
Common pasture of Crich	Wig Meadow Town Field [Ref: grant (Cart 551) to canons of 1 acre (of "Ten-Acres")]
Headland in Wigesbuttes	Wig Meadow Pingle
Ralph's Furlong	3 acres and part of Hays Land

TABLE D
SOME PRINCIPAL LANDOWNERS IN CRICH

Proximity of sites of their main allocations in the 1786 Enclosure Award

Proprietor	Location (see Figure 7)
Samuel Allen	Upper-Nether Common, Coddington Bank, Ludway Carr
Joseph Bowmer	Rue Cliff, Nether Common
John Bowmer	Nether Common, Wild Common
Hon. Nat. Curzon	Nether Common, Upper Common, Plaistow Green
Pheby Dodd	Nether Common, Nether Cliff
Duke of Devonshire	Wild Common, Leashaw, Coddington, Coddington Bank
Francis Hurt	Cliff, Thurlow Booth
G. & J. Marshall	Plaistow Green, Edge Moor
Rev. John Mason	Thurlow Booth, Coddington Bank
Peter Nightingale	Cliff, Wakebridge, Plaistow Green, Slacks
William Smith	Nether Common, Riddings
Earl of Thanet	Cliff
Richard Towndrow	Upper Common, Nether Common, Cliff, Plaistow Green
John Topham	Rue Cliff, Nether Common
Samuel Travis	Roughs, Hagg
James Turton	Plaistow Green, Dimple, Coast Hill
Sir Robert Meade-Wilmot	Plaistow Green, Edge Moor, Slacks
David Woodhouse	Cliff, Dimple, Nether Common, Upper Common
Thomas Woodhouse	Dimple, Fridings, Thurlow Booth, Upper Common, Coddington Bank
Nathaniel Wright	Plaistow Green, Coddington Bank

TABLE E
SOME PRINCIPLE LANDOWNERS IN CRICH

Proximity of sites of their main holdings on the 1847 Tithe Apportionment Survey

Proprietor	Location (see Figure 7)
John Bowmer	Roughs, Dimple, Millgreen, Mill Lane, Barn Close
Thomas Bowmer	Roughs
Butterley Co. Ltd.	Warner, Warmwell, Hilts, Lees
Duke of Devonshire	Coddington
Joseph Fritchley	Rue Cliff, Dam, Stones, Fishpond
Rev. John Hughes	Thorpe Hill, Culland, Parkhead
Francis Hurt	Crich Chase, Bilberry Wood
Richard Hurt	Crich Chase, Hagg
Robert Lee	Dimple
Mary Marshall	Plaistow
Wm. Nightingale	Leashaw, Shuckstone, Wakebridge, Glebe, Slacks
William Porter	Edge Moor, Lane Ends
Lord Scarsdale	Benthill, Lees, Nether Common, Plaistow Green
Ralph Smith	Nether Common
Wm. Shipstone	Fishpond, Kings Meadow
W. G. & J. Strutt	Cross, Coast Hill, Stones, Kings Meadow, Calvercroft

TABLE F
SOME LANDHOLDINGS IN THE PARISH OF CRICH IN THE 13TH CENTURY

(Index No. from Cartulary of Darley Abbey)

Date	Index No.	Owner or Occupier	Type	Size	Annual Rent	Description Given
Before 1220	544	Robert Culbil	Assarts Croft			The assarts called 'Le Housti' and 'Le Wro' - above Warmwell Le Caluecroft which lies over against the assart of Hacon beyond the waterfall
	548	Richard Culbil	1¼ Bovates Assarts Croft	-) -) -)	4s 0d	Le Hocsti and Le Wra Le Calvecraft over against Hacon's assart
Before 1220	547	Swain: son of Orm*		14½ acres	4s 6d	Between Thurlokebothe and Schardweie (The sunken way)
Before 1220	546	Canons of Darley	½ Bovate			Above canon's oven and stretching to cemetry near Hubert Fitzralph's orchard
Before 1220	543	Canons of Darley	Meadow	6 acres		By the road to Wessington between Farmanescroft and the ditch towards Moorwood
1250	550	Swain: son of Spegt	Field	17 acres		In Le Egge, near the road to Wessington

1253	470/565	Robert: son of Geoffrey of Plaistow	2 Bovates		8s 0d	One called 'Le Cost' and the other called 'Bastel'
	564	Robert: son of Sigerith	1 Bovate	12 acres		Lying between the mill of Crich and the village
1254	551	Hugh Gurney	Meadow	5 acres		Below Le Hey 4 acres between canon's meadow and village pasture called Sauvegeferth. 1 acre between canons meadow and common pasture
1248-1261	566	William Bylbot	Land with Meadow	4 ½ acres		In Le Lewes lying between land which John Culbil held and that of Ralph de Wakebridge towards Le Dumpel
1261-1275	567	Ralf son of Henry Hert of Crich	Toft and Croft	3 acres	4s 0d	2 acres in Le Stones ½ acre in Meduewell ½ acre in Le Scotteshachs

* Swain paid an initial fee of 10s 0d to get this land

TABLE G
COMPARISON OF NAMES OF MEDIEVAL HOLDINGS AND FIELD NAMES IN THE MID 19TH CENTURY

Names in Darley Abbey Cartulary (13th Century)	Crich Tithe Apportionment 1847 Field Name	Crich Tithe Apportionment 1847 Code No.	Approximate Map Reference (Figs. 2,3 & 7)
Waumwelle Warinwalle	Big Warmwell Little Warmwell Warmwell Close	1012 1042 1082	355544
Le Caluecroft Le Calvecroft	Calvercroft	1007	356546
Thurlokebothe	Thurlow Booth	1496	341536
Schardweie (Way thro' the gap)*	Chadwick Nick (possibly)	1277/1525	348532
Le Egge	Edge Moor	648 - 657	353556
Le Cost	Coast Hill Pingle Lower Coast Hill Upper Coast Hill	793 858 1327	348544
Le Hey	Hays Land	701;706	351549
Le Lewes	The Lees Lees Pingle Big Lees	992;993;995 990;994 1009	356544
Le Dumpel	Dimple Close Dimple House Dimple Croft Dimple	1047 1055 1056 1060	353540
Le Stones	Stones Little Stones Upper Stones Stones Closes	1345-48;1396; 1398 1361 1362 1349;1363-64;1395	345546
Meduewell	Well Meadow Upper Meadow	844;849 1333	346546
Le Scotteshachs	Scott Ashes	1340-1342	344547

* See Cameron, K. (1959) The Place Names of Derbyshire. Cambridge. Cambridge University Press.

TABLE H
WEEKLY MONEY INCOME
(d : old pence)

LABOURERS

Year	Amount (d.)	Source	Job
1290	6	Cp 109	Unskilled:country
1350	12-18	Fn 9	Day lab:farm
1420	18	Cp 121	Coventry scale
1530	18	Tn 102	Woman
1634	48	Cx3 239	Derbys Reaper/Thresher
1648	60	Cx3 239	——ditto——
1688	69	Tn 277	Labourer
1735	84	Ms 219	Lab:Oxon
1750	132-144	Ms 219	Lab:London
1762	108	Ms 219	Lab:Lancs
1785	120	Ms 219	Lab:Lancs
1785	96	Ms 219	Lab:Oxon
1794	102	Fy 185	Lab:Derbys
1814	144-180	PR 258	Farm Lab.
1822	108-120	PR 258	Farm Lab.
1830	180	Tn 471	Farm Lab.
1842	96-120	Ms 219	Farm Lab.
1842	216	Ms 219	Indust. Lab.

AVERAGE WAGES

Agriculture			General Industry		
Year	Amount (d.)	Source	Year	Amount (d.)	Source
1850	114	PR 264	1924	1000	PR 274
1860	132	PR 264	1936	1200	PR 274
1870	144	PR 264	1946	1440	PR 318
1924	336	PR 274	1970	6240	PR 318
1936	388	PR 274			

ARISTANS

Year	Amount (d.)	Source	Job
1290	18-24	Cp 109	Carpenter-Mason
1350	12-18	Fn 9	Carpenter
1420	24-30	Cp 121	Coventry:skilled
1634	72	Cx3 239	Derbys Carpenter/Bricklayer
1648	96	Cx3 239	——ditto——
1688	175	Tn 277	Artisan
1842	300-480	Ms 219	London:skilled
1842	240-300	Ms 219	Cotton:skilled
1857	288	Km 11	Carpenter:Lead mine

Symbols on Figure 5

▽ Labourers
△ Artisans Average
● Agriculture Average
■ Industrial
† Crich Vicar
☐ Lead Miner

Silk Workers (0 on Fig 10) are included as Artisans on Fig 5

STIPEND OF VICAR OF CRICH

Year	Amount (d.)	Source
1291	31	Cxl 35
1550	30	Cxl 50
1650	46	Cxl 50
1846	451	Bg 1846
1857	784	We 1857
1895	1125	Ky 1895
1941	1853	Ky 1941

Stipend of Rev. Lee of Calverton		
1570	18	Fn30

Sources of Data

Bg – Bagshaw
Cp – Clapham
Cx – Cox
Fy – Farey
Fn – Felkin
Km – Kirkham
Ky – Kelly
Ms – Mathias
PR – Parker-Reid
Tn – Trevelyan
We – White

TABLE J
WEEKLY MONEY INCOME : d (Old Pence)

FRAMEWORK KNITTERS

Year	Amount (d.) per week	Page Ref*	Job
1710	180	72	London hosier
1710	120	72	Country hosier
1750	360-720	83	Silk gloves
1770	360-432	102	Silk hose; Derby Frame
1776	120-144	117	Plain cotton:worsted
1776	120-168	117	Silk
1776	up to 192	117	Long hose, C&W eyelet work
1776	up to 204	117	Long hose, silk eyelet work
1810	84	231	Stockiner
1819	48-84	441	Framework knitter
1835	216	515	Hosier: silk
1840	96	515	Hosier: cotton
1844	72	516	Hosier: cotton
1844	63	119	Hosier: 20/22 gauge
1845	48-72	(B)	Country hosiers
1847	60	457	Hosier: 30 gauge & below
1847	93	457	Glover
1860	156	516	Hosier: silk
1865	126	516	Hosier: cotton
1880	216	(B)	Highest Class Framework Knitter

*References from Felkin (Fn)
(B) Bythell (Bl) p 93

Symbols on Figure 10

X   Framework Knitters: Cotton
O   Framework Knitters: Silk
△   Handloom Weavers
▽   Spinners: Doublers
■   Lead Miner

SPECIAL CLASSES

Year	Amount (d.) per week	Source	Job
1710	30	De 464	Lead Miner
1805	276	Ms 206	Handloom Weaver
1818	99	Ms 206	Handloom Weaver
1831	72	Ms 206	Handloom Weaver
1831	204	Fn 170	Spinner
1831	144	Fn 170	Doubler
1870	180	Km 11	Lead Miner

References   (Table I)

De   Defoe
Fn   Felkin
Km   Kirkham
Ms   Mathias

TABLE K
SOME FIELD-NAME GROUPS IN THE 1847-9 CRICH TITHE ASSESSMENT

Group	Name of Field	Code on Tithe Map	Approx. Map Reference	Zone in Parish (see Fig 7)
Furlongs	Nether Furlongs	1307	343539	Furlongs, Fridings and towards Stones
	Furlongs	1314	343539	"
	Furlongs	1316	344538	"
	Far Furlongs	1317	343540	"
	Furlongs Pingle	1319	347540	"
	Little Furlongs	1320	345541	"
	Furlongs Pingle	1321	346540	"
	Furlongs	1323	346541	"
	Furlongs	1324	346542	"
	Near Furlongs	1325	347542	"
	Furlongs	1330	346544	"
Lime Works etc.	Limefield	191	351566	Plaistow
	Limekiln Close	240	344574	Shuckstone
	Kilncroft	497	338549	Coddington
	Great Lime Flats	642	345555	Edge Moor
	Little Lime Flats	643	356554	Edge Moor
	Kilncrofts	741	350546	Cross
	(Road to) Limekiln	763	351545	Cross
	Kilncroft	796	349544	Cross / Coast Hill
	Oven Pingle	1000	354544	Hilts / Lees
	Upper Limekiln Close	1344	343546	Stones / Scott Ashes
	Nether Limekiln Close	1369	343546	Stones / Coddington
	Limeworks	1604	352520	Smiths Rough
	Limekiln Close	1638	355526	Hagg
	Limekilns	1648	352520	Smiths Rough
	Limekiln	1688	359523	Bullbridge
	Limekiln Close	1708	360524	Bullbridge
Windmills	Windmill Meadow	305	337563	Wakebridge
	Windmill Hill	306	337563	Wakebridge
	Windmill Close	587	352563	Plaistow
	Windmill Close	1332	344544	Stones
	Windmill Close	1399	341542	Coddington Bank

A History Of Crich

Fig 1

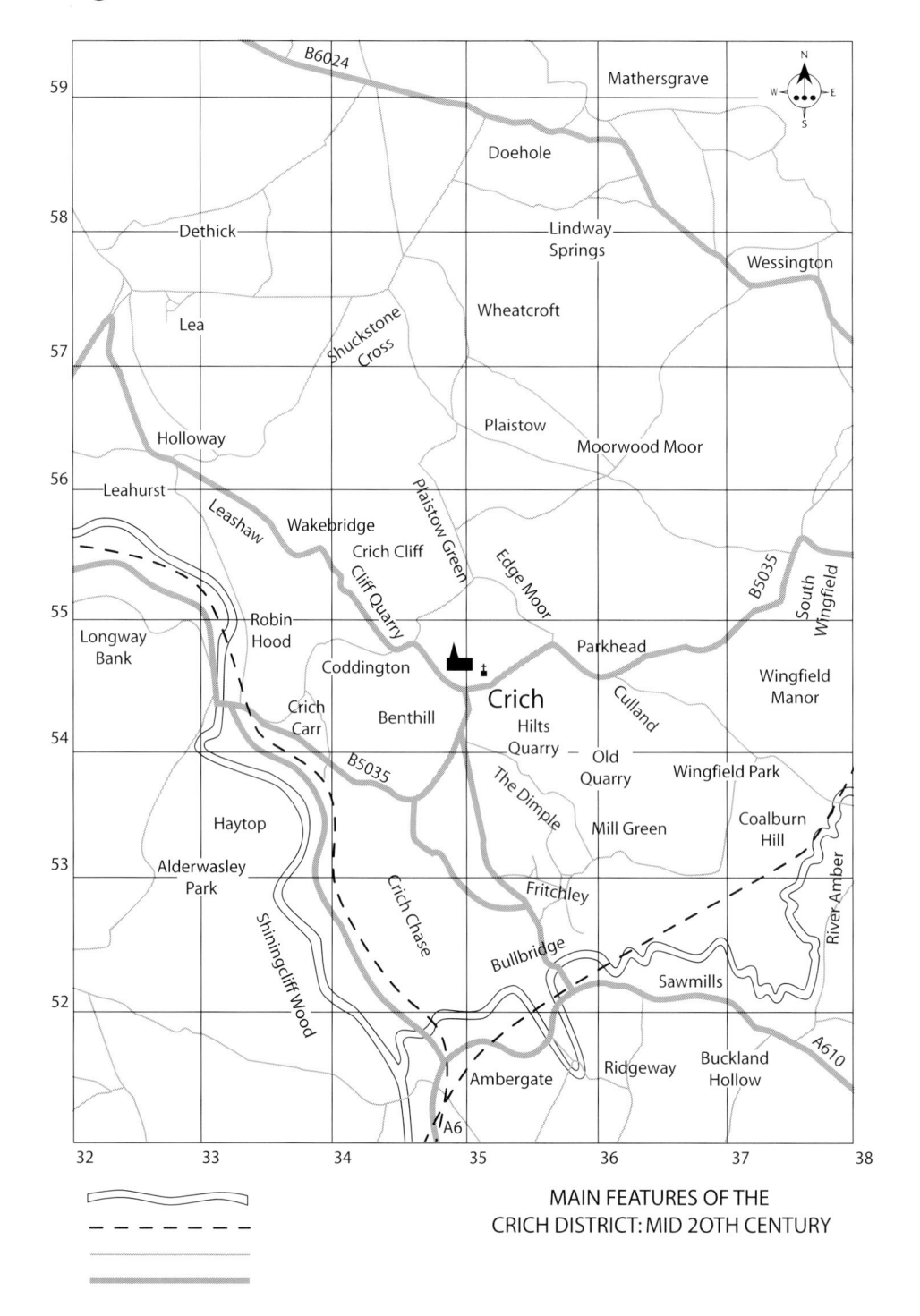

MAIN FEATURES OF THE
CRICH DISTRICT: MID 20TH CENTURY

Figures

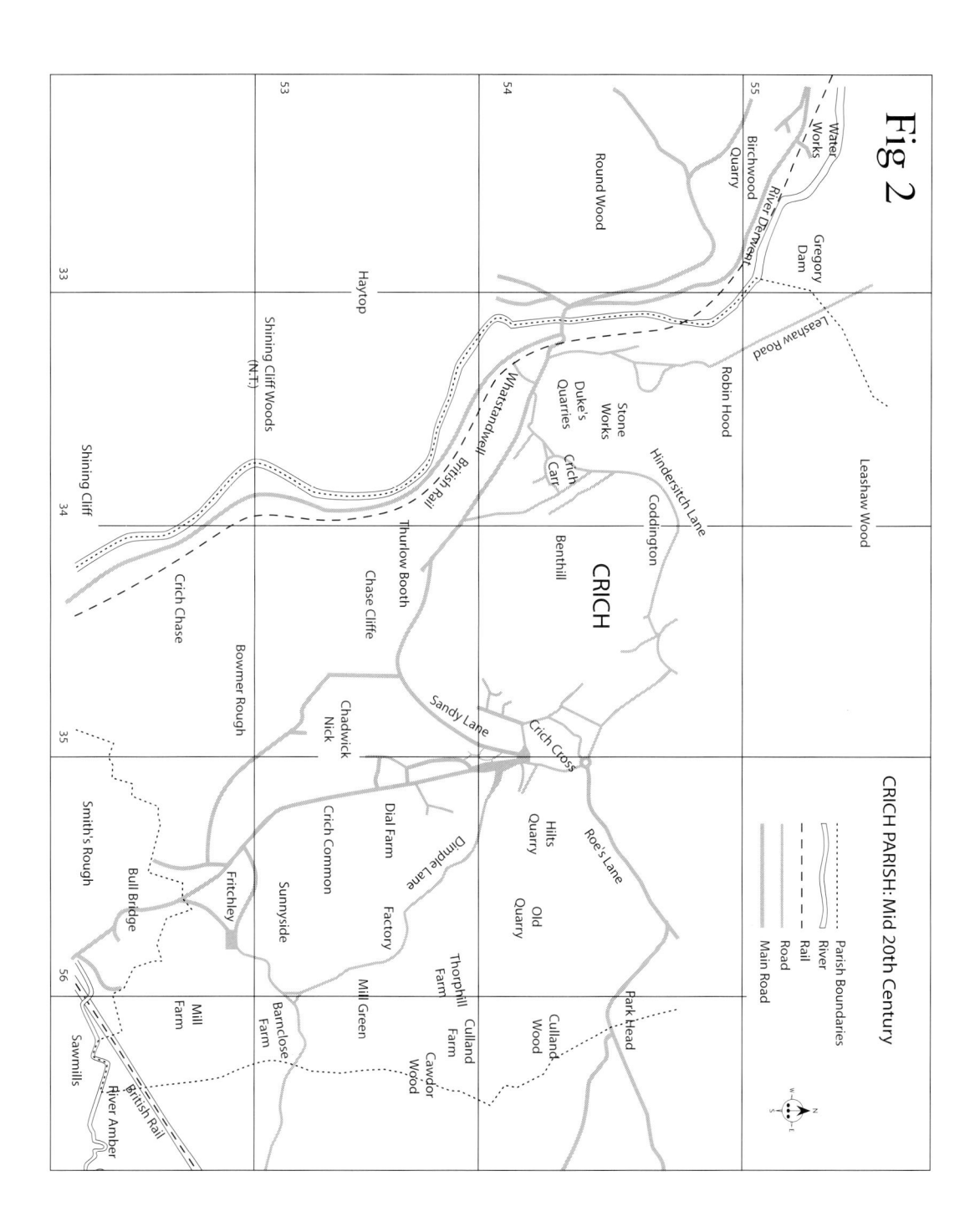

Fig 2

CRICH PARISH: Mid 20th Century

Legend:
- .... Parish Boundaries
- River
- – – – Rail
- Road
- Main Road

Labels on map:
- Water Works
- Birchwood Quarry
- River Derwent
- Gregory Dam
- Round Wood
- Leashaw Road
- Robin Hood
- Stone Works
- Duke's Quarries
- Haytop
- Whatstandwell
- British Rail
- Crich Carr
- Hindersitch Lane
- Leashaw Wood
- Shining Cliff Woods (N.T.)
- Coddington
- Benthill
- CRICH
- Shining Cliff
- Crich Chase
- Thurlow Booth
- Chase Cliffe
- Sandy Lane
- Crich Cross
- Bowmer Rough
- Chadwick Nick
- Dial Farm
- Hilts Quarry
- Roe's Lane
- Smith's Rough
- Bull Bridge
- Fritchley
- Sunnyside
- Crich Common
- Dimple Lane
- Factory
- Old Quarry
- Thorphill Farm
- Culland Wood
- Park Head
- Mill Farm
- Barnclose Farm
- Mill Green
- Cawdor Wood
- Culland Farm
- Sawmills
- River Amber
- British Rail

Grid references: 53, 54, 55, 33, 34, 35, 56

— 175 —

Fig 3

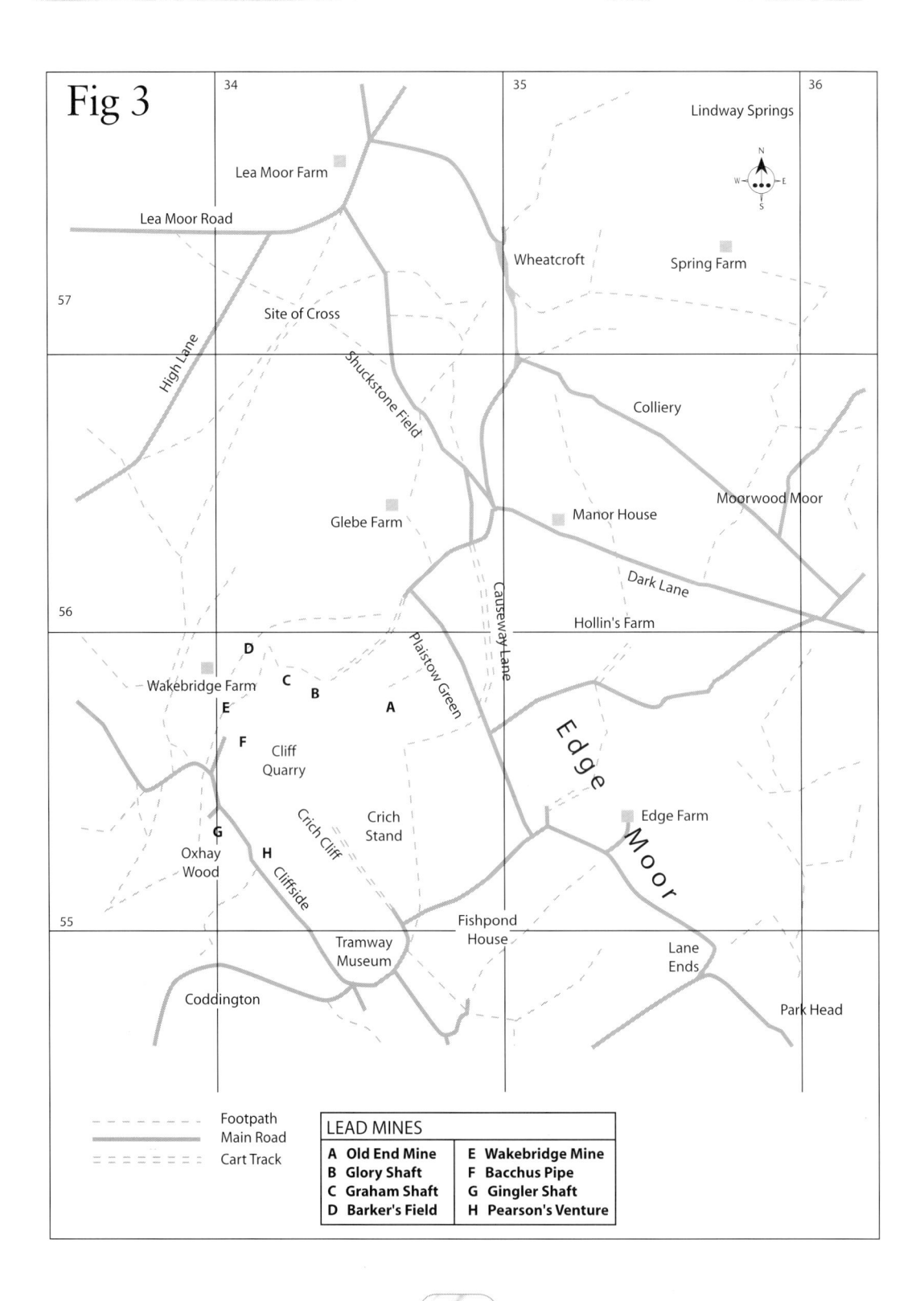

LEAD MINES
- A Old End Mine
- B Glory Shaft
- C Graham Shaft
- D Barker's Field
- E Wakebridge Mine
- F Bacchus Pipe
- G Gingler Shaft
- H Pearson's Venture

Footpath
Main Road
Cart Track

Fig 4

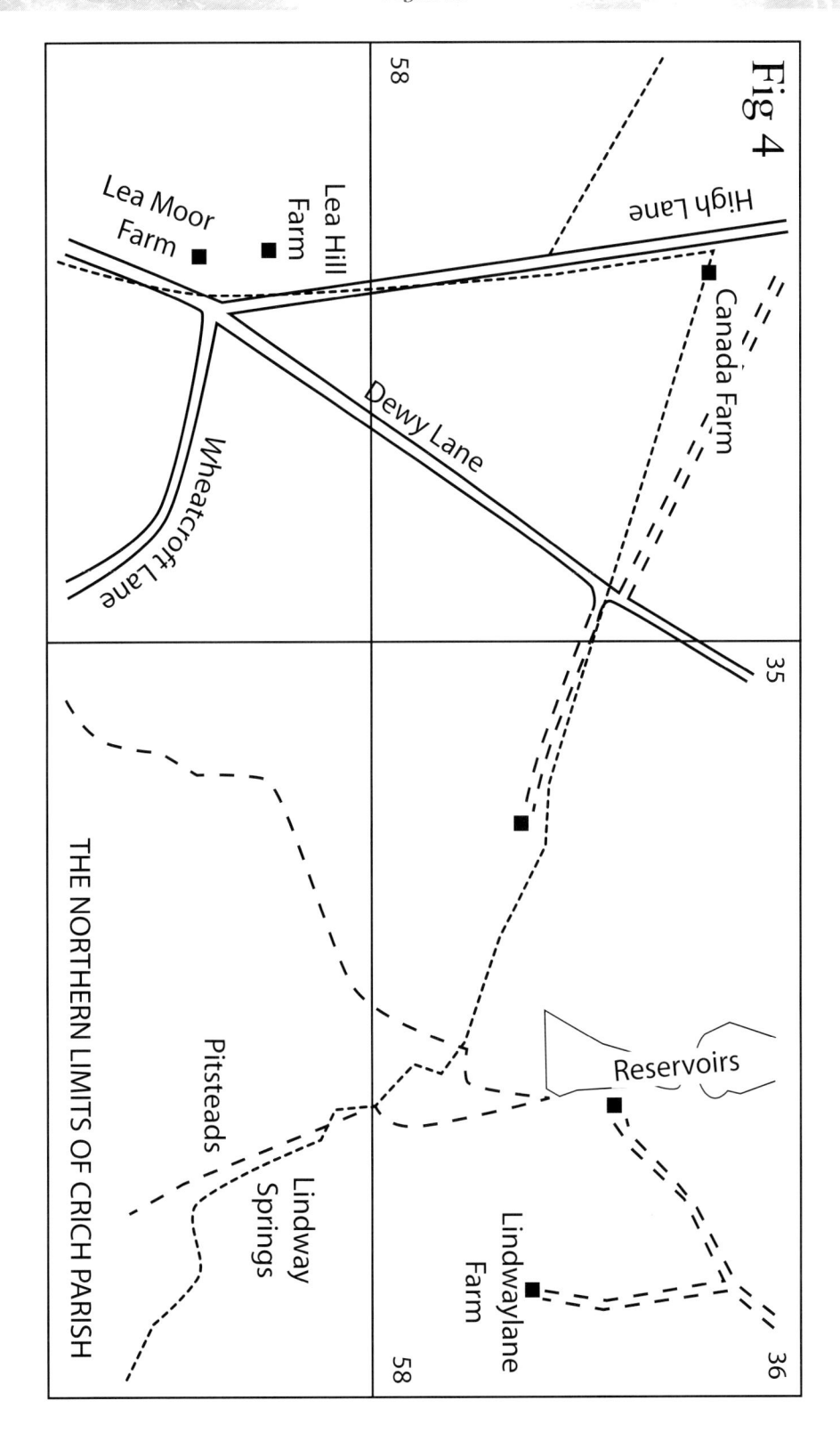

THE NORTHERN LIMITS OF CRICH PARISH

Fig 5

PRICE OF WHEAT
Lh. Scale
Shillings per Winchester Quart
Data from Beckman. 23

WAGES: Rh Scale
pence: d per week
— — Frame work Knitters (Fig 10)
† Stripend of Crich Vicar
▽ Labourers
△ Artisans □ Lead Miner
Average Wages
● Farm Workers
■ Industry

A - Domesday 1086
B - Black Death 1348
C - Dissolution of Monestries 1539
D - Civil War 1649
E - Arkwright Mill 1771
F - Waterloo 1815
G - Liverpool to Manchester Railway 1830
H - Great Exhibition 1851
I - Internal Combustion Engine 1876
J - Wright Flight 1903
K - World War I 1914
L - World War II 1939

WAGES AND THE PRICE OF WHEAT

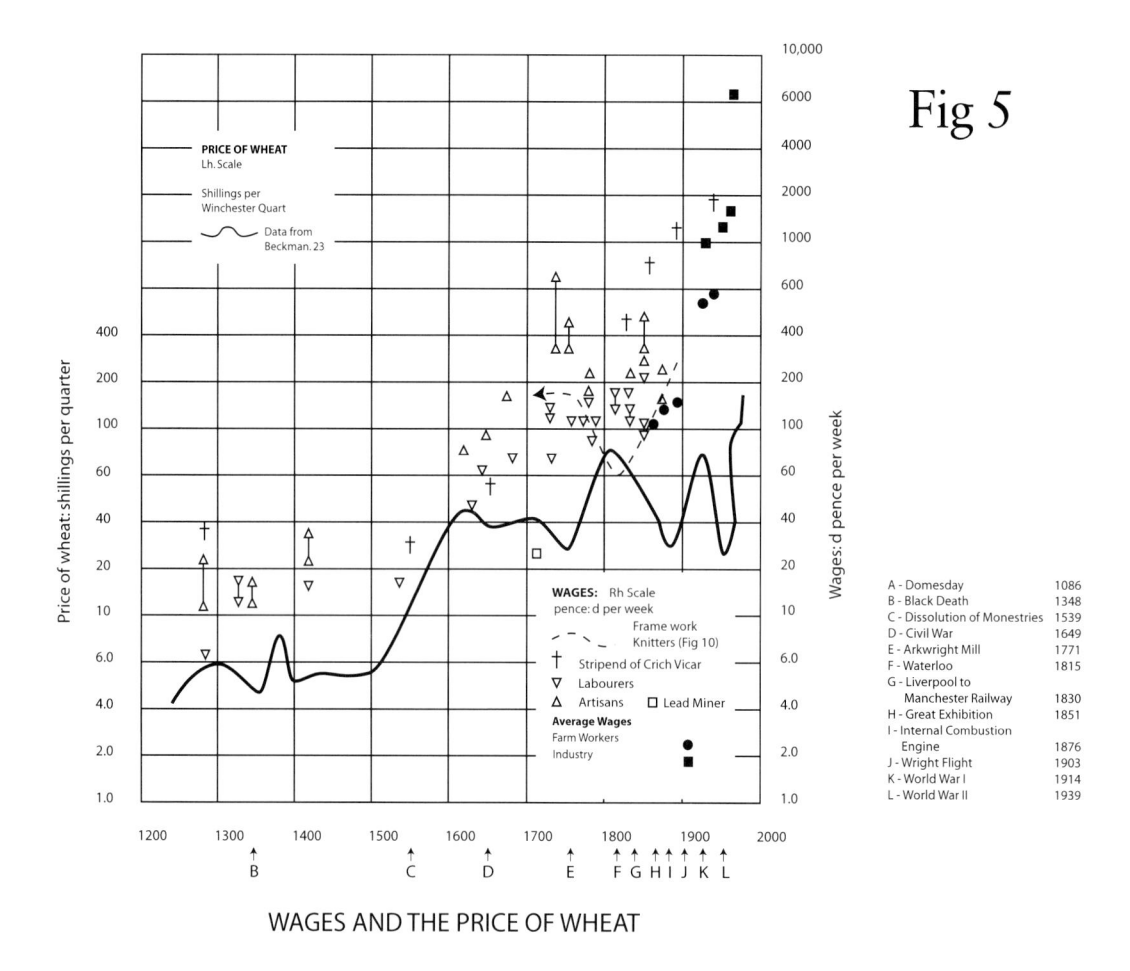

NOTE

The data given in Fig 5 for "wages" before about 1600 are, of course, rather tenuous and can only give an order of magnitude to the money wages available. Before 1700 or so, many people would not be completely dependent on such wages for the whole of their income. Produce from their crofts or the open field would help to sustain them (The Vicar would have his Tithe). Nevertheless the weekly wage is often derived from the day wage earned for six days each week. It may not therefore be too far from the "real" income.

After about 1780 workers like framework knitters - working long hours - would be entirely dependent on their money wage. If the "income" curve before 1600 could be drawn it might, indeed, be higher than indicated by the data on money wages i.e. further away from the "Price of Wheat" curve. The distance between that curve and the wage observations can be taken as an expression of the standard of living.

If after 1800 it is supposed that income is indicated by money wages - the increase in the standard of living since then is readily detectable.

On the same grounds, for humble work folk, the standard of living before 1770 was higher than it was from 1800 to 1840.

Figures

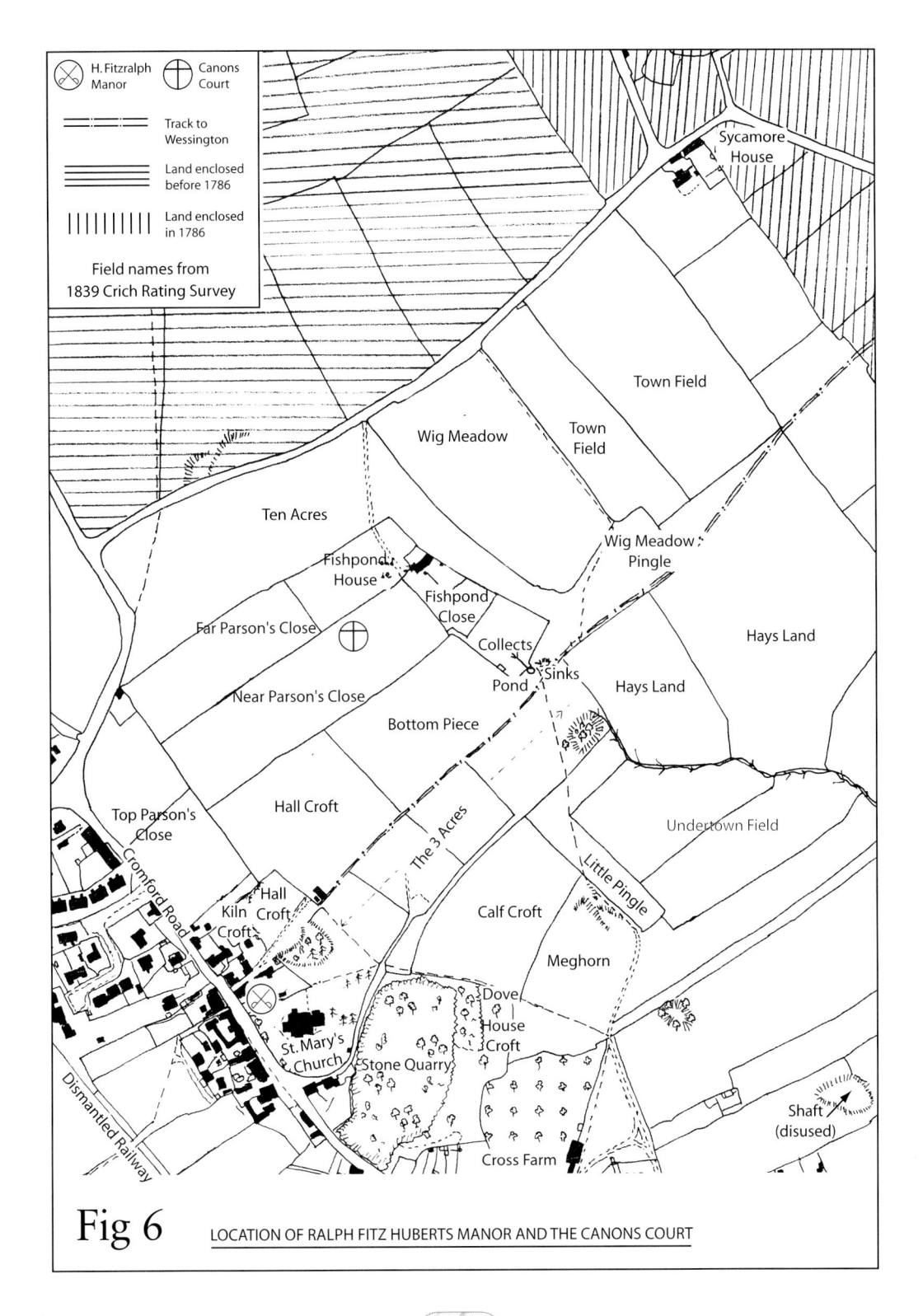

Fig 6 LOCATION OF RALPH FITZ HUBERTS MANOR AND THE CANONS COURT

Fig 7

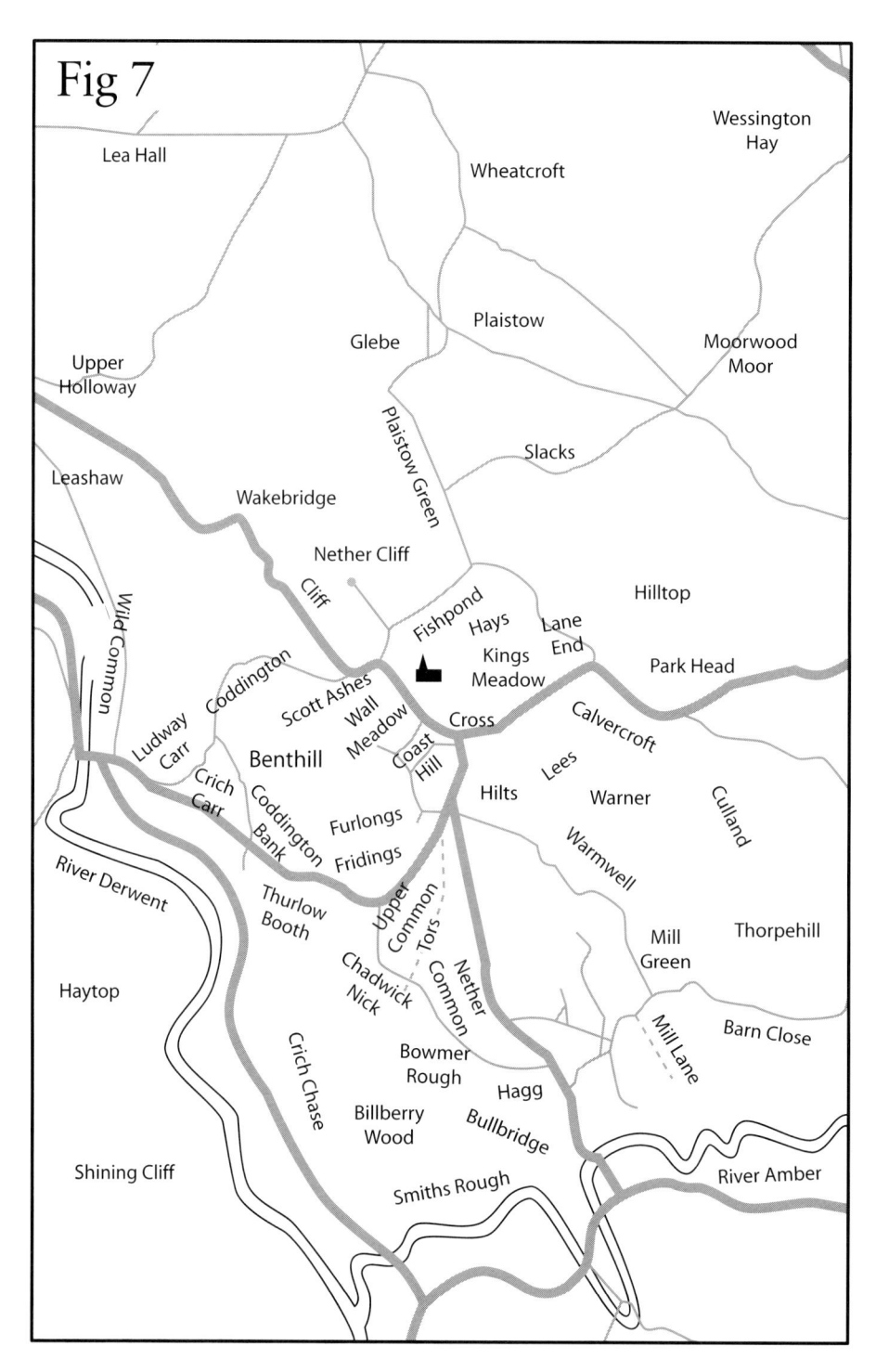

KEYS TO TABLES D & E : PRINCIPAL LANDOWNERS

Figures

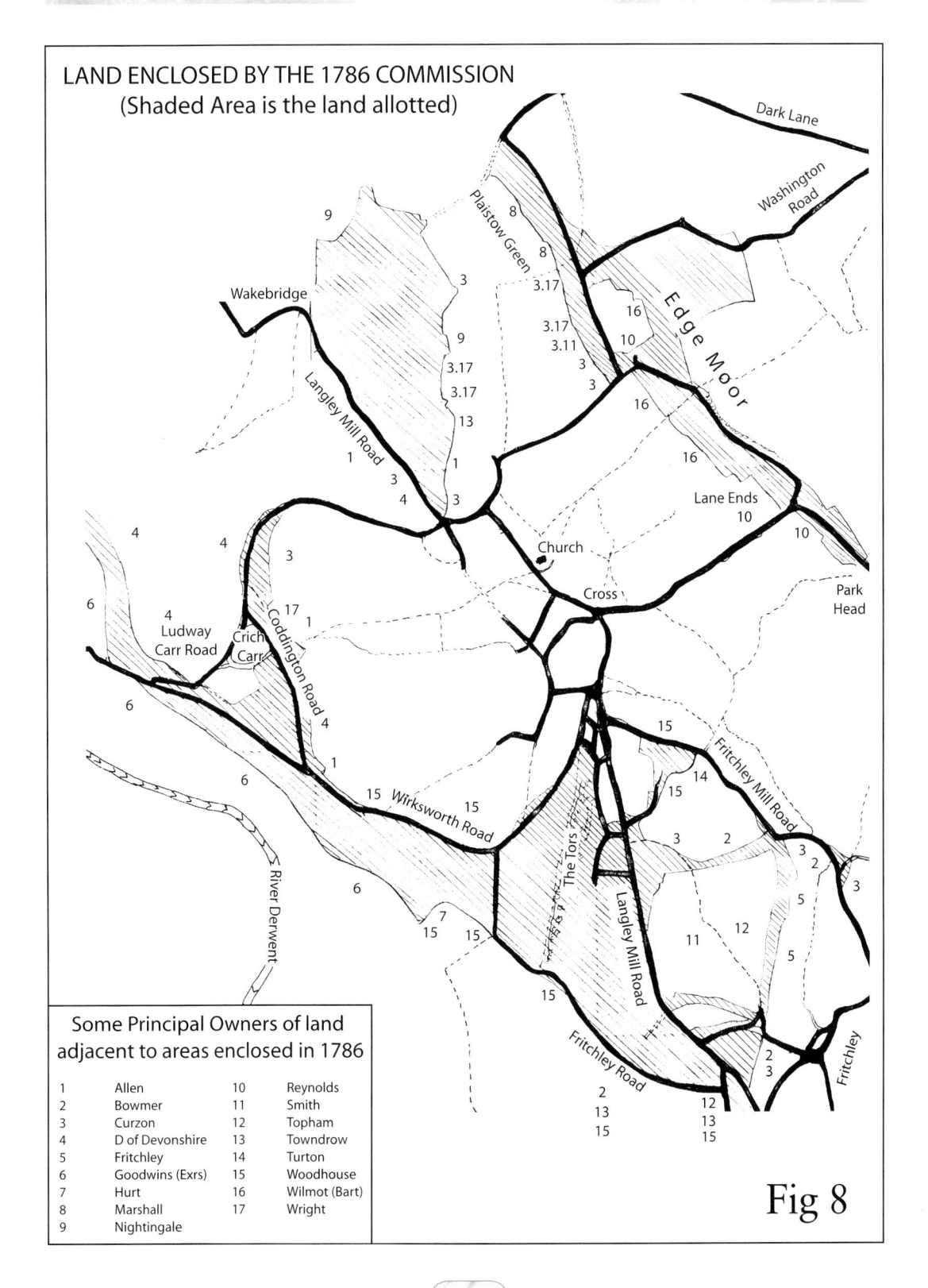

LAND ENCLOSED BY THE 1786 COMMISSION
(Shaded Area is the land allotted)

Some Principal Owners of land adjacent to areas enclosed in 1786

1	Allen	10	Reynolds
2	Bowmer	11	Smith
3	Curzon	12	Topham
4	D of Devonshire	13	Towndrow
5	Fritchley	14	Turton
6	Goodwins (Exrs)	15	Woodhouse
7	Hurt	16	Wilmot (Bart)
8	Marshall	17	Wright
9	Nightingale		

Fig 8

A History Of Crich

Fig 9

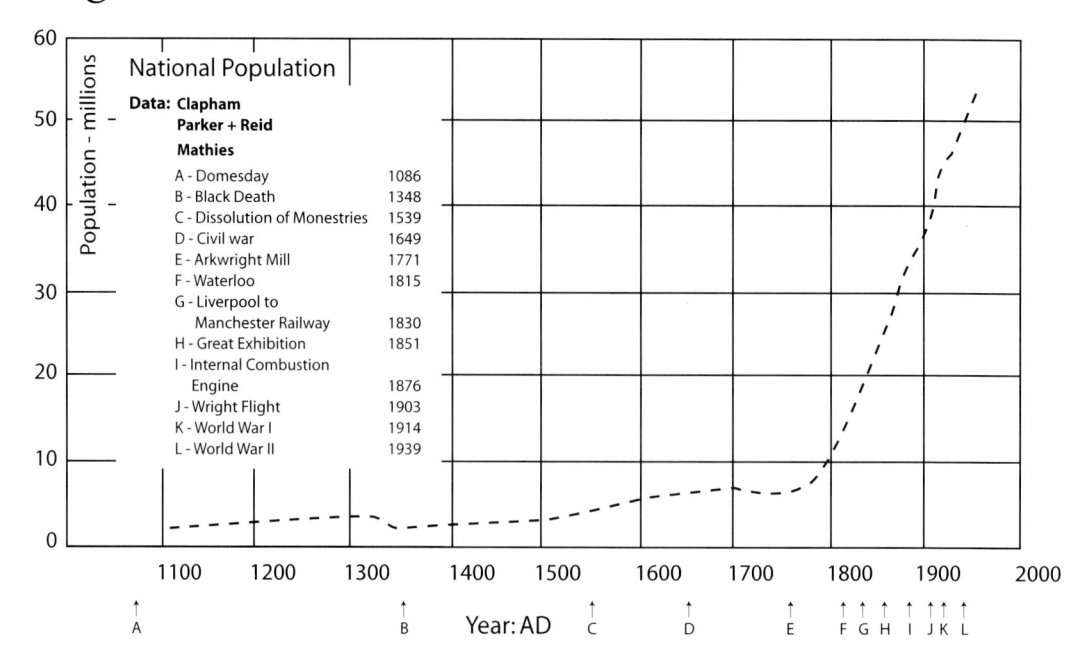

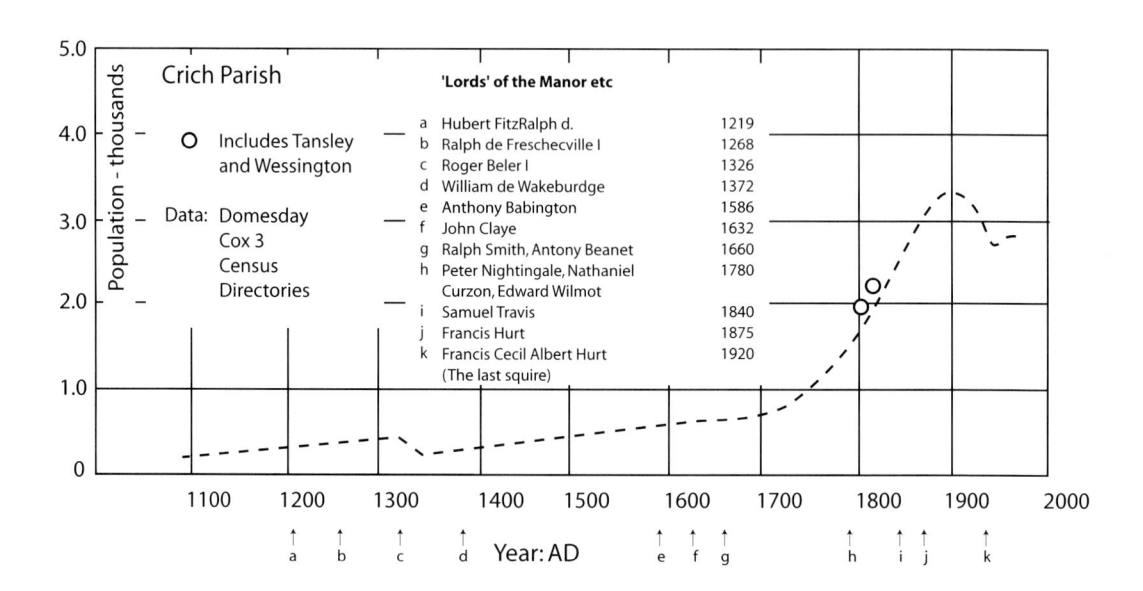

National Population

Data: Clapham
   Parker + Reid
   Mathies

A - Domesday — 1086
B - Black Death — 1348
C - Dissolution of Monestries — 1539
D - Civil war — 1649
E - Arkwright Mill — 1771
F - Waterloo — 1815
G - Liverpool to Manchester Railway — 1830
H - Great Exhibition — 1851
I - Internal Combustion Engine — 1876
J - Wright Flight — 1903
K - World War I — 1914
L - World War II — 1939

Crich Parish

○ Includes Tansley and Wessington

Data: Domesday
   Cox 3
   Census
   Directories

'Lords' of the Manor etc

a Hubert FitzRalph d. — 1219
b Ralph de Freschecville I — 1268
c Roger Beler I — 1326
d William de Wakeburdge — 1372
e Anthony Babington — 1586
f John Claye — 1632
g Ralph Smith, Antony Beanet — 1660
h Peter Nightingale, Nathaniel Curzon, Edward Wilmot — 1780
i Samuel Travis — 1840
j Francis Hurt — 1875
k Francis Cecil Albert Hurt (The last squire) — 1920

NATIONAL POPULATION + POPULATION OF CRICH

— 182 —

Fig 10

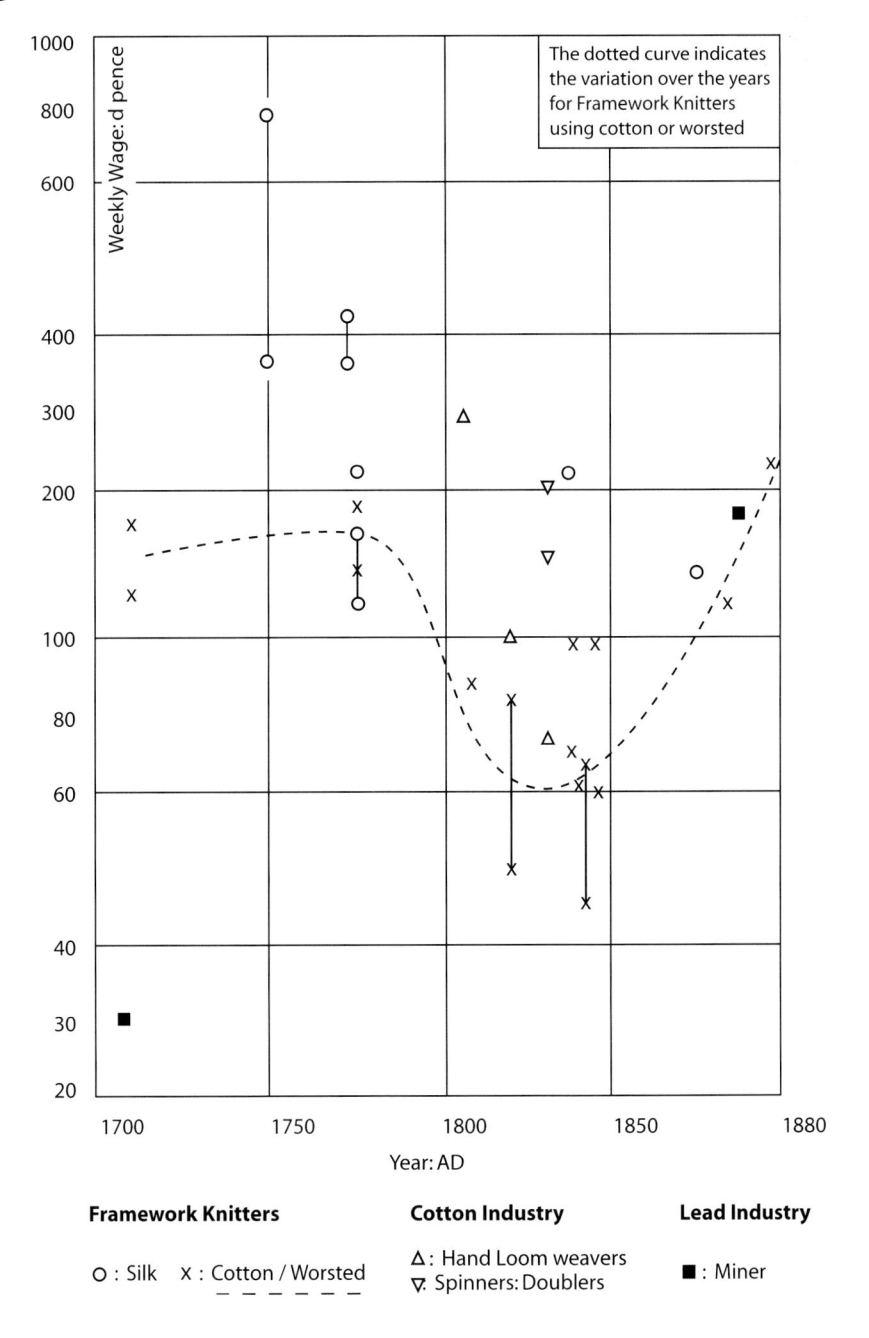

WAGE RATES (Local Interest)

Framework Knitters
O : Silk   X : Cotton / Worsted
– – – – –

Cotton Industry
△ : Hand Loom weavers
▽ : Spinners: Doublers

Lead Industry
■ : Miner

The dotted curve indicates the variation over the years for Framework Knitters using cotton or worsted

A History Of Crich

11. Crich Cliff
This view taken in 1907 from Carr Lane shows a very different landscape to the one we now know. The Cliff Inn is very recognisable but to the left are dramatic remains of lead mining with lofty spoil heaps and substantial buildings – all derelict and now completely overgrown with self-sown trees

12. Crich Cross
A view from the early years of the twentieth century which makes Crich look a very bleak place indeed. The blacksmith's shop was housed in the building on the left.

13. Whatstandwell
The station personnel (not forgetting the signalman at his window) in the 1890s

14. The Wesleyan Methodist Chapel, Crich
The first chapel built in the village was opened in 1765 and was twice visited by John Wesley himself – in 1766 and 1770. The pulpit he used is still in regular use.

15. Crich Market Place

Taken around the turn of the nineteenth century, this photograph shows that much of the Market Place was still under grass. The archway used to carry the mineral railway over Bulling Lane and was demolished in 1964

16. James Henry Dawes

Index

A

A., J. Jacoby 89
Aisle 15, 70, 71, 72, 74
Albinus 13
Alderwasley Park 19, 20, 48, 94
Alfreton 59, 60, 87, 128, 133, 151, 152, 159
Allen Lane 65
Allyn 26
Alsop, Luke 117
Amber Valley 10, 145
Amber View 61, 127
Amber Wharf 112
Anglo-Saxon 31, 32, 34
Anniversary 79, 88, 157
Arkwright, Richard 12, 19, 26, 44
Armistice Sunday 158
Ashlar 127
Ashover Grit 10
Assarts 93, 94
Australia 27, 28, 30, 76, 85, 136, 154

B

Babington, Katherine 25
Babingtons of Dethick 16, 18
Back Lane 86
Bacon, George 75, 128
Bag Men 135
Bakery 125, 154
Banks, Edward 112
Baptist Chapel 23, 78, 110, 111, 153, 156
Barge Building 127
Barker, George 101
Barlow 110, 126
Barmaster 117, 121
Barmote Court 116, 117
Barnclose Farm 59
Barnes, J. H. 82
Barnett, Absolom 51
Baron of Crich 12, 13, 15
Beardah, John 75
Beardmore, Isaac 134
Beardmore, Thomas 134
Beevor's Mill 129
Beighton, John 101
Bellringing 90, 158
Bells 59, 75, 158
Belper 12, 19, 29, 30, 52, 62, 65, 66, 79, 81, 90, 125, 132, 133, 135, 136, 141, 150, 151, 152
Belper to Cromford turnpike 66
Bembridge 26
Bennet, Anthony 18, 99
Bennets Lane 62, 90, 101
Benthill 10, 22, 89, 128, 146

Berrisford 26
Bess of Hardwick 15, 25, 53
Betty Kenny's Tree 19
Bilberry Wood 61, 103, 149
Bishop of Worcester 13
Black Death 12, 15, 23, 40, 95, 96, 97
Black Swan 65, 85, 86, 87, 94, 153, 154
Blackbird Lane 57
Blackmore, John 48
Blacksmith 124, 125
Bluebell Inn 85
Boamer 26
Bobbin Factory 78
Bobbin-Mill Hill 79, 81
Bobbin-Mill Woodyard 130
Bodencote 57
Bollington 26
Boole, Mr. 27
Bottom School 83, 84, 86, 154
Bottom Side 65
Bovate 31, 93, 96
Bower 23, 62, 80, 84, 86, 141
Bower, Alban 62
Bowmer 24, 61, 149
Bowmer Corn Mill 104, 129
Bowmer, Isaac 79, 107, 129
Bowmer, Thomas 24, 59, 75, 77, 102
Bowmer's Rough 103
Bownes, George 48
Bown's Hill 23, 24, 62, 74, 78, 85, 147, 155
Bradshaw, John 152
Brandreth, Jeremiah 136
Bricius 41, 53, 70
Brickworks 128
British Legion 154, 160
Brook Bottom 65
Browne, Gorge 72
Browne, Milescent 72
Bryan 86
Bryan's Steps 26
Bullbridge 10, 27, 57, 58, 59, 63, 66, 67, 85, 86, 87, 102, 103, 106, 111, 112, 113, 125, 126, 127, 129, 131, 146, 147, 148, 149, 150, 151
Bulling Lane 58, 60, 61, 65, 114, 128, 151
Bulls Head 66, 70, 76, 85, 86, 89, 153
Bunting 26, 45, 130
Bunting, Anne 130
Bunting, Joseph 130
Burdetts Map 125
Burglary 39, 86
Burials 26, 76
Burntlime 59, 112, 113, 114, 118, 126
Butchers 27, 124, 125, 155
Butterley Company 27, 83, 106, 111, 112, 113, 134

C

Caldwell Wood 86
Caluecroft 53
Canal Inn 85, 86, 125, 150
Canals 66
Candlemaker 124, 125, 146
Canons 13, 14, 22, 25
Canon's Furlong 21, 22
Canons Wood 22, 93, 100
Carriers 43, 66, 68, 109, 115, 122, 141
Castle Hill 11, 57, 60
Cattle 28, 58, 65, 92, 95, 96, 97, 98, 99, 102, 106, 107, 128, 129, 145, 146
Causeway 21, 58, 59, 60, 61, 65, 85
Causeway Lane 58, 85
Cawood, Mary 80
Chadwick, Edwin 51
Chadwick Nick Lane 41, 58, 61, 63, 65, 85
Chadwick, William 61
Chancel 17, 20, 70, 71, 72, 74, 152, 157
Chantry 14
Chapels 77, 80, 91
Charcoal furnace 125
Charge, John 117
Chase Cliffe 20, 87, 157
Chase Fields 53, 60, 153
Chatsworth Grit 10, 111
Cheetham, Thomas 130
Cherry House 127
Chesterfield 11, 25, 28, 37, 47, 55, 141
Chestnut Bank 81, 131
Chiddingstone Castle 23, 24, 86
Chief Constable of the Hundred 35, 37
Church of England 42, 73, 78, 81, 82, 154
Church of St. Mary 70
Church Quarry 76, 111, 114, 160
Church Registers 26
Church School 78, 81, 83, 157
Churchwarden 39, 40, 144
Churchwardens 42, 43, 71, 72, 75, 76, 152, 158
Churchyard 23, 75, 76, 102, 116
Cinema 155, 157
Civil War 12, 13, 18, 26, 45, 73
Classis 73
Clay Cross 69, 113, 114, 149
Clay Cross Company 83, 114
Claye, John 12, 16, 17, 18, 22, 23, 24, 45
Cliff Inn 21, 53, 61, 85, 153
Cliff Quarry 61, 76, 113, 114, 115, 120, 121, 127, 154, 159, 160
Cliff side 21
Clubs 88, 153
Co-op 27, 28, 155
Coal miners 155
Coalburn Hill 57, 136
Coates, Peter 77
Cockayne, Joe 122
Cockermouth 78, 130

Coddington 10, 74, 93, 100, 111, 126, 153
Common Farm 27, 106
Commonwealth 43, 45, 72, 73, 77
Comrades Club 86, 154
Congregational Chapel 78, 154
Cooper 74, 91, 102, 152
Cooper, John 152
Corn 18, 34, 41, 67, 92, 93, 94, 96, 97, 98, 99, 100, 101, 102, 103, 104, 105, 129, 133, 155
Cornmill 129
Cotton Mill 86, 129, 130, 134
Cotton Spinning Factory 129
Cotton weavers 51
County rates 39, 40, 51
Courts leet 32
Cow 28, 86
Cowper Lane 61, 65
Crecy 15
Crich 10, 11, 31, 32, 33, 34, 35, 36, 37, 38, 41, 43, 44, 48,49, 51, 54, 56, 57, 58, 59, 60, 61, 62, 63, 65, 66, 67, 68, 70, 72, 73, 74, 75, 76, 77, 78, 81, 82, 83, 84, 85, 86, 87, 88, 89, 90, 92, 93, 94, 95, 96, 97, 98, 99, 100, 101, 102, 103, 105, 106, 110, 111, 113, 114, 116, 117, 118, 119, 126, 127, 128, 130, 131, 133, 135, 136, 137, 138, 139, 140, 141, 144, 145, 146, 147, 150, 151, 152, 155, 160, 161
Crich Athletic 153
Crich British 84
Crich Brook 128
Crich Carr 10, 78, 86, 89, 94, 110, 155
Crich Carr National 84
Crich Chase 13, 20
Crich Church 13, 14, 15, 17, 18, 20, 21, 22, 23, 24, 58, 75, 76, 79, 83, 96
Crich Cliff 11, 26, 115
Crich Co-operative Society 27
Crich Common 28, 80, 85, 89, 150
Crich Cricket Club 84, 153
Crich Fair 28, 89, 102, 107, 124, 145
Crich Mining Laws 38
Crich Rangers 153
Crich Rating Survey 20, 29, 55, 68, 91, 120, 141
Crich Reading Room 89
Crich School 80
Crich Sough 120
Crich Stand 19
Crich Tithe Apportionment 56, 68, 102, 103, 109
Crich Tithe Map 52
Crich Tramway Village 160
Crich United 89, 153, 154
Crich United Silver Prize Band 154
Crich Wood 13, 14
Cromford Bridge to Langley Mill Turnpike 65
Cromford Canal 28, 61, 66, 112, 113, 114, 121, 126, 127
Cromwell, Lord Ralph 12, 15
Cross 58, 60, 62, 65, 78, 80, 81, 85, 100, 102, 111, 114, 125, 147, 156
Cub Pack 154
Culland 10, 11, 14, 19, 53, 86, 93, 95, 100, 103, 110, 111, 120, 128, 129
Culland Park 18, 22, 95, 99
Culland Wood 112, 126
Cupolas 120
Curzon, George 25
Curzon, Joan 25
Curzon, John 24, 133
Curzon, Nathaniel 21, 24, 25, 44, 74
Curzons of Kedleston 12, 25
Custom 36, 40, 74, 75, 89, 116, 139, 146, 157, 158

D

Daddy Haywood 157
Dakin, John 17
Dames Schools 80
Dances 154, 156
Dark Lane 16, 23
Darley Abbey 13, 14, 20, 21, 25, 28
Darley Abbey Cartulary 20, 52, 58, 93, 95, 128
Dawbarn 125, 146
Dawes, J. 67, 79, 84, 89
Dawes, John 144, 147, 152, 153, 157
Dawes, Thomas 125
Daws 26
Deacon family 157
Debanke, Joshua 133
Defoe, Daniel 37, 118
Delphs 126
Demesne 33, 92, 93, 94, 95, 96, 97
Denman Mason 26, 27, 52, 67, 68, 77, 79, 84, 88, 89, 100, 106, 107, 120, 128, 145, 150
Derby 10, 11, 16, 17, 25, 28, 29, 30, 37, 45, 48, 53, 55, 56, 130, 134, 135, 137, 140, 141
Derby Jail 77
Derby Mercury 65, 69, 80, 83, 85, 86, 87, 102, 108, 109, 130, 134, 141
Derby Museum 55, 108, 140
Derby Rib 135
Derwent Dams 149
Derwent Hotel 85
Derwent Valley 10, 117, 145, 148, 149
Derwent Valley Aqueduct 149
Dethick 10, 13, 16, 18, 58, 84, 149
Dethick Common 57, 145
Dial Farm 27, 61, 146
Dimple 10, 14, 21, 25, 46, 57, 61, 65, 85, 111, 113, 128, 129, 131, 133, 134, 146, 151, 159
Dimple Green 23, 57, 128, 146, 147
Dimple House 79, 80, 144, 159

Dimple Villas 146
Dingle Farm 77
Dissolution of the Monasteries 16 25
Dixie, Beaumont 17
Dixie-land 24
Dodd, Thomas 128
Dole 42, 51
Domesday Book 12, 28, 33, 34, 55, 92, 108, 122
Dovecotes 94
Dower-house 41
Downall, William 123, 133
de Draycote, W. 70
Droving 36, 58
Druid's lodge 84
Duffield Frith 11, 19
Duke of Devonshire 24, 44, 53, 60, 83, 111
Dukes Quarries 60, 111, 126
Dutchman, Jovial 27, 85, 88, 106, 114, 147
Dyson, H. 89

E

Earl of Newcastle 18, 25
Earl of Thanet 25, 46, 101, 113, 117
Earls of Shrewsbury 12
Edge Moor 10, 11, 14, 16, 22, 24, 27, 57, 58, 66, 74, 86, 110, 111, 126, 128, 129, 146
Edward of Salisbury 13
Electricity 131, 147
Else, Guy 150, 151
Enclosure Award 19, 25, 29, 53, 57, 58, 62, 63, 66, 68, 74, 109, 115, 128, 141
Enclosures 21, 24, 53, 99, 100, 101, 132
Eyam 17, 59, 62, 77

F

Farming community 103, 145
Fawne 19
Felkin, William 138
Fernside 79
de Ferrers, Robert 13
Fireclay 127
Firing range 48
Fishpond House 21, 22, 27, 58, 93
Fitz 113
FitzEudo, Ralph 13
FitzHubert, Ralph 12, 13, 33, 34
FitzRalph, Hubert 12, 13, 15, 21, 22, 25
Flamsteed, John 18
Flax 41, 42, 103, 125, 130, 131
Flower Meadow 159
Fluorspar 122
Flynte 26
Folds Yard 22

Font 70, 74, 133
Football teams 153
Four Lane Ends 65
Framework knitters 51, 87, 135, 136, 137, 138, 139, 140
France 15, 47, 101, 104, 120, 132
de Frecheville, Ralph 13, 15, 20, 23
Frecheville 12, 13, 15, 20, 22, 23, 25
Frederick, Albert Hurt 44, 47
Freeman 31
Fridensti 53, 57, 60, 93
Fridesseford 60, 61
Friendly Societies 87, 88
Friends 17, 59, 62, 142, 159, 161
Fritchley 10, 18, 20, 21, 24, 26, 57, 59, 61, 63, 65, 66, 77, 78, 79, 85, 96, 100, 102, 103, 111, 120, 126, 127, 129, 130, 134, 137, 140, 145, 146, 147, 150, 151, 153, 154, 157, 161
Fritchley (National) School 78
Fritchley Green 61, 63, 151, 155, 157, 158
Fritchley Lending Library 153
Fritchley Level 120, 128
Fritchley Mill Road 63, 65, 100, 125
Fritchley Mission Church and School 20
Fritchley National 82, 84
Fritchley Road 63, 65
Furlongs 93, 100, 103, 128

G

G. Wheatcroft and Sons 67
Gameinge 36
Gamekeepers Cottage 61
Ganister 122
Gas mains 77, 147
General Highway Act of 1835) 43
George 67, 113, 144, 159
Gilbert, 7th Earl of Shrewsbury 15
Gin mill 118
Gingler Mine 122
Gisbourne's Charity 152
Glen Road 86
Glory Mine 120
Godwin the Saxon Earl of Wessex 12, 31
Grange 120
Grant, John Sargent 78
Graves 75, 76
Gray Lane 60
Greehough 26
Greyhound 76, 85
Grocers 124, 155
Grooves 116, 118
Grove House 62
Gunpowder 61, 118
Guns 36, 94

H

Hagg Lane 58, 65
Halton, Immanuel 18, 44, 60
Halton, Timothy 95
Hardwick, S. 136
Harrison, Enoch 129
Harrison Mill 129
Haslam 26, 72
Haslam, John 72
Hat Factory 112, 123, 128, 129, 130, 131, 134
Hawking 36
Hawks 94
Hay 20, 41, 59, 92, 93, 98, 99, 103, 106, 107
Haynes, John 125
Hays Land 21, 53
Haytop 19
Heage Firs 57, 60
Hemp 41
Henry, James Dawes 125, 144, 147, 150, 151, 153, 155, 157, 160
Henry, Sir Sacheveral Wilmot Bart 53
Hepworth, Mrs. 136
Hilts Cottages 128
Hilts Quarry 60, 111, 112, 113, 134, 151, 159
Hindersitch Lane 41, 61
Hob Hall 20, 53
Hog Nick 20, 21, 53, 58
Holden, Jas. 79
Hollingsworth, Sam 154
Hollins Farm 120
Holloway 79, 84, 89
Holloway School Board 84
Holly Lane 57, 60
Holmes 26, 124, 125
Holywell Pump 146
Homesford Cottage 148
Horse 35, 45, 46, 59, 65, 66, 76, 86, 99, 106, 111, 112, 115, 119, 121, 129, 141, 155
Horse and Groom 65
Hosiery 135, 137, 138, 139, 140
Houses of Correction 42
Howard, Henry 18, 27, 74
Howards 24
Hudson, George 26
Hue and cry 31, 35, 37
Hundred 25, 31, 32, 33, 34, 35, 37, 40, 47, 48
Hundred Court 33, 35
Hundred of Scarsdale 25
Hungry Forties 105
Hunt's Barn 136
Hurt 61, 146
Hurt, Charles 44, 46, 48
Hurt, Francis 19, 44, 46, 65, 67, 86, 104, 125
Hurt, Nicholas 19, 44, 46
Hurts 12, 19, 20, 24, 26

I

Independent Friendly 78, 87, 91
India 74, 97, 135, 160
Industrial Revolution 38, 73, 100, 106, 111, 120, 138, 162
Infields 92
Iron Gates 86
Ironworks 20

J

Jessop, William 44, 66, 102, 112
Jimmy Tommy Lee 154, 156
John, Sir Gell 18
John, Sir Pole 12, 17
Joiner 124, 125, 146, 154, 155
Joseph, Sir Banks 44
Jubilee 62, 89, 90, 91, 110, 141, 143
Jury 32, 35, 71, 93
Justices of the Peace 35, 38, 39, 40, 42, 43, 44, 45, 54, 64, 144

K

Kenyon, Luke 19
Kidder, Thomas 123, 132, 133
Kilns 103, 111, 112, 113, 114, 159
King (Edward II) 14
King George VI 158
King John 13
Kings Arms 18, 62, 85, 147, 155, 156
King's Court 13, 14
Kings Mead 25
Kirk, E. 89
Kirkham Lane 57, 129, 130
Kirkland, John 74, 94, 152
Knights 13, 14, 33, 39, 45, 95

L

Lambs 41, 53
Landowners 53, 64, 73, 104, 117
Last Drink Out 85
Le Hey 21, 53, 94
Le Lewes 14, 53, 111
Le Scotteshaches 53
Lea 12, 13, 19, 23, 84, 86, 128, 129, 132, 135, 139, 141, 149
Lea Bridge 65
Lead 10, 11, 13, 14, 26, 27, 46, 57, 58, 59, 60, 61, 62, 64, 65, 67, 68, 86, 110, 113, 116, 117, 118, 119, 120, 121, 122, 123, 124, 125, 128, 131, 132, 141, 148
Lead mine 13, 14, 27
League 153
Leam, Joseph 66
Leashaw 60, 65, 125
Leofric 31
Leonia 13
Leonoth 31

Lime-burners 64, 111, 126
Lime-wash 126
Limestone 10, 68, 110, 76, 111, 112, 113, 114, 120, 121, 128, 150, 159
Lindway-Spring Wood 10
Linford 60
Lister, William 134
Little Chester 11
Little Eaton 59, 62, 77
Littlewood, Charity 73
Lockett, William 137
London 28, 29, 30, 42, 53, 55, 56, 64, 68, 78, 87, 88, 89, 90, 98, 108, 109, 113, 115, 117, 120, 122, 123, 127, 132, 134, 135, 141, 142, 143, 146, 150, 151, 156, 157
Long Wood 57
Looms 129, 130
Lord Nelson 85
Lord, Thomas Beler 14
Lowe, Anthony 19, 45
Lowe, Edward 152
Lowndes, Walter 79
Luddite Riots 136, 138
Ludlam 26, 120, 136, 137
Ludlam, Isaac 136
Ludlams 65
Ludlam's lane 120
Ludlow, Mrs. 130
Ludway Carr 86
Lutadorum 11
Lynam, John 77

M

Mainpieces 57, 77, 103, 104
Malt Offices 102
Manners, John 17
Manor Hotel 65
Manor of Alderwasley 12, 19, 24
Manor of Shining Cliff 19
Manor of Wakebridge 12, 15, 19, 23, 52
Manorial Courts 32, 33, 34, 40
Manors 12, 15, 19, 25, 26, 31, 41
Mansion House 24, 74
Manufacture 26, 126, 127, 128, 129, 133, 134, 135
Market Place 23, 27, 28, 36, 38, 62, 63, 65, 78, 84, 85, 86, 93, 110, 114, 124, 125, 128
Marshall, Mary 23, 27, 67
Marshall, William 27, 75
Martyn 26
Mary, Dame Dixie 24
Mary Leam 66
Mary, Queen 19, 25
Mary Queen of Scots 15, 23, 127
Mason, Edwin 27, 84
Mason, John 27
Masons 127, 155
Mather, Joseph 71, 80, 117
Matilda 13

Matlock Bath 67, 88
Matlock Bridge 67
Meadow 14, 21, 41, 53, 92, 93, 99
Medieval mill 128
Meerbrook Sough 148, 149
Meeting House 78, 79, 91, 142, 161
Melbourne 27, 49
Melkridge House 120
Memorial 16, 19, 59, 70, 71, 72, 74, 90, 122, 161
Mercaston 16, 49
Merewelsiche 21, 22
Middle Moor 57
Midland General Bus Company 151
Mill 18, 34, 57, 86, 91, 92, 103, 104, 113, 117, 118, 125, 128, 129, 130, 131, 132, 133, 134, 141
Millgreen 25, 57, 93, 125, 129
Millstones 102, 110, 126, 129
Mine 115, 116, 119, 120, 121, 122, 128
Mineral railway 59, 62
Miners Hack 85
Miners Welfare 153
de Montfort, Simon 19
Moorwood Moor 99, 126, 127
Morderns Map 100
Moris, Mary 72
Moris, Patrick 72
Morley Park 125
Morley, Thomas 24, 127
Morleystone Litchurch 25
Mount Tabor Chapel 60, 78, 81, 82, 83, 111
Musters 24, 45, 46
My Lady Coach 151

N

Napoleonic Wars 38, 103, 137
Nave 70, 74, 154, 157
Navy 47, 102, 103
Nether Black Swan 85, 86, 94
Nether Common 49, 61, 62, 63, 65, 146, 157
Nevile, Richard 25
Nightingale 44, 76, 83, 86, 101, 117, 128, 132
Nightingale, Florence 83
Nightingale, Peter 12, 19, 23, 44
Non-Anglicans 76
Non-conformism 77
Norman Conquest 12, 31, 34, 70, 144
Nottingham 66, 78, 85, 94, 117, 127, 134, 135, 136, 137, 138, 139, 140
Nottingham Castle 127
Nottingham to Newhaven Turnpike 64
Nunsfield 25
Nuttal, John 101

O

Oakerthorpe 11
Oakhurst 60
Offering, Easter 41, 53
Old Quarry 10, 21, 53, 59, 112, 113, 128, 134, 160
Open fields 93, 96, 99, 100
Orchard 93, 116, 129, 130
Orme, Samuel 93
Out-workers 51, 139
Outfields 92, 94
Outram, Joseph 101
Over-grazing 98
Overseer of the Poor 39, 56, 104, 109, 141
Oxen 43, 62, 92, 97
Oxhay Wood 60

P

Packhorses 59
Parish Meetings 40,
Parish Room 35, 54, 70, 78, 85, 87, 88, 90, 137
Park Farm 57, 136
Parkhead 10, 14, 60, 65, 100, 149, 150
Parliament 13, 14, 15, 17, 18
Parochial 81, 82, 83, 84
Peacock 86
Peakrills 119
Pearson's Venture 119, 121
Peasant 33, 93, 96, 97, 99, 119
Peat, Wm. 130
Peel, Robert 38
Pello House 127
Penfold 35
Pennine 10, 148
Pentrich 11, 49, 88, 102, 103, 116, 136, 137, 142
Pentrich Revolution 136, 137
Percy, Peter Taylor 156
Perry, Ann 59
Petitpas 93
Petts, Isaac 59
Phyllis' Brook 128
Piggin 26, 79, 114, 124
Piggin, John 114
Pigs 41, 95, 97, 101, 106, 107, 125
Pigs of lead 11
Pilkington 11, 68, 122, 132, 142
Pippin Bus Company 151
Pitsteads 10
Plaistow 10, 14, 21, 22, 57, 71, 86, 94, 96, 152
Plaistow Green 16, 21, 24, 74, 93, 100, 103, 150
Plaque 17, 70, 74, 102, 127, 140
Plough 12, 43, 47, 58, 92, 97, 98, 99, 103, 104, 107, 125

Poaching 94
Pole, German 12, 17, 18, 25, 44, 45
Poles of Radbourne 16
Police station 147
Pony and trap 27, 67, 145, 150
Poor House 48, 49
Poor Rate 42, 44, 48, 51
Poplar Cottage 128
Porch 22, 70, 71, 74, 75
Pot House 16, 23, 27
Presbyterian 72, 73, 77
Primitive Methodists 78
Privy Council 39
Prospect Terrace 101, 102, 139, 155
Public Houses 85
Punchon 79
Puritan 18, 75, 77
Pusey, Timothy 17, 18
Pye, Thomas 159

Q

Quaker 29, 59, 68, 77, 78, 79, 81, 90, 91, 130, 142, 150, 153, 158, 159, 161
Quarries 10, 86, 110, 111, 112, 126, 127, 160
Quarter Sessions 35, 36, 37, 39, 43, 144
Queen Victoria 110, 140
Queen Victoria's Golden Jubilee 89
Queen's Room 16, 23

R

Radford 26, 27, 45, 106
Railways 53, 66, 67, 106, 107, 124, 126, 127, 131, 145, 146, 149, 150, 162
Rakes 10
Ray, Timmy 156
Reading Room 24, 89, 90, 153
Recreation Ground 60, 153
Red Lion 57, 85
Red-lead mill 18
Redfern 26, 128
Reeve 31
Reformation 41, 42, 72, 158
Reginald 16
Relief of the poor 41, 42, 52, 54
Repeal of the Corn Laws 105
Reservoir Corner 65
Reservoirs 148, 149
Retailers 124
Reverberating furnaces 120
Reynolds 49, 75, 80, 141
Richard, Duke of Gloucester 25
Richard Johnson and Nephew 146
Richard, son of William Bylbot 14
Rickman, Matilda 79, 80
Riddings 89, 100
Ridgeway 21, 57, 58, 60, 61, 79, 119, 121, 125, 129
Ripley Advertiser 114

Rising Sun 147, 153
Robbery 39, 86
Robert, Sir Meade Wilmot 24, 44, 53
Robin Hood 10, 11, 60, 94, 110, 125, 146, 160
Rodney Mine 121
Roe 65, 76, 78, 85, 111
Roger, Sir Beler 12, 14, 23
Roger, the Bishop of Worcester 13
Rogues 36, 38
Roman Catholics 76
Romans 11, 57, 58, 64, 110
Rosskeen 147
Royal Oak 85, 137, 140, 143
Royal Oak Terrace 137, 140
Rue Cliff Quarry 61, 127
Ryknild Street 11, 57, 60, 65

S

Sabbath 36, 76, 158
Sandy Lane 62, 65, 89, 151, 153
Sawmill 130
Saxton, John 74
Scarsdale, Lord 25, 44, 46
School 17, 25, 37, 70, 71, 78, 79, 80, 81, 82, 83, 84, 86, 90, 91, 140, 150, 151, 152, 153, 154, 155, 156, 157, 162
School Board 44, 81, 82, 84
Scott, Mr. 82, 83
Scout Troop 154
Scutage 13, 33
Sellars 26
Serf 33, 97
Seven Years War 64
Sewers 131, 147
Shales 10
Shaw, Bernard 150
Sheep 22, 28, 34, 92, 93, 95, 96, 97, 99, 102, 106, 107, 120, 145
Sheldon Pingle 60, 152
Sheriff 17, 24, 31, 32, 33, 39, 40, 45, 46, 94, 99
Sheriff's Court 33
Sherwood Forest 15
Sherwood Foresters memorial 19
Shire-reeve 31
Shoemaker 78, 124, 125, 136
Shore's Wood 86
Shoulder of Mutton 85
Shuckstone 10, 11, 57, 58, 60, 61
Sideweie 31
Sir Sadler 16
Smedley, John 132
Smelting Works 120
Smerwick Clarke 72
Smith 18, 26, 27, 36, 72, 75, 77, 78, 79, 90, 99, 100, 106, 116, 124, 125, 133, 159
Smith, Donald 159
Smith, John 72

Smith, Ralph 18, 27, 78, 99, 100
Smith, William 133
Smiths Rough 58, 103, 145
Smithy 125
Snowdrop Valley 61, 62, 63, 128, 146, 157
Sokeland 33
Sokemen 33, 92
Sough, Ridgeway 121
South Wingfield 12, 14, 15, 38, 44
South Wingfield Association of the Prosecution of Felons 86
Southampton 62, 117
Special trains 67
Spinning of yarn 131, 132
Spoil dumps 120
Squire Nightingale's 28
Squire Wass 28, 120, 121
St. Thomas' Mount 14, 20, 21
Statute of Bridges 42
Statute of Labourers 15, 40
Statute of Winchester 34, 35, 39, 40, 54
Steam joinery works 125
Steep 114
Steeple Grange 60, 65
Stephenson, George 113, 159
Stephenson, Robert 26, 67, 115
Stevenson's Dye Works 131, 146
Stockiners shop 137
Stone Age 10
Stone working 26
Stones 20, 100, 128
Stonewell, Walter 60
Storer, John 79, 80
Straw hats 123, 132
Street Lane 57, 60, 65
Street lighting 147
Strips 92, 93, 96, 100, 101, 106
de Stuteville, Robert 13
Sudbury, William 19
Sulley, Henry 140
Sumner, W.T. 82
Sunday School 78, 80
Sunnyside 129, 130
Surveyor of highways 39
Swillington 12, 14, 15
Sword 35
Sycamore House 21

T

Talbot, George 15
Talbot Papers 17, 29
Talbots 12
Tansley 10, 13, 45
Tanyard 125, 136
Taylor, Benjamin 89
Ted the Post 139
Ten-Acre-Lane 21
The Barn 41, 58
The Bowmers 24, 102

The Briars 130, 150
The Common House 27, 77
The Crich Tales 27, 29, 84, 90, 122, 139, 143, 144, 161
The Hill 10, 68, 131
The King's Peace 31, 39
The Smiths 12, 24, 27, 28, 102, 117
The Victory 86
Thomas 14
Thomas Bowmer 102
Thomas, Rev. Shelmardine 77
Thorpe Hill 19, 129, 137
Thorphill Farm 57
Thos., Rev. Cornthwaite 152
Thurlow Booth 10, 60, 61, 65
Tithe Barns 41
Tithe Farm 94
Tithes 16, 17, 25, 40, 41, 52, 53, 105, 144, 159
Toft 14, 92, 97
Tomb 15, 17, 71, 74, 75, 102
Tomes, Edward 159
Tomlinson, Henry 136
Tommy, Jimmy Lee 154, 156
Top Hagg Lane 58
Top Lane 61, 62
Top Side 65
Topham 19, 26, 66
Tors 10, 58, 61, 62, 65, 66, 90, 110, 114, 126, 128, 146, 148, 149, 151, 153, 155
Tors Spring Company 146
Tors Steps 61
Tower 19, 23, 70, 75, 160
Town End 65, 66, 85, 147, 151, 157
Town Fields 21
Towndrow Harrison 74
Towndrow, Samuel 19
Towndrow, Thomas 19, 113
Towndrows 12
Tractor 145
Tradesmen 37, 43, 125
Tramway 112, 113, 114, 134
Travis, Samuel 19, 26, 74, 113
Travises 12
Trent 13, 31, 64, 77
Trent Bus Company 151
Tudor 12, 16, 17, 23, 28, 29, 36, 39, 45
Tudor, Mary 16
Turbutt, Gladwyn 44
Turner, William 136
Turning Mill 125
Turnpikes 43, 57, 63, 64, 65, 66, 101, 102, 118, 124, 126, 133, 135
Turton Cotton Mill 129
Turton, James 111, 133, 134
Turton, John 44, 46, 133, 134
Turton, Thomas 48, 133, 134
Turton, William 44, 134
Turtons 12
Tything 31, 32

U

Undertown Field 21
Underwood 103
United Methodists 78
Upper Common 62, 65
Urinal 147

V

Vagabond 38, 41, 42
Vagrancy 42
Varden, Richard 72
Veins 10
Vestry 39, 44, 70, 72
Vicarage 53, 128, 153, 157
Vicarage 41
Vicarage Croft 157
Victoria House 153, 154, 159
Victoria, Queen 140
Victory Cottage 86
Vill 31, 32, 34
Village lock-up 35
Villeins 33, 34, 43, 54, 92, 97

W

W., Ralph Smith 27, 78
W., T. Evans 83
Wager, Jasper 48
de Wakebridge, Peter 15, 41
de Wakebridge, William 12, 14, 15, 17, 23, 39, 40, 44
Wakebridge 10, 11, 12, 14, 15, 17, 18, 19, 21, 23, 41, 58, 60, 61, 65, 70, 85, 96, 103, 116, 121, 122
Wakebridge Mine 120, 121
Wakes 28
Walker, John 80
Walker, W. 80
Walmsley, Joshua 26
Walter, Abbot 13
Walter, Sir Raleigh 16
Walters, Robert 136
Wapentake 31, 33, 34, 60, 116
Warner 59
Warner Quarry 127, 159
Warrens 94
Water Corn Mill 18
Waterhouse, David 75
Watkins, Arthur 130
Watkins, Edward 130, 131, 146, 159
Waumwell 53
Weathercock 75
Weaver Brook 114, 128
Weightman, George 136, 137
Weir Mill 57, 60, 103, 136
Well 36
Wesley, John 27, 77
Wesley Methodist Chapel 61, 62, 76
Wessington 13, 14, 21, 49
Westmorland 25, 162
Wetton 26, 84, 124, 160

Whatstandwell 10, 60, 65, 67, 78, 85, 106, 114, 121, 125, 145, 150
Wheatcroft 10, 23, 74, 78, 94, 96, 124, 126, 127, 152
Wheatcroft, German 127
Wheatsheaf Inn 85, 114
Wheatsheaf Lane 85, 114, 128
Wheeldon House 23, 27, 62, 78
Wheeldon, Ralph 27, 74, 75, 78
Whist drives 156
Whit Monday 63, 88, 154, 157
White coal 65
White Swan 85
Whitsuntide Walks 88
Wig Meadow 21, 22
Wightman 78, 130
Wigwell Grange 58, 60, 112
Wild Common 60
Wild, Ralph 86, 93
de Wilde, Robert 93
Wildgoose, R. 89
William Marshall 27
William the Conqueror 14
Willington 49, 103
Willoughbys of Wollaton 12
Windmills 103
Windy Gap 65
Wing 57, 136
Wingfield Gate 65
Wirksworth 11, 29, 48, 60, 61, 65, 66, 73, 77, 108, 114, 116, 117, 132, 133, 148, 150, 151
Witham, Joseph 66
Wolstan, Sir Dixie 17, 18, 24, 46
Wolstenholme, Hugh 137
Womens Institute 154
Wood, Tommy 160
Woodhouse 74, 101, 102
Wool 41, 42, 53, 97, 100, 130, 131, 132, 135
Woolley, William 111
Workers Educational Association 154
Workhouse Row 49, 62, 152
Workhouses 48, 49, 50, 52
Wragg, Joan 140
Wright, John 44, 74
Wright, Thomas of Fritchley 18
Wyld, John 73
Wylde 26, 73

Y

Yeoman farmer 97, 98
Yeomanry 47, 48
Yorkshire 25, 33, 57, 137, 152